Forza Ferrari

Forza. Ferrari

HOW **F1**'S MOST FAMOUS TEAM CAN **WIN** AGAIN

NATE SAUNDERS

Aurum

Quarto

First published in 2025 by Aurum Press,
an imprint of The Quarto Group.
One Triptych Place, London, SE1 9SH,
United Kingdom
T (0)20 7700 9000
www.Quarto.com

EEA Representation, WTS Tax d.o.o., Žanova ulica 3, 4000 Kranj, Slovenia

Text copyright © 2025 Nate Saunders
Design copyright © 2025 Quarto Publishing plc
All pictures in plate section copyright © 2025 grandprixphoto.com

Nate Saunders has asserted his moral right to be identified as the Author this Work in accordance with the Copyright Designs and Patents Act 1988.

All rights reserved. No part of this book may be reproduced or utilised in any form or by any means, electronic or mechanical, including photocopying, recording or by any information storage and retrieval system, without permission in writing from Aurum Press.

Every effort has been made to trace the copyright holders of material quoted in this book. If application is made in writing to the publisher, any omissions will be included in future editions.

A catalogue record for this book is available from the British Library.

ISBN 978-1-8360-0282-6
Ebook ISBN 978-1-8360-0284-0
Audiobook ISBN 978-1-8360-0618-3

10 9 8 7 6 5 4 3 2 1

Typeset by SX Composing DTP, Rayleigh, Essex SS6 9HQ
Publisher: Richard Green
Editor: Frank Hopkinson
Senior Production Controller: Rohana Yusof

Printed by CPI group (UK) Ltd, Croydon, CR0 4YY

Dedicated to the memory of my friend, Katie Shapiro
Also for my mum and dad, Vicky and Frank, and my beloved Italian 'nonna' Maria

Contents

	Acknowledgements	ix
	Foreword	1
	Introduction	3
1.	Enzo's Team	7
2.	Di Montezemolo	24
3.	Dream Team	40
4.	Schumacher	57
5.	Maranello	82
6.	The Iceman Cometh	89
7.	Felipe, Baby, Stay Cool!	104
8.	Abu Dhabi 2010: Debacle in the Desert	119
9.	Glory Days…	137
10.	2014: Fatally Flawed	153
11.	Two Sides of The Same Coin	171
12.	Vettel Falters	187
13.	Leclerc, Binotto and a Thirsty Engine	200
14.	False Dawn	213
15.	Red Fred	224
16.	'Amilton	232
17.	Il Predestinato	242
18.	Winning Again	254
	Index	259

Acknowledgements

This book would not have been possible without the co-operation and input from the following F1 luminari who offered their own first-hand experience of working for, or in some cases competing against, Scuderia Ferrari: Luca di Montezemolo, Fred Vasseur, Stefano Domenicali, Mattia Binotto, Chris Dyer, Rob Smedley, Laurent Mekies, Iñaki Rueda, Sabine Kehm, Guenther Steiner, Christian Horner and Jacques Villeneuve. Special thanks to Luca Colajanni for his guidance on all things Ferrari.

Thanks to my fellow journalists Lawrence Barretto, Laurence Edmondson, Maurice Hamilton, Julianne Cerasoli, Carlos Miguel and Carlo Vanzini for providing their own insights at various points. Other quotes came from my own reporting for ESPN over the years, while driver quotes came from both FIA press conference and open media sessions held in Formula 1 paddocks across the course of a race weekend. Thanks also to my agent Mel Michael-Greer, Quarto publisher Richard Green and my editor Frank Hopkinson, and to some of my closest friends in the F1 media centre, including Chris Medland, Luke Smith and Ben Hunt, for their continued support and encouragement on the project.

FOREWORD

Ferrari has been, after my family, the most important thing in my life. The sport of Formula 1 would not be the same without Ferrari – that is as true today as it ever was.

I am proud to have helped Ferrari win again in two different periods of my life and to have done it with some of the team's greatest champions. First, when Enzo Ferrari himself asked me to be sporting manager and we won the Drivers' Championship with Niki Lauda in 1975 for the first time in 11 years.

After a long time away from Formula 1, I came back as president in December 1991 and my job was to rebuild the F1 team from top to bottom. Step by step, brick by brick we managed to do that; by 1999 we won the Constructors' Championship and then, with Michael Schumacher in 2000, we won the Drivers' Championship for the first time in 21 years. We won five titles in a row with Michael and another with Kimi Räikkönen in 2007.

My Ferrari did not win every year, but it was almost always in the position to win. I consider myself a fortunate person to have seen the success we had. I won 19 championships, between constructors' and the drivers' with Niki, Michael and Kimi. I also lost many World Championships at the last race of the season: Once with Niki, a few times with Michael, once with Eddie Irvine, once in Brazil with Felipe Massa, and then twice with Fernando Alonso. But whether we won or lost at the end, my Ferrari was the team the others – Williams, McLaren, Renault, Red Bull – had to beat to be World Champion. That remains my proudest achievement at Ferrari.

Today, I still consider myself the number one *tifoso*, even after all this time. So my love and my heart for Ferrari is still as strong as it has ever been, but I'm sad to see the team has not been in that same condition to fight for a Drivers' Championship since I left 11 years ago. The last time a Ferrari driver arrived at the final race of the season with a chance to win the championship was Fernando at the 2012 Brazilian Grand Prix.

But I am hopeful for the future. Ferrari is coming to an exciting new era, as we saw from Ferrari's race wins in 2024 and its battle in the Constructors' Championship with McLaren. The team also has an exciting new partnership this season.

Lewis Hamilton has been and remains one of the greatest drivers Formula 1 has ever seen. A career is not complete until a driver has had the chance to race in the red of Enzo's team. If he wins another title with Ferrari his name will be in the history of Formula 1 like no-one else before him. And there is also Charles Leclerc, a super talent, a Ferrari talent – after six years at the team, it is his time to win also. These are two superstar drivers both ready to be champion for Ferrari.

Like all *tifosi* in Italy and around the world, I feel sure one of these two great drivers is the one who can end the long wait for another Ferrari driver's name to be on the World Championship trophy.

I know it is a question of when, not if, and hope the when is very, very soon indeed.

—Luca di Montezemolo

INTRODUCTION

Everyone has 'that moment' when it comes to sporting fandom: in Formula 1 terms, mine was standing on the track after the 2006 Italian Grand Prix at Monza, staring up at Michael Schumacher celebrating victory on the podium. Monza's podium is impressive regardless of who stands on the top step – when a Ferrari has won the Italian Grand Prix the ceremony is magical. The race track becomes jam-packed with fans, crushed together in a ball of noise, flares and flags, celebrating the most Italian of things: Enzo Ferrari's team winning on home Tarmac. I've been lucky enough to experience that both as a fan and, years later, as a journalist.

In 2006, Michael Schumacher had won and title rival Fernando Alonso's Renault engine had gone bang in the final laps, blowing their championship battle wide open. Monza is perfect for a celebration in those circumstances. The podium juts out over the track, inviting fans to gather underneath. Getting there had been a story itself. With my dad Frank and my childhood friend Simon Lewis – still an ardent member of the *tifosi* today – I had been watching from the infield with general admission tickets. Being an English teenager with the surname Saunders did not suggest an obvious affinity for Ferrari but Dad and I were like Simon in where our allegiances lay – my paternal grandmother, Maria, emigrated from Piacenza after the war and met my grandfather, Dennis. Dad forgave me for supporting England in football, but supporting Ferrari was non-negotiable. Luckily, the pull of the famous red team was irresistible.

After watching most of that race from the entry to Parabolica, we had followed one man who claimed he knew a place we could get on the track right by the podium itself. We followed – our progress slowed briefly by a roar of noise and the sight on screen of Alonso's smoking Renault coming to a halt at Turn 1. True to his word, our random Italian had found a tunnel, just before the paddock entry and off limits to us, it went under the circuit and back up the other side. Once through we did a U-turn, scaling the slope that ran alongside and diving under a fence being held up by another man decked out in Ferrari red. Then we found ourselves in the unlikeliest of positions – clinging on to mesh fencing, next to the main grandstand and opposite the start–finish straight, as Schumacher's beautiful red and white car appeared from the right and flashed by to secure the win.

Almost as soon as he was past, people around us were climbing the fence and spilling onto the race track. We were not sure the race had even finished but we followed anyway, arriving on the race track as the giant red flag with Ferrari's Prancing Horse logo in the centre of it was unfurled like a giant parachute. Celebrating as if Schumacher had won the title already, the crowd grew thicker and thicker. Strangers hugged each other. A man near us wept uncontrollably. Italy had won the World Cup a few months before but it felt like it was happening all over again. When Schumacher – a German by birth but an adopted Italian to everyone there – finally appeared, the noise was deafening. The national anthem was not sung, it was roared, before Schumacher threw his hat into a throng of people not far away – my immediate regret at not catching it disappeared when I saw the ruck of people descend on the person who did.

Ten years later, I returned to Monza in a different capacity. On my first day back to the circuit, driving a hire car, I suddenly had a sense of déjà vu.

INTRODUCTION 5

Now working for American sports channel ESPN and there to cover the race, as I flashed my FIA (Fédération Internationale de l'Automobile) media accreditation lanyard at circuit staff I was directed to drive down a small tunnel which went under the circuit and to the infield. I recognized it immediately. There to the right was where the three of us had crawled under the fence all those years before – the fencing appeared to have been reinforced, confirming my suspicion we should never have been able to do that in the first place. Every time I go back I drive under the same tunnel, which leads to parking for the media among the trees, and have the same memory of being a teenager overwhelmed at witnessing a Ferrari win at that most atmospheric of venues.

That 2006 victory was symbolic of changing times. Schumacher and his team still had a feeling of invincibility, built from a decade of being the benchmark everyone else had to beat. By that Sunday evening the headlines had changed – Schumacher announced after the race he was retiring, with McLaren's Kimi Räikkönen set to take his place. No-one at Monza knew it then but, even with a Räikkönen championship coming the following season, Ferrari was at the beginning of a slow decline which would trickle into the next decade. The glory days were grinding to a halt. By the time I came back to Monza in a professional capacity Ferrari was no longer the dominant force in Formula 1, having been replaced by Red Bull, who in turn had been displaced by Mercedes. Räikkönen's 2007 title remains the last by a Ferrari driver.

Since becoming a journalist I have covered only championships for Mercedes, Red Bull and, as of their Constructors' Championship in 2024, McLaren. Many people ask you who you cheer for as a journalist – the honest answer is you try to be impartial, often simply rooting for the best story. Social media has poisoned a lot of discourse around sports and the most common retort I get in response to posts is that lazy old trope: classic British media bias. I always laugh at that, remembering the giant Ferrari flag on the wall next to my bed as a kid. Although never outwardly rooting for any team or driver, the joy and the despair linked to individual results are always at their most extreme around the performance of Ferrari's red cars. A whole generation of Formula 1 media and fans have not experienced a Ferrari championship and most of us would tell you we don't want to leave the sport until we have ticked that off. I am no exception.

This is the tale of motor racing's greatest team, an inside look at its near collapse in the 1980s, its revival in the 1990s, dominance and then decline in the 2000s and its missed opportunities of the 2010s, with the resurgence and renewed hope of recent years rounding the story off for good measure. Lewis Hamilton's arrival in 2025 promises to be memorable, whether a glowing success or unmitigated disaster, and it has been hard lately not to get swept up in that most dangerous but intoxicating of feelings in the Formula 1 paddock: the Ferrari hype train. That feeling has burned plenty of people before. Here is the story of how we arrived here and how a team as big and famous and talented as Ferrari could be entering a 17th season since it won a championship title.

1
ENZO'S TEAM

'It's like being in the French legionnaires or the SAS, or something similar to that – you carry it with you forever. It's like you've done it, you've survived it, you've maybe even thrived in it. It's very different to anywhere else you'll find in Formula 1.'

Rob Smedley

Charles Leclerc presses his foot to the floor, blasting the Ferrari SF-24 race car out of Portier towards F1's most famous tunnel.

Tears start to well up in his eyes.

'Not now, Charles' he tells himself, letting his eyes flicker to clear his vision. But it's hard not to feel emotional in this moment. These are the streets he grew up on, where he fell in love with Ferrari and Formula 1. He has been unlucky here in the past and fate is always waiting to intervene. He is listening for every noise from his Ferrari 066/12 engine.

People had been calling it a curse for so long Leclerc had even started to wonder if it might be true. But he can't dwell on that now – he knows well enough that this place owes him nothing, even if he feels like it should.

Five more corners. So close now, as he navigates through the famous harbourside chicane one last time. No time to think about past Ferrari heroes who have come to grief at this very spot – Ascari, Hawthorn, Collins, Bandini.

Four more corners, as the Rosso Corsa-coloured car swings left through Tabac tantalizingly close to the massed gallery willing him onwards.

Three more corners, as he flicks the car into the first swimming pool chicane; *two more corners*, as he sweeps through the second. His hands grip tightly around the steering wheel. 'Stop thinking about it!'

One more corner, as his car turns uphill through Rascasse and towards the final right-hander, where he used to catch the bus to school.

And there it is. Leclerc looks ahead and sees outstretched red sleeves, pumping fists and the most beautiful sight of all – the chequered flag. It takes a moment for it to sink in, and then the emotion finally escapes.

'YES! YES! YES' Leclerc screams on team radio, over and over again.

The tears come back and this time he doesn't try and stop them. No matter what happens from now until the end of time, he can call himself something he always dreamed of being.

Lifelong Honour

When it was announced that Lewis Hamilton would join Charles Leclerc at Ferrari in 2025 he was taking on a share of the burden of racing for the most mythologized and – in the recent period of F1 – most frustrating team in motor racing. The arrival of the seven-time World Champion proved one thing: despite some underwhelming years the magnetism of Italy's most famous brand was stronger than ever. Hamilton's old rival Sebastian Vettel spoke prophetically about the pull of the red car in 2016: 'Everybody is a Ferrari fan, even if they're not; they are a Ferrari fan. Even if you go to the Mercedes guys and they say, "Oh yeah, Mercedes is the greatest brand in the world," they are Ferrari fans.'

In order to join Vettel on the list of drivers to have raced for Enzo Ferrari's great creation, Hamilton walked away from Mercedes and the sport's most successful driver–team partnership ever – he scored 84 wins and six Drivers' Championships with the Silver Arrows – to join a team that last won the drivers' title in his rookie Formula 1 season, 2007. They had last won the Constructors' Championship in 2008. Both he and his team-mate had the same overarching goal – to emulate what Michael Schumacher was able to do at the start of the millennium and put their names in the history books, not only as a Ferrari World Champion, but as drivers who ended a long and painful wait for a championship. For Leclerc, a title would be vindication of Ferrari's long faith in him and his long faith in them. For Hamilton, a title would move him clear of Schumacher, perhaps the driver most singularly associated with Ferrari, into unchartered waters as an eight-time World Champion and what would surely be an unrivalled claim to the title of greatest driver of all time. Both compelling scenarios and fitting for a team so wrapped up in the history of the sport that it can be difficult to separate fact from much-repeated fiction. A status held by few drivers awaits Hamilton or Leclerc if and when they can bring the championship back to Maranello. While the burden of that task might seem unreasonable to some, its existence begs a deeper question: what is worse, to race for Ferrari but never win a world title in one of its cars, or to never race for Ferrari at all?

Despite the trophy drought of more than a decade, it would be difficult to find a driver who would not like to drive for Ferrari at some point in their career, who didn't adore driving for Ferrari during their career, or who doesn't harbour a regret that they didn't get the chance. The Italian team is unique in that its worldwide fanbase is known by a single name: *tifosi*. That collective is as important to Ferrari as any other factor. 'I've been lucky enough to stand on the podium at Monza when Ferrari have won and there's no better sensation than that,' said Ross Brawn, the technical director of Schumacher's superteam of the early 2000s. 'Seeing the huge crowds and the emotion and passion of the fans. I'd walk through the airport at Bologna and I'd get abused or I'd get praised and that doesn't happen anywhere else in the world.' A group defined by unbridled passion and unquestioned loyalty, they are the gatekeepers of a special club.

While he has won a single championship for McLaren and six for Mercedes, Hamilton's affiliation with Ferrari might define him in a different way altogether, with or without a championship at the end of it. 'It's a lifelong honour,' said Rob Smedley, who worked for the Scuderia between 2002 and 2013, most famously as Felipe Massa's race engineer. It was a role he held when Hamilton snatched the championship away from the Brazilian driver and Ferrari at the final corner of the 2008 Brazilian Grand Prix. 'It's like being in the French legionnaires or the SAS, or something similar to that – you carry it with you forever. It's like you've done it, you've survived it, you've maybe even thrived in it. It's very different to anywhere else you'll find in Formula 1. Nothing else even comes close, but you don't know that until you've been there and done it.' Former Ferrari team principal and current Formula 1 boss Stefano Domenicali put it to me more simply about Hamilton's prospects: 'He may not have thought about it but the world will see him differently when he is dressed in red. Maybe what is different for Ferrari is that the *tifosi* cheer for Ferrari first, then cheer the driver coming to Ferrari second. You are joining something very special.'

Ferrari's stature in Italy is undeniable – it is a national institution, akin to a second religion. It has competed in every season since the World Championship started in 1950 and has more race entries, wins, podium finishes and pole positions than any other team. Ferrari boasts 15 drivers' titles and has won the Constructors' Championship – given to the team with the most points every year since 1958 – 16 times: it gets an annual bonus payment (estimated at $125m/£100m every year) just for showing up, while it maintains a seldom-used historical veto on certain rule changes. For this to be true in any sport would be astounding. For it to be the case amid the fierce rivalry in the 'Piranha Club', where teams protest rival car designs to the millimetre, is astonishing. Ferrari's unique position has survived the test of time. But that's Ferrari.

It was once said Formula 1 would not survive without Ferrari and that Ferrari would not survive without Formula 1. While both are debatable, what is certain is that neither would be the same without the other. While teams have come and gone (and sometimes, like Mercedes, come back again) Ferrari has stuck around through it all, through its good, its bad, its winning streaks and its title droughts. Even Ferrari's rivals marvel at the special quality the red team and its Prancing Horse logo possess. 'Ferrari is old school,' reckons Red Bull boss Christian Horner. 'It's still got a gentleman racer's attitude to it. It's rarely outspoken. It holds its counsel. It's a national team, not just a team. When you beat Ferrari it is extra rewarding because of all of that history.'

It is that history which Hamilton and Leclerc are looking to write their names into. Since Räikkönen's 2007 drivers' title and the highs of the 'dream team' put together by former president Luca di Montezemolo, Ferrari has endured heartbreak after heartbreak. There was Massa's 2008 title defeat before Fernando Alonso suffered agonizing near-misses at the final races in both 2010 and 2012, and then Sebastian Vettel blew a big chance to win the championship in 2018. While academy graduate Leclerc has experienced great highs, like his wins in Monaco and Monza in 2024, he has suffered his own string of calamitous moments – like the team's implosion in 2022 when he and Ferrari appeared to be title favourites. Momentum is everything in F1 and Hamilton arrived at Maranello at the perfect moment. Under team boss Fred Vasseur, (Lewis's former GP2 boss) Ferrari took the Constructor's Championship fight with McLaren to the wire in 2024 only to lose out in Abu Dhabi. But as the *tifosi* know all too well, being in the hunt and actually winning a championship are two very different things.

The Man From Modena

Explaining the story of Ferrari, the team he was most successful with, Ross Brawn once said: 'Enzo Ferrari didn't sit down and say, "Right, I'm going to create this empire and this is how I'm going to do it". It just evolved and became the world-famous racing team and car manufacturer it is today. To be a small part of that was very special. But I love all the phases of Ferrari. The intrigue and the mystery behind it is all part of it.'

Enzo, known for most of his life as *Il Commendatore* (The Commander), was born on 18 February 1898 in Modena, a small industrial town in the northern Italian province of Emilia-Romagna. By the time he died ninety years later folklore and legend were as much a part of his story as that of the marque he had built. Later in his life, it was often said, he was the most influential and most important Italian behind the Pope.

Despite being synonymous with motorsport today, Enzo's company pre-dates the 1950 creation of the F1 World Championship by several decades. You can trace a line back to pivotal points in its history: Enzo being hired as a race driver for the Alfa Romeo team in 1920; the first entry of the 'Scuderia Ferrari' in the 1930 grand prix season running Alfa Romeos; Enzo Ferrari taking over Alfa Romeo's works team in 1933; his rift with Alfa Romeo boss Ugo Gobbato in 1939 which prompted him to cut ties completely and form Auto Avio Costruzioni (intended to be a car-building entity until the Second World War started); and in 1947, when that company was renamed Ferrari.

As a boy Enzo was often woken to the sound of clanging hammers from his father's workshop below the bedroom he shared with his brother Alfredo Jr. After a successful career as a driver he realized his passion lay in building and running cars, not driving them himself. He had been shocked by the death of national hero Antonio Ascari (father of Alberto) in 1925 and with the birth of his own son Alfredo 'Dino' he resolved to quit driving. His team's success with Alfa Romeo customer cars in the 1930s alongside the works team's relative failure got him the job as the marque's official entrant. From 1933 Enzo oversaw Alfa's entire motor racing operation including multiple wins in the sports car races Mille Miglia and Targa Floria. The high point was Scuderia Ferrari driver Tazio Nuvolari, a memorable figure of the era, claiming one of racing's great upset victories at the 1935 German Grand Prix against the Nazi-Government-funded Mercedes and Auto Union cars.

The lasting achievement of that stage in his life was not a single result or performance, but an emblem he created to race with. It first appeared on the Alfa Romeo machinery he raced himself and then on his own cars. The origin of Ferrari's iconic badge is still contested but the most popular story goes that Enzo had visited the parents of a famous flying ace, Francesco Baracca, who had flown with his brother Alfredo Ferrari Jr. (both Alfredo Jr. and Sr. died in a 1916 Italian flu epidemic). Baracca used to fly with a black horse rearing up on its hind legs, painted on the side of his warplane. The Prancing Horse (or, as it is more strikingly known in Italian, *Cavallino Rampante*) would evolve from its first use and, once Enzo had added the canary yellow of his home town Modena's flag as the background, and the Italian tricolour stripe along the top, the most famous logo in the automotive industry was born.

An argument with Alfa Romeo boss Ugo Gobbato resulted in Enzo leaving the company in 1939, saddled with an exit clause that restricted him from racing or designing rival cars for four years. Even so, he found a way to produce two cars for Alberto Ascari and Lotario Rangoni to race in the 1940 Mille Miglia. The Second World War put an end to his new company Auto Avio Costruzioni's business of supplying racing parts to other teams. AAC were tasked with producing equipment for Mussolini's army from their factory in Modena. After it was severely damaged by Allied bombing, they relocated to Maranello and another piece of the Ferrari jigsaw fell into place. Enzo founded Ferrari S.p.A. in 1947.

In the postwar recovery years Enzo Ferrari's goal was quite simple: to build great racing cars and to beat his former paymasters at Alfa Romeo. In 1946 an offshoot of governing body the FIA codified a set of rules for different categories of single-seater racing. The premier category of these was to be known as Formula 1.

Initially the rules were balanced between cars with different engine capacities, allowing non-supercharged, 4.5-litre cars to race against 1.5-litre supercharged cars known as '*voiturettes*'. With a lack of racing machinery on hand and scarce resources in the wake of hostilities, grids needed all the cars they could get. There had been European championships in the 1930s, and teams would pick and choose which races they attended depending on prestige and prize money. The FIA brought together the most important grands prix to decide a World Championship for the first time in 1950.

Although presenting a huge opportunity for the Scuderia Ferrari, Alfa Romeo were still a force to be reckoned with. They continued their early postwar success with the dominant Alfa Romeo 158/50, which in the hands of Juan Manuel Fangio and Giuseppe Farina won all six races of the debut season – Farina taking the drivers' title. A year later and it was Fangio who scored three wins out of seven in the 1.5-litre Alfa 159 to take the drivers' crown.

However, in 1951 Enzo Ferrari put his faith in a 4.5-litre engine and the skills of established driver Alberto Ascari and new-to-the-team José Froilán González. In that second season of the new championship, at the British Grand Prix at Silverstone, Argentinian driver Froilán 'the Pampas Bull' González wrestled his Ferrari 375F1 to the Scuderia's first official F1 grand prix victory. Enzo had beaten the all-conquering Alfas with his own car. Reflecting on that first win, Ferrari would later write: 'I cried for joy. But my tears of enthusiasm were mixed with those of sorrow because I thought, today I have killed my mother.' It might have been a histrionic response, but Alfa Romeo's demise was closer than even he realized.

Ferrari would build on that Silverstone success with two further wins for Ascari, in Germany and the elation of his home race at Monza. The momentum continued. In 1952 Italian racing icon Ascari claimed Ferrari's first championship, winning six of the seven races that year – Ferrari's domination was so complete that team-mate Piero Taruffi won the other while Ascari was away competing at Indianapolis. Finally beaten and unable to finance its F1 programme, Alfa Romeo then shocked the racing world by withdrawing at the end of the 1952 season, leaving Ascari and Ferrari virtually unopposed for another championship the following year. Ferrari had supplanted the great racing company as its nation's premier team.

Ferrari's dominance of the Italian racing landscape didn't stop at the boundaries of the race track; even visually, Ferrari remains closely associated with the colour red. Rules first written for the Gordon Bennett Cup in the early 1900s had national teams in specific colours: France in Blue, Germany in White and Italy in Rosso Corsa red. Late-to-the-party Britain had to opt for Shamrock green, later to be defined as British Racing Green.

The way Ferrari came to supplant Alfa and all other Italian car makers was best summarized by motorsport journalist Denis Jenkinson's obituary for Enzo in 1988: 'When you spoke of Ferrari you could be referring to the man, to his cars or merely the image of Italian racing, and red racing cars at that. An exciting-looking red car in the street would bring only one word from an Italian enthusiast: 'Ferrari' – even though it might be a Maserati, an Alfa Romeo, a Lancia, a de Tomaso, an Iso Rivolta or a Lamborghini.'

An all-red F1 car that was not a Ferrari would be bordering on sacrilege. Even when Alfa Romeo returned to F1 in 2019 as the title partner of the Sauber team, it would mix red with large chunks of white and black on its liveries.

A Deadly Obsession

Ferrari biographer Brock Yates wrote: 'If Enzo Ferrari did nothing else, he built racing cars that were stronger and safer than they needed to be'. For a man consumed by speed, Enzo prided himself on building what he deemed to be the safest cars. Yet Ferrari's World Championship and sports car success came at a terrible human toll. Tragedy became interwoven into the story of the great team, fuelling a legend that drivers were willing to drive beyond the limits of what was safe or possible to satisfy *Il Commendatore*. Despite losing Alfa Romeo team-mates Ugo Sivocci and Antonio Ascari, Enzo would display a cold indifference to many of his drivers. They were employees like anyone else – the cars were his creation, his pride and joy; the men sitting in them could be replaced.

One well-told story sums up this attitude better than most. In 1957, popular Italian Eugenio Castellotti, known at home simply as *Il Bello*, was killed driving a Ferrari sports car he was testing at the Modena Autodrome, an accident portrayed vividly in Michael Mann's 2023 film *Ferrari*. After hitting a kerb at high speed he was thrown nearly 100 metres (330 feet) from the car and died instantly. Peter Collins, star of the Ferrari F1 team who was viewing the test, went to check on Castellotti and then came back to update Enzo on his condition. Collins would later recall that, after a moment of sombre reflection, Enzo looked up at him and said simply: '*E la macchina?*' ('And the car?').

It was not until the late 1960s that seat belts were universally adopted by F1 drivers; most raced without being strapped in. Better to take your chances being thrown from a car, the logic went, than to be trapped inside a burning one. Peter Collins was thrown from his Ferrari after clipping a bank at 100 mph (160 km/h) at the Nürburgring during the 1958 German Grand Prix and never regained consciousness. That same year, Luigi Musso, angered at the friendship of Ferrari's British team-mates Collins and Mike Hawthorn, which he felt bordered on a conspiracy against him, had been thrown from his car after driving too hard to catch Hawthorn in the French Grand Prix at Reims.

And all this in the wake of Alfonso de Portago's catastrophic death in the 1957 Mille Miglia. Less than 75 miles (about 120 km) before the finish, de Portago and long-time friend and co-driver Ed Nelson driving a Ferrari 335S were spun at 150 mph (240 km/h) into a roadside crowd by what is believed to have been a burst tyre. Ten spectators died including two children hit by a concrete milestone that was ripped from the ground by Portago's car and thrown into the crowd. Italy mourned, the Mille Miglia was cancelled indefinitely and many blamed Enzo Ferrari for pushing his drivers to race on worn tyres, although a post-race inquiry found that the tyre had more likely been cut by striking a cat's eye in the road.

A certain hostility had grown towards Enzo Ferrari in the Italian media by this point. *Il Commendatore* was soon being compared to the Roman god Saturn who, the great tales of the past said, had survived by raising and then devouring his children. It was a charge Enzo could not escape because it kept happening. At the Italian Grand prix of 1961 Ferrari drivers Phil Hill and Wolfgang von Trips, the son of German nobility, were racing each other for the title in the famous 'Shark Nose' Ferrari 156. Von Trips was slow off the line and immediately involved in midfield battles.

On the opening lap, racing down towards Parabolica, Jim Clark, slipstreaming in the Lotus, looked to make a move down the inside. Just as the Scotsman went for the inside line, von Trips moved over – the rear wheel of the Ferrari 156 car touched the front of Clark's Lotus, sending the German's car violently to the left and into the outside embankment. Von Trips was fatally thrown from the car, which would continue in an uncontrolled spin through the air and into the crowd. It claimed the lives of 14 spectators, injuring countless others. The race was not stopped. Similar to the Le Mans tragedy of 1955 organizers did not want the approach roads jammed with spectators leaving the circuit when ambulances needed to attend the scene. Italians being killed by a Ferrari at the Italian Grand Prix sent the national press into a frenzy.

A similar reaction followed the 1967 Monaco Grand Prix, when Italian driver Lorenzo Bandini died in horrifying circumstances. Having lost control of his car on the exit of the tunnel section, Bandini's car hurtled towards the corner where Ascari had taken the plunge into the harbour over a decade before. Once it came to a stop, Bandini's car was resting upside down on straw bales and on fire, with the Italian trapped in his car. The popular Italian suffered extensive burns and after several days of unimaginable agony Bandini died in hospital. As with the Le Mans tragedy, the inadequacy of the circuit design and the trackside safety provisions were to blame, but the fury of the press was largely aimed at Enzo and a team many Italians were starting to think was plagued by some dark hoodoo. The following year Enzo decided Ferrari would not show up at the Monaco Grand Prix, as he felt the circuit was not safe enough.

Plenty of drivers of the time were killed racing for other teams, but the story of it happening to Ferrari drivers seemed to take on a deeper meaning for people. Phil Hill, who had become America's first World Champion after von Trips's accident suggested why: 'There was something about the ambience at Ferrari that did seem to spur drivers to their deaths. Perhaps it was the intense sibling rivalry atmosphere Ferrari fostered, his failure to rank the drivers and his fickleness with the favourites.' While it was said in the 1950s and 60s that the men NASA needed for America's space programme needed 'the right stuff', this was perhaps also true of Ferrari and its team. Enzo's drivers needed to put it all on the line to win. Anything short of winning was failure.

There is one final tragedy to recount from the early 1980s and one which may well have touched the remote *Il Commendatore*. When Niki Lauda had walked out of the team two races before the end of the 1977 season the Scuderia had moved quickly to sign a Canadian wildcat who McLaren thought was going to prove too expensive. Gilles Villeneuve had dutifully played back-up to Jody Scheckter in his 1979 championship-winning year. In 1981 he had scored improbable victories in the ill-handling Ferrari 126CK at Monaco and Jarama, despite it being 'a big red Cadillac', but in 1982 the car was handling better, things were looking up. His teammate was Frenchman Didier Pironi and they seemed to be getting along fine . . . until they reached Imola for the San Marino Grand Prix. The race at Maranello's closest circuit had limited entrants due to a stand-off between some of the teams and the governing body. Only 14 cars would compete, so Ferrari's drivers reasoned they should put on a show for the home crowd. A gentleman's agreement had, Villeneuve believed, existed before the race that whichever of them led into the first corner would win the race. It had been Villeneuve. Late in the race, after several laps of swapping places, Pironi passed Villeneuve for the lead and held on to it, claiming the race win. A fuming Villeneuve swore he would never speak to his French team-mate again.

It was a promise that came to pass. In a practice session ahead of the next race, the Belgian Grand Prix at Zolder, Villeneuve, still angry beyond the point of reason and determined to beat Pironi's lap time, went out to set a new mark of his own. At one corner he approached Jochen Mass, who had moved off the racing line to let Villeneuve through just as the French Canadian, with his foot firmly kept in, went the same way. Villeneuve's car went up in the air and he was flung into trackside catch fencing, dying almost instantly. Villeneuve is still considered to have been one of 'the old man's' favourites and a picture of the two men sharing a laugh together greets youngsters who walk into the Ferrari Driver Academy building at Maranello. How do young Ferrari drivers like Leclerc or Oliver Bearman feel seeing such an image on arrival? What message does it send? The aura and the suggestion is that here are two Ferrari men, laughing at caution, united in glee at the desire to question what's possible; to just go a little bit faster.

Pironi, who now seemingly had an open path to the championship, would shatter both his legs a few months later when he drove into the back of Alain Prost's Renault during a rainy practice session at Hockenheim. The injury ended Pironi's title hopes and his driving career on the spot. It would fall to Keke Rosberg (father of Nico) to claim the drivers' title for Williams by five points, with only a single race win all season. Ferrari had the consolation of picking up the 1982 constructors' trophy and again in 1983 with Arnoux and Tambay – but it would not be until 1999 that they picked up another top prize at the end-of-season FIA gala. While Pironi was recovering in hospital from injuries that had almost necessitated a double amputation, he received flowers and gifts from Enzo with the words, 'to the 1982 World Champion'. Pironi would be killed in a powerboat racing accident several years later off the Isle of Wight, a crash that killed all three crew.

Veni, Vidi, Vici, Veto

After toppling Alfa Romeo, witnessing the alarming rise and sudden departure of Mercedes and the fading away of Maserati in the 1950s, Ferrari's ascendency continued. Enzo may have been knocked off his stride by the British *garagista* teams and the arrival of lightweight, rear-engine cars, but bounced back with Carlo Chiti's beautiful Ferrari 156, which won a title for Phil Hill in 1961, and the Ferrari 158 designed by Mauro Forghieri, which gave John Surtees his only world crown in 1964. A decade later it was Forghieri's 312T which Niki Lauda used to maximum effect claiming the 1975 and 1977 drivers' titles only losing out in 1976, the year in which he survived an almost unsurvivable fiery crash at the Nürburgring. Jody Scheckter followed that up in 1979, Ferrari's last Drivers' Championship of the twentieth century.

Ferrari sports cars enjoyed success at Le Mans, dominating the race in the early 1960s and engaging in a fierce duel with the Ford GT40 in 1966.

Ferrari were unequivocally the biggest brand in motor racing, and that gave Enzo Ferrari considerable power.

In the late 1970s Brabham team owner Bernie Ecclestone, who had bought Jack Brabham's team in 1971, was beginning to organize the other team bosses to lobby the governing body. His Formula One Constructors Association (FOCA) wanted a better distribution of the money, a bigger share of F1's commercial rights. The manufacturer teams, such as Ferrari and Renault who had major corporate backing, sided with the FIA's race organizers, the Fédération Internationale du Sport Automobile, or FISA. They preferred to be on the side of the sport's rule-makers. As the factions politicked their way through the 1980 season, threatening or boycotting races and even rendering the 1980 Spanish Grand Prix result ineligible for the World Championship, the hostilities were dubbed the FISA vs FOCA war.

Peace only broke out after the signing of a Concorde Agreement in 1981 (named for the FIA office address in Place de la Concorde, Paris, as opposed to the sentiment of the meeting). Ecclestone had long since recognized that F1 was almost meaningless without the inclusion of Ferrari and thus the Scuderia were able to exact two major concessions from their Concorde negotiations. They would end up with a bonus simply for showing up and lending the cachet of Ferrari's name to the World Championship, and they would have a veto.

The sport remains bound by cycles of similar deals. The most recent Concorde Agreement was signed in 2021 and runs until the end of 2025. Any entrant wishing to compete and take a slice of Formula 1 revenues in 2026 and beyond will need to sign up to the terms laid out in the next one. The 1981 version was significant in that it enshrined Ferrari's right to veto any rule change the team thought did not serve their best interests. The veto itself is a remarkable piece of business in a belligerent sport like Formula 1, but Ferrari has been remarkably cautious in how it has exercised this power over the decades. It has also made it clear there is no world in which it would continue to race without it. Recent uses – or threats of use, which carry just as much weight – include in 2015, over setting a maximum price customers could be charged by manufacturers for engines and gearboxes, or in 2021 over the suggestion that Mercedes boss Toto Wolff might become Formula 1 CEO. The role instead went to former Ferrari team boss Stefano Domenicali.

When the clause remained a part of the most recent Concorde Agreement, the eighth in the series, company chairman Louis C. Camilleri alluded to his perception of Ferrari's position in the sport, the power of the veto and its contention among some of the team's rivals all at the same time. Speaking to the *Financial Times*, Camilleri said: 'We have retained the veto rights and those are critical not just for Ferrari but for F1 as well. Will we ever use it? I doubt it. Just the fact of having it, does it get people's attention? I think so. It's something I think is important. Some of the teams think it's anachronistic and shouldn't be there but on the other hand some think it's a good idea to have an "adult" in the room.'

It's tricky to argue with the idea of a veto that's in place with the complicit agreement of the other F1 teams – but deep down, it seems contrary to the idea of fair play and a level playing field. And does such elevation help Ferrari or, as we've seen in recent years, hinder it? Ferrari's consistent lack of championship titles in over a decade seems so much more visible, so much more pronounced, because of the name and the history. Any athlete in the world will tell you that no amount of legendary status will bring you track victories; only hard work, talent and ability do that. Ferrari have certainly accomplished that in their time.

In this book, we'll be looking precisely at how the Ferrari team has won, lost and rebuilt. We'll be examining what 75 years of racing has brought to Ferrari and modern Formula 1. Only one team can cite the drivers Ascari, Fangio, Hawthorn, Hill, Surtees, Lauda, Scheckter, Schumacher and Räikkönen – World Champions all – in their history. Or the names of Prost, Mansell, Vettel and Alonso, World Champion drivers who could not bring a title back to Maranello. Only one team can lay claim to a vast number of 'firsts' in the sport. Only one team can rise again, and again, and again.

2

Dı MONTEZEMOLO

'Enzo Ferrari built the myth of Ferrari, Luca di Montezemolo marketed it. He made the Ferrari we know today.'

Guenther Steiner

Much has been made of Ferrari's current championship drought, but the team of the late 1980s and early 1990s found itself in a far deeper funk than the modern equivalent has ever experienced. Between Jody Scheckter's title in 1979 and Michael Schumacher's in 2000, two decades passed without a Ferrari driver winning the championship. Worst of all, roughly halfway through that lean run the inevitable happened.

Enzo Ferrari's death in August 1988 plunged his company into an existential crisis. As was the case with titans such as Henry Ford and Walt Disney, great companies synonymous with their larger-than-life founder one day have to face the reality they are no longer around to lead. Decisions that once rested on their shoulders start being passed on to people operating in the shadow they left behind.

Some immediate relief came in the short term – less than a month after Enzo's death, Gerhard Berger led team-mate Michele Alboreto in a hugely emotional and fortuitous one–two finish at the Italian Grand Prix, denying McLaren a clean sweep of victories that season. It was a win that seemed to have been predestined from on-high: Ayrton Senna had been leading until two laps from the finish when he collided with hapless Williams stand-in driver Jean-Louis Schlesser. But the win was the one bright spot in an otherwise dismal season on track.

Enzo's control over the empire he built had diminished in the last two decades of his life. In 1969, Fiat had purchased 50 per cent of the company – the caveat to the deal was that Enzo would remain in sole charge of the racing team. By the year of his death, Fiat's controlling stake had risen to 90 per cent. By the time of his passing, things were looking bleak. The F1 team had slipped off the perch of the late 1970s and early 1980s as the benchmark for the rest to beat. The road car division, which had been taken off his hands, was financially strapped as the global economy stuttered. Some felt the core value of Ferrari's brand, the key to its continued success and popularity, was waning. Without Enzo, that problem was only felt more keenly.

Replacing Enzo with someone who encapsulated his personality, his drive and his passion would not simply happen at the click of a finger. Current Formula 1 CEO Stefano Domenicali joined Ferrari in 1991, rising through almost every department in the race team to eventually become team boss. He remembers the uncertainty which touched every part of the business when he arrived. 'It was a company that was clearly in a situation of evolution,' Domenicali recalled, politely. 'Every year there was someone new coming in, resetting. There was not a clear strategy on the product point of view, on the marketing point of view, on the sporting point of view. It was a very, very difficult period for Ferrari at that time.'

In *The Story of Ferrari*, author Stuart Codling put it more succinctly: 'Enzo's death had left a power vacuum, with all the petty manoeuvrings that entailed. Another strong leader was required.'

Fortunately, a popular figure from the team's past, one who had both experience of Formula 1 success and the blessing of Fiat's Agnelli family, was waiting in the wings. Gianni Agnelli quickly realized that to replace

Enzo he needed a character who inhabited many of the founder's same qualities – the blinding will to win, the utter devotion to the Ferrari brand and the experience of building successful racing teams. Who better than a man Enzo had personally picked to run the race team in the past? Enter Luca di Montezemolo, who had been team manager for Niki Lauda's first championship season in the mid-1970s.

'When I returned, it was big trouble,' remembers di Montezemolo. 'Big, big trouble. A lot had to change to make the team successful and to rebuild what Ferrari had been before.'

The decisions di Montezemolo would make in the 1990s would help rebuild the sport's greatest marque. Arguably, he created the shadow under which the modern Ferrari team still competes today. To understand di Montezemolo and the situation he found Ferrari in when he returned as president in December 1991, a rewind back to his first stint in charge is required.

Summoned to Maranello

While Agnelli's call in 1991 would reshape the destiny of Ferrari in Formula 1, it was another phone call which put di Montezemolo on the radar of Enzo Ferrari in the first place. Born into the Italian aristocracy, it would have been easy to paint him as a child of immense privilege and unearned opportunity, such was the scale of his rise to prominence in Formula 1. But di Montezemolo's personality and his leadership qualities are what immediately set him on a course to the top. He had a brief stint as a rally driver for the Lancia team in 1971 with Daniele Audetto as his co-driver, but his chosen profession was law. After graduating from Rome's Sapienza University with a degree in law, he studied for a Master's in international commercial law at New York's Columbia University. But it was a stint working with a local radio station in Italy that would put him on the radar of the most revered Italian in the world.

'During a radio show I had this big polemic with a guy who said racing was dangerous and a sport for rich people,' di Montezemolo told me. 'Enzo Ferrari was listening and he called the live transmission and he wanted to meet me, at least on the phone. He said, "Congratulations, you have the balls to answer in this way to this guy", and he invited me to go to Maranello. I was in the process of going to the United States and Columbia University. When I came back [to Italy] for a few days, I went to see him. At the end of the meeting he said, "I need a guy like you, because I'm in the prison of the engineering technicians. They can tell me a lot of bullshit." You have to consider at that time Ferrari had not won a championship for years, the last one was John Surtees. So when I finished university in July 1973, I made a non-stop flight from New York to Italy, and went straight to Maranello to start working for him. I started to work as Enzo Ferrari's assistant. After a few months he made me team manager.'

Fresh out of university to leading the most famous F1 team in the world. By any standards, it was a remarkable appointment. To add some context, in 2024 Alpine appointed the 36-year-old Oliver Oakes, who was labelled the second youngest 'team principal' in F1 history behind Christian Horner, who became Red Bull boss at 31. Di Montezemolo shadowed Enzo Ferrari for the rest of 1973, a season in which the team failed to score a single podium. Rising to team manager the following season, he found himself working with a known entity in Swiss racer Clay Regazzoni, as well as another new signing, a relatively unknown Austrian driver named Niki Lauda. He and di Montezemolo would strike up what turned out to be a lifelong bond.

'It was quite unusual to have someone who was 25 years old as the manager of one of the most important teams in the world,' di Montezemolo said. 'That's why Niki and I grew so close, we both started very young at Ferrari with a lot of pressure and a lot to manage. He became one of the best friends of my life.'

The respect was mutual. In Lauda's compelling biography *To Hell and Back* he wrote 'Montezemolo, Ferrari's team chief, was a fully fledged protégé of the Agnelli (Fiat) dynasty; he was very young but he was good. Because of his social background he was largely proof against the daily round of intrigue and that meant that he could concentrate on the real job in hand, something of a privileged position for a Ferrari chief. Off the top of my head I can't think of anyone in that position before or after who enjoyed the same freedom.'

As team manager, di Montezemolo set about cleaning up a messy organizational structure. Enzo's team was loaded with great minds and passionate disciples to the cause, but was dogged by in-fighting and – as Lauda alluded – petty politics. Designer Mauro Forghieri, the Adrian Newey of his era, was given the overarching role of technical director. Beneath him were two figures, a head of the engine department and a head of the chassis department, not too dissimilar from the kind of structure most teams operate with today. 'Before I arrived there were a lot of polemics between the chassis and engine teams. No-one really wanted to take charge, so I made those roles more clear,' di Montezemolo explained. It would be a philosophy that would serve Ferrari well in both of his stints at the team.

'My relationship with Enzo Ferrari was not good, it was fantastic,' di Montezemolo said. 'He hired me, totally out of Formula 1, a completely different world, but he trusted what he saw in me. And then he put me in the best condition to succeed. He backed me all the time, whatever decision I made. I learned a lot from him and to be honest, in the second half of the 1970s Ferrari was like what we eventually had in Michael's [Schumacher] time, a dream team.'

To succeed in an environment like Formula 1, at a team as scrutinized as Ferrari, clearly required a certain something. 'He had this aura about him,' veteran journalist Maurice Hamilton said. 'He was a handsome-looking man, well-bred, well-mannered. Utterly charming and with a reasonably good grasp of English. He was easy to understand, spoke well. He spoke with this dramatic way . . . you would be mesmerized by him, quite honestly.'

Success with Lauda and di Montezemolo was swift. At the fourth race of 1974, the Spanish Grand Prix, Lauda would claim his first F1 win. A famous picture from this event shows Lauda's car approaching the man waving the chequered flag. To his left is di Montezemolo, dressed in a sharp dark blue suit, leaping off the ground, his arms aloft straight up in the air. The young team manager's exuberant personality became a common theme, as Hamilton recalled. 'At Brands Hatch later that season Niki got blocked in the pit-lane and [di Montezemolo] went berserk, in typical Italian fashion throwing his hands around. He was just wonderful to watch.'

Lauda was runner-up in 1974 and then won the championship in 1975. He likely would have won the title again the following year were it not for the fiery crash at the Nürburgring which almost claimed his life and left him severely burned. By that time, having re-set the structure of the team, di Montezemolo had left the company, promoted within the Fiat organization. Daniele Audetto, his former rally co-driver at Lancia replaced him.

Niki Lauda was uneasy at the winds of change. 'The first hint of trouble came in 1976 with the departure of my friend and ally Luca Montezemolo who had to make a career for himself and couldn't afford to stay on the lower rungs of the ladder as team chief indefinitely,' he wrote in his autobiography. 'His successor, Audetto, as fraught a personality as any surrounding Ferrari, promptly got involved in the day-to-day intrigues in an effort to carve out a niche for himself.'

It was Audetto who was in charge when the F1 championship reached the Nürburgring in the summer of 1976. Lauda, who was leading the championship by more than two race wins, tried to organize a boycott of the event on safety grounds, but lost the drivers' vote by one. His argument was that the Nürburgring was just too long to be marshalled safely. The eerie footage of Lauda's crash was repeated in Ron Howard's biopic *Rush* – the Ferrari 312T2, loaded to the brim with fuel, spins out of control and into a barrier, immediately erupting into flames before being hit by another car. Lauda was trapped in the flames. Four drivers stopped to help, but it was Arturo Merzario, who had knowledge of Ferrari's Klippan seatbelts, who was able to get Lauda free from the blazing wreckage. The Austrian, severely burned, was given the last rites in hospital but remarkably, 33 days later, complete with newly transplanted eyelids, lined up to race at Monza.

With rain pouring down at the Japanese Grand Prix, the final race of the season, Lauda retired his car early on, handing the championship to McLaren's James Hunt. Lauda claimed a second championship in 1977, but it was not the same with di Montezemolo gone from Maranello. The Austrian's relationship with Enzo Ferrari changed after his aborted 1976 race at Mount Fuji. 'He reacted like any other team boss who sees his chance slipping away,' he wrote in *To Hell and Back*. 'There was none of the Ferrari greatness about him. Officially he supported me and accepted my decision. But even the telephone conversation I had with him from the airport lounge in Tokyo was non-committal, heartless . . . he never seemed to want to understand the anxiety felt by a driver who had been through a serious shunt, never gave any indication of wanting to go on together towards a new and better season.'

Indeed Enzo signed Carlos Reutemann to be the No.1 Ferrari driver for 1977, believing that Lauda had lost it. After three races in the next season the Austrian had already put Enzo's favourite Argentinian 'in his place'.

A Very English GTO

The structure di Montezemolo put in place served the team well. After Niki Lauda's drivers' title in 1977, Ferrari backed it up with a championship for Jody Sheckter in 1979 and constructors' titles in 1982 and 1983. Patrick Tambay was drafted in to replace his good friend Gilles Villeneuve in 1982 and he was subsequently replaced in 1984 by Italian driver Michele Alboreto who had won races for Tyrrell despite the team struggling with normally aspirated engines. Alboreto led the championship in mid-1985, but his challenge faded at the end of the year. In 1986, with the bulky and cumbersome Ferrari F1/86 car, Alboreto and Stefan Johannsen failed to claim a win, pole position or fastest lap.

Formula 1 was changing in a major way. As teams abandoned the 3.0-litre, naturally aspirated engines for 1.5-litre turbocharged units, two British teams rose to prominence: McLaren, powered by the TAG-Porsche engine, and Williams-Honda. Ferrari's first V6 turbo engine in 1981 and 1982 had been the envy of the field but by 1985, the unreliability of the same unit helped unravel Alboreto's title charge. Enzo Ferrari had grown irritable with the events of the new decade. The company founder saw a potential saviour in McLaren's superstar car designer, John Barnard, an engineer revered by his peers. 'Barnard not only raised the bar, he raised the game,' wrote F1 technical journalist Giorgio Piola for *Motor Sport* in 2021. The Englishman's work was often groundbreaking: his McLaren MP4/1 was the first F1 car to be built with a carbon fibre chassis, a landmark moment in terms of safety in the sport and something quickly copied by rivals – carbon fibre chassis are standard in F1 today.

In mid-1986, *Il Commendatore* dispatched new team manager, Marco Piccinini, to lure the Englishman over to the team. The desperation to steady the ship can probably be gauged by the remarkable concessions Ferrari was willing to make to get their man.

'I'm at McLaren, it's 1986 and I start getting phone calls from a guy in London saying there's a team in Europe that wants you to work for them,' Barnard told the *Beyond the Grid* podcast in 2020. 'My answer was very simple, "Thank you, no, I don't want to go to Europe". That's all he said, "a team in Europe". Back then there was Ferrari, Alfa, Matra, ATS. So theoretically there were those options. Eventually it's pretty obvious it's Ferrari.

'I go to London, go and see who it is. It's Marco Piccinini. Even then, I was not predisposed to do it. They'd been throwing all these numbers at me, big pay cheque, but I didn't want to do it. Then eventually Marco came back and said, "What about if you could set up something in England?" I said, "Well, that's interesting, that's a different take." So it was actually them who suggested it.'

Given the option of staying put at home, Barnard accepted the big-money offer. The most famous Italian team would now be building the majority of its F1 car in Surrey, just north of Woking, the long-time home of rivals McLaren. Barnard set up shop on the river in Guildford, in a facility which created a bizarre method of working between two countries. Working from the carefully named Guildford Technical Office, (giving it the acronym GTO), Barnard and his team faxed their completed designs page by page through to Maranello, where they were painstakingly assembled. Barnard was a pioneer of many things and that includes remote working.

Alboreto would later liken the Guildford and Maranello set-up to a doctor performing brain surgery over the phone. The Guildford Technical Office was a huge step away from anything the team had done before. This was a team founded by a man who rarely left Emilia-Romagna, a man who had always been wary of the *garagistas* in the UK. Now an Englishman was guiding the production of Enzo's F1 cars from an English facility.

'I ended setting up more in England than they anticipated because I think they assumed I just wanted a few guys and a drawing board,' Barnard said. 'As it turned out I produced a whole factory, with a complete composite facility, a machine shop. In those days we were making the chassis, the suspension. All that stuff. The bodywork was made in

Maranello but all the serious stuff was done by us because I didn't trust anyone else to do it.'

It immediately set Barnard against the majority of Ferrari's workforce in Italy. The motorsport press, so used to writing about the grid's most passionately, unashamedly Italian squad, had to come to terms with its sudden move towards dual nationality. The *tifosi* were initially overjoyed at Barnard's arrival, and he was soon dubbed *Il Mago* (The Magician). But his insistence on operating from the UK had already created a working condition that could not last long term. 'There was great suspicion,' Barnard said. 'I don't care who you are or what you're doing, there's always the fallback option of – "well this wasn't done here, that was done there". If you have a problem it's easy to immediately start looking at the other lot and say – well it's them, not us [at fault].'

The new set-up created a toxic work environment. His cars were not the problem. Gerhard Berger won the final two races in 1987, although just the singular Monza victory followed in 1988. Barnard always maintained that his first proper race car, the one which had been the focus of most of his attention, was the 1989 F640 – the final product was gorgeous, a red car featuring striking black front and rear wings. It was the first to feature a semi-automatic gearbox operated by two paddles on a steering wheel – another Barnard innovation which has filtered through to all kinds of racing and road car machinery. New signing Nigel Mansell dubbed *Il Leone* (The Lion) by the Italian press, took the roaring 640 with its V12, to victory on debut in Brazil. Even so, McLaren remained the dominant force and Mansell and Berger managed just one win apiece after that. The 1989 car's successor, the F641, continued the trend of being the best-looking car on the grid. Along with the Museum of Modern Art in New York, which holds one of the beautiful chassis, there was a future team boss who was a fan.

'That John Barnard Ferrari was stunning, absolutely stunning,' Red Bull boss Christian Horner told me, recalling a trip to a circuit as a teenager.

'I loved those cars. I loved the cleanness. The red cars, the black wings. I remember going to watch a tyre test, it would have been in 1990, and Ferrari had the V12 . . . it was like an orchestra. It was completely different to anything else. There's always been that mythical specialness to Ferrari and those Barnard cars captured that perfectly.'

Mansell had been the last driver personally invited to drive for Ferrari by Enzo, although his debut was at the beginning of 1989, meaning his two seasons at the team were at the most tumultuous and uncertain point in the team's history. On a personal level, he was just what the team needed. 'They loved him,' added Horner, who grew up supporting Mansell in whichever colours he raced in. 'I mean, a Brummie being called *Il Leone*! They took him to their hearts because he drove with real passion, he was a real fighter.'

But Mansell and team-mate Alain Prost's passion for Ferrari quickly waned – something which would happen to other big-name drivers brought to the squad in later decades. Even the combination of supreme talent in the car and Barnard's prowess outside of it could not get Ferrari a title. Prost might have won the championship were it not for one of the most controversial championship deciders in the sport's history.

At the 1990 Japanese Grand Prix, Prost lined up alongside old McLaren team-mate Ayrton Senna. A year earlier at the same Suzuka circuit Prost had won the title when their two Marlboro-liveried McLarens had collided at the final chicane. Senna's had continued and finished the race, only to be disqualified afterwards for cutting the chicane. An incensed Senna never forgot the slight against him. Twelve months on, Senna lined up on pole position, which FIA President, Frenchman Jean Marie Balestre insisted should be on the inside of the grid and not on the racing line. Senna's protests were batted aside, just as his appeal had been squashed the previous year. But it was the Ferrari man who got the better start. Senna had already decided what he would do. If Prost got the better start, neither car would be exiting Turn 2. As Prost entered Turn 1 ahead, Senna, who had the points lead in the championship, simply went straight on and took himself and Prost out of the race, making himself World Champion.

Regardless of the outcome of the championship, the highs and lows of that 1990 season had proven to be the breaking point for the two-country experiment for Ferrari, with tensions behind the scenes reaching nuclear proportions. Former Lancia rally manager, now promoted to Ferrari team boss, Cesare Fiorio decided the UK operation could no longer continue and gave an ultimatum to Ferrari's chief designer. 'It couldn't work, a series of dynamics had been triggered that for me were unacceptable: when things went well it was thanks to the UK, when things went badly it was Maranello's fault. I asked Barnard to move to Italy, but he refused so we said goodbye.'

While the Guildford hub complicated the workflow and effectively set two sides of the same team against each other, to many, the request to set up shop in England was a line crossed. Maurice Hamilton, who has covered Ferrari throughout his long career, suggested Barnard's insistence on working from the UK meant he was doomed to fail from the beginning. Hamilton used the example of the man Barnard replaced when he accepted the contract, fellow Englishman Harvey Postlethwaite, who departed Ferrari at the start of 1987. 'Harvey was as different to Barnard as you could be in terms of dealing with Ferrari. Harvey went there and immersed himself in Italy, became fluent in Italian, lived locally,' Hamilton said. 'I went to a restaurant with him near Maranello once and it was like royalty was arriving. It was extraordinary. He said, "Oh, this happens all the time". They loved him because he became one of them. He was a Ferrari man, a member of the club. Barnard wasn't. Ferrari people never saw him as one of them and that was a bit of a slap in the face.'

Mansell followed Barnard out of the door at the end of 1990, upset that the team had rallied around Prost's championship ambitions that year (at one point Prost had believed Mansell's chassis to be faster and had got the team to secretly swap it over, but Nigel spotted the change). Mansell was so broken by his two years at Ferrari he announced his retirement, only to be snatched up by Frank Williams the following year – in 1992, Mansell would finally win the world title for the Williams team.

Hand-Picked by Enzo

'When Ferrari died, there was a moment in which Fiat felt obliged to put Fiat people in charge of the team. And this is a quite different job to that,' said di Montezemolo, who in 1985 had been named manager of the organizing committee for the 1990 World Cup in Italy. He had stayed in good favour with Fiat boss Agnelli but had not been directly involved with the company for a while. Fiat had installed Piero Fusaro as president after Enzo Ferrari's death – Fusaro's name has not reverberated through the pages of F1 history like that of his successor. His job was an unenviable one: to guide Ferrari through the wake of Enzo's death and the uncertainty that had come with it. Fusaro was seen as someone with limited influence and his time at the helm was marked by tension and in-fighting, and not just from the Guildford set-up which had so bitterly split the team.

Like Mansell a year earlier, by 1991 Prost was discovering the limits for his love of the Prancing Horse, a situation exacerbated by the 'truck' of a car the team built that year. A divorce was looming, and many close to the team recognized why. 'I could see what was coming,' former driver Alboreto said in an interview at the end of 1991. 'The Fiat men were beginning to arrive, taking over, and I didn't like what I saw, the way things were being done.'

Fusaro and sporting director Fiorio were also at odds. The latter had approached Prost's bitter rival Senna about a potential 1991 contract but had found the talks immediately stopped from above. 'We had agreed on everything,' Fiorio would tell *La Stampa* years later. 'But Fusaro opposed it. Perhaps it was to avoid antagonizing [Prost], or perhaps because he wanted to make me understand that he was in charge.' Fusaro, for his part, has suggested Prost got wind of the Senna talks and went straight to the Agnellis to get it snuffed out. One other interviewee I spoke to for this book suggested Fusaro's account is the correct one but whatever the truth, there is perhaps no better example of the vacuum of power which existed after Enzo's death.

Fiorio would be sacked in the middle of the year, but little improved on track. Ferrari would not win a single race in 1991 – worst of all, they never came close. As seemed to be the case for this part of Prost's career, a decisive flashpoint came at Suzuka's Japanese Grand Prix. After finishing 40 seconds off the lead and having spent the race fighting a car with heavy steering around one of the most technically challenging circuits on the calendar, a fed-up Prost gave an interview that has gone down as one of the most infamous in Ferrari lore. 'It was like a horrible truck to drive,' Prost said. 'No pleasure at all.'

The quote poured petrol on an already fiery situation. Prost had broken the *omerta* which had always existed around Ferrari and the team's competitiveness. It bordered on sacrilege to suggest the car was the issue, even if it was so obviously the case. 'To be at Ferrari with a good car is fantastic; otherwise, everything is the driver's fault,' Alboreto said. 'I understand very well how Alain felt.'

The national press had a field day – the Frenchman had insulted Italy. In 1981, Gilles Villeneuve had got away with calling his car a 'big, red Cadillac' because of its brute force and terrible handling, but he had taken his Cadillac to a win at the most unlikely of places, Monaco. Prost was immediately sacked and replaced by Gianni Morbidelli at the final race and by Ivan Capelli for the following season. Weeks after Prost's departure, Agnelli stepped in decisively. Having seen how rudderless the Ferrari team was and how it was being torn apart from within, he knew decisive leadership was needed. Fusaro was sent packing, shuffled back into a role within the wider Fiat empire and was scarcely heard from in F1 circles again. Luca Colajanni, who had worked for di Montezemolo on the World Cup project and would become head of communications for Ferrari later in the decade, said there was no-one else his replacement could have been.

'In 1991, it was complete turmoil,' Colajanni told me. 'Mr Agnelli understood he needed a leader. And di Montezemolo was the right man, because if there's something di Montezemolo showed since the very beginning, it's the capacity to be a leader. Also he understood the capacity to interpret the values of Ferrari, the values that the founder of the company always pushed for, in the right way. He was the right man to properly succeed Enzo Ferrari. He was the right person because he worked with Enzo Ferrari when he was young, he was hand-picked by him. He also had certain of the same characteristics, not all, but certain characteristics which made him perfect. He understood crucially we needed to update ourselves and that's what we did.'

Di Montezemolo officially took the new job in December 1991, with the lessons of his first stint still firmly in his mind. He often talks about the conditions needed to win – the Ferrari of 1991 had very few of them. He found a team with some talented people, but with a messy organizational structure, no clear sense of who was in charge of what and a thick layer of fear stopping anyone from taking accountability.

'When I arrived, I remember I went to Maranello. I gathered people together and I asked, "Who built this car?" A simple question. But everyone just looked at each other.' Di Montezemolo quickly realized the key element of the Ferrari team which had existed in the mid-1970s needed to be quickly injected back into the team. In 2003, he explained his philosophy in an interview with American broadcaster Charlie Rose: 'I tried to identify priority goals. I tried to give motivation to the people. I tried to put the right people in the right positions, with a clear organization in term of responsibilities. I tried to push passion, creativity and, particularly in the difficult moments, said to them "Go ahead". When you enter into a company like Ferrari you need to be immediately involved in the culture, the history. It's like if you enter into a club, you need the badge. Enthusiasm, passion, this is our culture.'

Like few others before him, di Montezemolo understood that final point. Winning on track was one thing, but the pull and mystique of Ferrari was something few other teams could boast. Adding to the scale of his task was Ferrari's falling road car sales, which had become a victim of the global economy. In his mind, this only doubled the importance of getting the race team back on stable footing. 'There is not a direct victory in racing and increase in volume [of car sales], not at all,' di Montezemolo said. 'But it adds fuel on the Ferrari fire, the Ferrari myth. This is important.'

Over the next two decades, di Montezemolo would re-establish that myth. The winning days would return on the track. The road car business discovered a new lease of life. The aura of Ferrari grew to a level greater than Enzo ever achieved in his own lifetime. His influence still resonates today, even to those who never worked with him.

'To me, the guy is the king,' is the view of former Haas boss Guenther Steiner, who grew up in Italy's South Tyrol making him an ardent Ferrari and Niki Lauda fan. 'What he did for that company is incredible. It's why I always say – Enzo Ferrari built the myth of Ferrari, Luca di Montezemolo marketed it. He made the Ferrari we know today.'

To re-build the mystique, di Montezemolo first needed to get a handle on the race team. The blueprint already existed in the form of the 1970s team he had been part of. To recreate it, he first needed to find a version of himself – a loyal, committed team boss whose personality would drive the team. He needed a Mauro Forghieri, or two, but also a structure in which those brilliant and innovative minds could work freely and efficiently. And once that was all in place, he needed a version of Lauda, a driver who could make the crucial difference on the race track once all the other conditions were set. Fortunately, good candidates for each of those roles existed and, as 1991 rolled into 1992, di Montezemolo set about assembling what would become the greatest team the sport had ever seen.

3

DREAM TEAM

'It doesn't matter if the cat is black or white, as long as it eats the mouse.'

Luca Colajanni

With Luca di Montezemolo back at the helm of Ferrari, patience was the name of the game. The Formula 1 team he walked back into in December 1991 was completely different to the one he had arrived at in the mid-1970s. Formula 1 had also changed dramatically and Ferrari had fallen behind in terms of resources and results.

'My first feeling in 1991 and the start of 1992 was that it was a big disaster, because I saw people not at a level that was necessary,' di Montezemolo said. 'No clear rules, no mentality, no team spirit. So my first job was [to work out] why have we not been successful from Jody Scheckter until now? Why? We have got the drivers – don't forget, we had Mansell, we had Prost . . .'

Fiat boss Gianni Agnelli had given Ferrari's new president the blessing to approach rebuilding the Formula 1 team in a slow and methodical fashion. 'It was like Lego. Brick by brick, piece by piece,' di Montezemolo added. 'I knew I had to take the time. We were not going to win anything for a few years and that was okay.'

The Frenchman

Top of his list early on was finding a new version of himself. Recalling his days in charge of Enzo's team, di Montezemolo now found himself in a reversal of roles. 'I said we need one person who can be the number one without being an engineer. The same decision that Ferrari took with me in the 1970s. Not a technician, but an organizer and manager. That was my first priority.'

Having brought order to chaos in his first stint, di Montezemolo had been one of the few Director Sportives who had a memorable tenure in charge of the race team. Marco Piccinini had been another, leading the team to the drivers' title in 1979 and the constructors' title in 1982 and 1983. He was also the key architect of Ferrari's highly beneficial Concorde Agreement. Piccinini left on the eve of Enzo's death. After him, and in the void left by the founder's passing, Ferrari lost clear leadership. Piccinini's successor had been Fiat man Pier Giorgio Capelli, but he was only ever a stopgap. Cesare Fiorio had arrived with real pedigree from the successful Lancia rally team and appeared to have the right stuff to lead, but the antagonism between him and John Barnard's GTO, which he inherited from Piccinini, and his falling out with Alain Prost saw him kicked to the kerb. His replacement, Claudio Lombardi, also from Lancia, was at the helm when di Montezemolo took over.

Di Montezemolo knew he had to look further afield. He wanted someone with ambition and a character who could cut through the politics and identify which areas needed addressing immediately. He wanted someone who could manage and act as a shield from the press and their high expectations of Ferrari. Fortunately, someone who fitted the bill perfectly was out there, in a familiar role.

After years of petty internal squabbles and spats with the wider Fiat group, it was not surprising that di Montezemolo sought someone outside the orbit of both companies and outside of Formula 1: diminutive

Frenchman Jean Todt. He may not have been Italian, but he shared the same rallying background as di Montezemolo, Audetto and Fiorio. As a rally co-driver, he had competed between 1966 and 1981 with the Talbot/Peugeot team, finishing runner-up with Guy Fréquelin in the 1981 World Rally Championship. But it was away from the track he made a name for himself, branching out into management in the latter stages of his co-driving career and representing the team in the sport's main commissioning body. Nerves of steel are a prerequisite for a rally co-driver, but his organizational skills and his no-nonsense approach to most matters earned him a fierce reputation and he soon was placed in charge of Peugeot's entire motor racing division. On his watch Peugeot returned to the World Rally Championship in 1984 and won it the following two seasons, clinched the Paris–Dakar rally four consecutive times and, in 1992, won the Le Mans 24 Hours race – a rare triple success across rally, cross-country and world endurance racing. It was a colossal achievement. In a short time, Todt had re-organized what had been a flailing company and led it to a period of incredible success.

There was only one obvious category left for Peugeot: Formula 1. Plans were drawn up for an entry, spearheaded by Todt, but the company eventually backed out of the idea and elected to enter the sport as an engine supplier. It was this process that brought Todt into contact with Formula 1 boss Bernie Ecclestone, who brokered what would turn out to be a historic meeting between the Frenchman and Ferrari's president.

'I decided to hire Todt for three reasons,' di Montezemolo said. 'He was not a *mercenario*, he did not jump from one team to another. He had been his whole career in Peugeot. This was important because he was always with the same company, and also it is a car manufacturer closer to us at Ferrari than to the English racing teams in terms of philosophy. Second reason was that I knew him from rally times; everyone told me he was a good navigator and organizer. And third, in my first meeting with him he showed to me that he really loved Ferrari since he was a child. So for these reasons I decided to hire Todt, despite the fact he had zero experience, zero, in Formula 1.'

With Peugeot's F1 plan dead in the water, Todt had told his bosses he wanted to move away from racing altogether and was being prepped for a wider job within the Peugeot Group when the Ferrari approach came. Only one company could make him change course.

'Maybe it's a paradox because I went to Ferrari to run Formula 1, but simply because Ferrari was special to me,' Todt told *Beyond the Grid* in 2020. 'Ferrari was the halcyon of motor racing. I was never expecting to get this challenge offered to me. That's why I loved it. [I knew] bringing Ferrari back to the highest level of success in Formula 1 would be a special achievement.'

As di Montezemolo's first important hire it was a major statement. The Italian press had two easy lines of attack: his job history and his nationality. Recalling the reaction to the appointment, Luca Colajanni said: 'The arrival of Todt, it was a very brave move . . . to call someone without experience in Formula 1, French, already known for being a character. I think he was properly the first non-Italian to run the team.'

Di Montezemolo took it on the chin: 'I was criticized for hiring a non-Italian, but I never had any doubt he was the right man.' The significance of Todt's nationality cannot be understated. While it seemed alien to many to have a foreigner leading the most Italian of brands, it gave him a key degree of separation. His long past at Peugeot meant he arrived untainted by the company's politics and came with a different cultural perspective to the one that permeated behind the scenes. It is easy to draw parallels between Todt and the modern-day Ferrari team principal, Fred Vasseur, who has thrived in an environment where he has been unaffected by some of the pettier aspects that come with the role.

Fittingly, Todt started on 1 July 1993, at the French Grand Prix, before he had even stepped into his office at Maranello. It was a race that showed the task at hand: Jean Alesi's engine failed while running in the points and Gerhard Berger finished 14th, two laps down on the leaders. Ferrari's jilted ex, Alain Prost, who had taken a year out after leaving the team and landed at Williams, won the race in a year he would comfortably claim the championship. Around that same time, Prost had given his fellow countryman some stark advice as he embarked on his new job: 'You will not be able to resist [quitting] more than a year and a half, two years.' As had been the case the previous season, Ferrari did not win a race in 1993.

Todt had heard the rumblings of how bad Ferrari was – the tumult behind the scenes had become part of motor racing lore in the early 1990s. 'When I arrived, first I tried to make my own opinion to analyze the situation. If you are a doctor you see the patient, you then try to define the right prescriptions …. At the time there was not unified analysis [of what was wrong]. Chassis people were saying the engine was not working. Engine people were saying it was the chassis. Then everybody was saying we didn't have the proper drivers. It was honestly a mess.'

Jean Todt was an easy scapegoat if things did not immediately go to plan and di Montezemolo was determined not to expose his carefully chosen team manager to the darker side of life at Ferrari. 'At the beginning, it was like having a dog,' di Montezemolo said of Todt. 'For a few months I kept the dog very close to me because I didn't want to let him think he was an expert. For me it was necessary for him to wait day after day to enter into the mentality of the team and know the people. At the beginning I gave him, week after week, a little more power. I gave full power when I understood that he was in condition, really, to run the team. Of course we were used to talking three, four, five times a day. At the beginning I wanted to be sure that his introduction to Formula 1 was proper – he was French, he was not an expert of Formula 1, so I had to wait. Even with the press, with the *tifosi*, with everybody. When I was sure he was able to run the team, I left him much more alone than at the beginning.'

The Factory

To make progress, sometimes you have to take a step back. 'In 1992 we had the Ferrari F92A, my first launch of a car,' Luca Colajanni explained. 'The car was three seconds slower. No-one else but Williams had the active suspension. And we were nowhere.' This was the year that Nigel Mansell flattened all opposition with Adrian Newey's outstanding Williams FW14B. 'We scored 21 points that season. So [di Montezemolo] understood that we needed to speed up and renew ourselves from a technological point of view. Then he asked again for John Barnard to work for Ferrari. That's when the second Guildford experiment happened.'

Those years operating across two countries had left Maranello ill-equipped to deal with the design requirements at that time. Williams had aerodynamic specialist Adrian Newey, rock solid engineering from Patrick Head and electronic innovation from Paddy Lowe's team.

'What we needed was a technological shock,' Colajanni recalled. But the English side of the equation had been terminated. The Guildford Technical Office was no more – Ferrari had sold the building to McLaren, of all companies, who used it in the production of their Gordon Murray-designed F1 road car.

'The first factory we'd set up was on a brand new, hi-tech estate, right by the river, right by Guildford. Beautiful.' Barnard told *Beyond the Grid* in 2020. 'What Ferrari needed was a good presence, a high-end type of building. Then the building on the estate next to it becomes available and I had to do it up again. I was like, this is unreal!'

Barnard's new factory, next door to the old GTO, was given the less-memorable acronym FDD, for Ferrari Design and Development. 'It was almost back to where I started the first time,' Barnard added, 'but without the clout of having in my contract – Technical Director'.

By 1994, the new system was fully in operation. Todt, now fully off the leash, was clearly making progress with the team and Gerhard Berger would win the 1994 German Grand Prix, just over a year after Jean Todt had taken over. It was the first Ferrari win in almost four years.

Di Montezemolo had been shocked at the state of Maranello's dilapidated facilities and over the next decade the company embarked on what became a €200m rejuvenation project. International architects Renzo Piano and Jean Nouvel were brought in to redesign Ferrari's ageing racing division, the Gestione Sportiva. The end product was the stunning red building which sits opposite the old factory gates, with imposing dark windows lining the walls in every direction. But the work done inside the building was equally important. Years of splintered leadership and bitter political in-fighting had turned the famous old factory into one built on eggshells, with a suffocating fear lingering in every corner. It had stopped being a place where people could innovate.

So as the building changed on the outside, so it did on the inside. Di Montezemolo slowly implemented what became known as 'Formula Uomo'. The idea was simple: empower Ferrari's employees and make them enjoy coming to work again. State-of-the-art lighting and air-conditioning units which could adapt to the time of day were placed inside the building. Trees and plants were placed in green areas around the factory. A fitness centre was built on its grounds. Di Montezemolo saw the best way to unlock the passion underpinning everything at Ferrari was to create a workforce who felt driven to succeed from the moment they walked into the building until the moment they left. By the end of the 1990s, Ferrari was regularly winning 'best workplace' awards in Italy, something di Montezemolo still points to as one of his proudest achievements from his tenure in charge.

Before long, it was obvious Ferrari should be conducting all its business from its spiritual home. Everything they needed was right there, the factory, with a newly invigorated workforce, the Fiorano test track right next to Enzo's old house. Once again, Barnard was asked to move to Italy. Once again, he declined.

Todt did not view the FDD episode as a complete failure. 'It was crucial for a number of Italian engineers who spent time there, who lived and breathed what was going on from a technological point of view in the UK from motorsport. The experience they gained there when they came back to Maranello, it worked. After a longer time, it was clear that we had to bring back design and development together with the factory, together with the engine guys. For many years that was the advantage, that we had everyone together.'

Though short lived, Barnard's second stint with the team would see the design of two cars: the 1995 and 1996 challengers. The latter would be given to the man tasked with taking Ferrari back to the promised land.

The Driver

Michael Schumacher is today as synonymous with Ferrari as just about anything else. But his route to the team – and indeed, his success on arrival – might have looked very different had events of the decade played out in a less tragic way.

At first, the driver had been the least of di Montezemolo's worries, given the scale of the rebuilding job. 'At first the priority was to have a competitive team and a competitive car,' he said. 'If I had hired Superman, or somehow a driver who was a mix between Senna, Schumacher, Juan Manuel Fangio and Jim Clark, in 1993, 1994, 1995, it would have made no difference. It would have been a mistake.'

One of those drivers seemed like the only logical solution, providing Ferrari could wrestle him out of his contract. Ayrton Senna had moved to Williams in 1994, looking to emulate what Mansell and Prost had each done in the preceding two years by winning a title in a dominant car. Senna had joined expecting to have another class-leading Williams but the move had not gone according to plan. Schumacher and his Benetton team had emerged favourites in the rapid B194, designed by South African Rory Byrne. Senna, who had grown suspicious that the Benetton was illegal, failed to finish at the opening two races in an erratic Williams car far from his liking. Making matters worse, Schumacher won on both occasions. Senna, who had been in talks with Ferrari at the start of the decade which came to nothing, was already souring on Williams. Overtures were made to Ferrari once again and, ahead of the third race of the year, the San Marino Grand Prix at Imola, Senna drove to Bologna to see Ferrari's president.

'Ayrton . . . he came on the Wednesday night to have dinner with me,' di Montezemolo recalled, speaking slowly, as if remembering their encounter as he spoke. 'My home is 40 minutes from Imola. He told me, "I want to close my career with Ferrari. I want to win with Ferrari".'

Senna had been so desperate to make the move he was willing to rip up his contract altogether. 'We offered him a switch to Ferrari in 1995, but he was pushing for 1994,' Todt said years later. 'We already had two drivers under contract, Jean Alesi and Gerhard Berger, so we couldn't satisfy his request, and when Ayrton asked why, I explained the situation to him. He didn't give up, telling me that in Formula 1 contracts don't count, but I replied that for me a contract has to be respected. So we offered him a deal for 1995, but unfortunately we know what happened.'

Fate would deny them the opportunity. The 1994 San Marino Grand Prix was one of the darkest in the sport's history. Rubens Barrichello sustained life-threatening injuries in a crash during practice before Roland Ratzenberger was killed in a high-speed qualifying accident the following day. On Sunday, 1 May, just days after dinner with di Montezemolo to discuss a potential future working together, Senna would be killed when he crashed out at the Tamburello corner at the start of the seventh lap.

With Senna gone, Schumacher remained the only option who could satisfy Ferrari's craving for a top driver. The German had been a phenomenon from the moment he stepped into an F1 cockpit at the 1991 Belgian Grand Prix for Jordan. He was deputizing for Bertrand Gachot, who altered the course of F1 history on the eve of the event by getting into an altercation with a London cab driver and landing himself in jail for two months. Schumacher impressed on his debut and was signed by Benetton for the next race. He claimed the first of his 91 career wins exactly one year later on the return to Spa-Francorchamps. 'Schumacher has a degree of talent seen only once or twice in a generation,' *Autosport*'s long-time grand prix correspondent Nigel Roebuck wrote in 1993. From the beginning, Schumacher was lightning fast, but he possessed a ruthless streak in him which manifested itself in a take-no-prisoners style of racing. By 1994, Schumacher and Benetton, a team run by marketing man Flavio Briatore and with a technical department led by Englishman Ross Brawn, were ready to win the title. Damon Hill took up Williams' title challenge in Senna's stead and might have won were it not for a controversial collision with Schumacher at the final race in Adelaide. The German driver ran off the race track fatally wounding his car, before rejoining the circuit and ramming into Hill. In early 1995 it was clear Schumacher and Benetton were cruising to another championship. Ferrari won just once that season – Alesi claiming his only F1 victory in Canada – but di Montezemolo felt the time was right to invest in who would be inside the cockpit.

Schumacher signed after a meeting with Todt at the 1995 Monaco Grand Prix, committing to join the following year as team-mate to another new signing, Ulsterman Eddie Irvine. Schumacher's signing coincided with di Montezemolo's growing confidence in the squad he was putting together. 'We were ready in 1996. By 1997 we knew we would have a completely new wind tunnel. We had a list of things to do, it was very long, but very clear priorities. It was: we need to do this in the next six months, this in the next 12 months. The driver was not high on that list to start with. Then we arrived at the moment which was 1996, which is when I thought, "Now is the moment to have the right driver. Now the driver could make a difference." That's when we started with Michael in 1996.'

For di Montezemolo, it was the key piece of the puzzle. For Todt, who had seen on his arrival the engine and chassis department pointing fingers at each other and at the drivers in the cockpit, it was important for another reason. Years later, he would tell *Autobild*: 'When things go bad, Italians tend to blame each other . . . There was always an excuse. By signing Michael, I solved at least one of the problems. Nobody could tell me that he was not a good driver. After all, he had just become World Champion twice.'

It was clear from Schumacher's first test how different his mindset was going to be. His first appearance as a Ferrari driver left a lasting impression on a young Mattia Binotto – the Swiss-Italian engineer who would rise through the ranks, becoming team boss in 2019. 'I started in 1995, when Jean Alesi and Gerhard Berger were the drivers,' Binotto told me. 'My first engineering job at the test team was with those two drivers and Nicola Larini as test driver. When we went to the test events, the drivers would come in last minute, put the helmet and overalls on, do an installation lap and then start to discuss the programme with the engineers. Then, end of 1995, Michael joined and the first test was in Fiorano and then Estoril. I remember arriving at the race track with the entire team. He was already there, waiting, wanting to do the meeting before we started. He pointed to his watch and said, "8 a.m. guys, we have the meeting". So the next day the whole team had to be there at 8 a.m. So we arrived earlier than normal the next day and he was already there again. And there was not a single test he was not participating in. And if he was there, you had to be there as well, whatever time it was.'

The Estoril test was impressive for other reasons. Driving the V12-engined 1995 car, Schumacher posted times quicker than his predecessors Alesi or Berger had ever got close to, lapping nearly two seconds faster. With Ferrari set to switch from a V12 to a V10, and due a whole new car for the 1996 season, it left a lot of people at the team wondering what might have been. John Barnard, who was present at the test, recalled: 'I remember him saying, "I could have won the championship easier in this car than I could in the Benetton". That was his comment. Take it for what it's worth, but that was his comment.'

While he felt he could have done something with its predecessor, the 1996 car Schumacher climbed into for his debut season was a dud. Compared to a bathtub by the press, the chunky, high-rise cockpit looked especially cumbersome and, when paired with large, squared-off side pods, made the F310 one of the worst looking Ferrari's of the era. 'That car should never have won a race,' wrote Andrew Benson for the BBC ten years later.

If there was any doubt that Schumacher was the right man, it evaporated four races into his debut season. Schumacher's standout moment came at the 1996 Spanish Grand Prix at the Circuit de Catalunya. Already known as a master of wet conditions from the early years of his career, Schumacher's status as *Der Regenmeister* (The Rainmaster) was never more apparent.

Starting third, Schumacher quickly found his way to the front. Hill, on his way to the world title, spun in the dominant Williams. On Lap 13, Schumacher caught and passed Hill's team-mate Jacques Villeneuve. From that point he disappeared into the distance, regularly lapping an astonishing three seconds quicker than anyone else for most of the contest. Schumacher was on another planet to his rivals. While Todt publicly tried to cool the hype, many at the team realized immediately they had witnessed one of the best drivers in the sport's history. 'This is not the time to talk of the dawning of a new age,' he said, in what has to go down as one of the understatements of all time. 'We have won one race. Our objective is to continue improving.'

Schumacher finished 45 seconds clear of Alesi, who had swapped places with him at Benetton, with Villeneuve three seconds further back. No other driver finished on the lead lap. 'It was not a race, it was a demonstration of brilliance,' racing legend Stirling Moss said afterwards. 'The man is in a class of his own . . . there's no one in the world anywhere near him'.

Another part of the puzzle had dropped into place – similar to the mid-1970s when di Montezemolo had forged a strong partnership with Niki Lauda, Schumacher and Todt quickly forged an almost unbreakable working relationship.

In an interview years later about this Ferrari dream team, Bernie Ecclestone would recall: 'One day we were sitting together, and I asked Michael, "Who is leading this team?" And he answered: "I am going to do that." He did that really well. He could get the best out of the people. He earned the respect of the people; they listened to him. Whenever he said something, they knew it was correct. Whatever Michael said, Todt followed it.'

'Michael was made exactly of the same material [as Todt],' Colajanni said. 'He was another person who was only seeing the victory. Michael and Todt, being so tough and so uninterested to please people and to please the world outside, needed someone like di Montezemolo to protect them from the pressure that always came from Fiat, from the shareholders. Especially from Italian public opinion. Di Montezemolo in this was a genius. He was able to moderate certain things and to create the right circumstances for Todt.'

The Supporting Cast

'For me, it was necessary to pick up a few people from outside, not many, but people who can make the difference,' di Montezemolo said about his hiring philosophy. 'They can arrive in Maranello with a different mentality. So to make the story short, I opened the window to fresh air to come into the team.'

Two key names would follow the breeze from the UK across Europe and into Maranello's freshly air-conditioned factories with Schumacher. With the Barnard set-up dismissed for a second time, Schumacher pointed to his old team for Ferrari's next moves. Ross Brawn, the technical mastermind of his Benetton team, was hired in late 1996, but getting the Benetton B194 designer Rory Byrne to follow him was not a foregone conclusion.

Like Todt years earlier, Byrne had considered himself done with motor racing after leaving Benetton in 1996. At the end of December that year he had left the UK and flown to Thailand, intending to set up a scuba diving business on the island of Koh Lanta. It was a short-lived venture – less than two months later, a call from Europe reached the remote island. 'It was Jean Todt from Ferrari,' Byrne said. 'He explained that after many years the consultancy agreement with John Barnard just hadn't produced the results for Ferrari and they'd hired Ross Brawn and would I like to join and design the cars, just like I'd done at Benetton? Michael had been there a year at that stage. I said I'd think about it.' Faced with a return to the cut-throat and competitive world of F1 or his new life on the beaches of Thailand, Byrne was another who could not resist the pull of the Prancing Horse. 'It didn't take a lot of thinking,' he said. 'Ten days later I was in Maranello. That was the briefest retirement ever, six weeks!'

Byrne and Brawn were two of the most important signings Ferrari ever made. When Michael retired (the first time) in 2006, Schumacher had claimed 87 of his 91 career F1 victories in cars designed by Byrne.

'Once I joined Ferrari we found ourselves in a very tough situation,' Byrne said. 'For a start, Ferrari had in Italy a very good race team, they had a good manufacturing base, but they had absolutely no design or research facility. All that was done by John Barnard and his group of engineers and his company in England. Of course once they'd parted company with Barnard they had no infrastructure. So there were several tasks at hand. First was to make the 1997 car competitive, which had already been designed and they were testing. It was off the pace so we had to make that competitive. We then had to build up the infrastructure, employ all the engineers, get the wind tunnel programme started, start building up all the simulation tools. It was a huge job. At the same time, from about mid-season onwards I had to start designing the 1998 car. The rules had fundamentally changed for 1998 so it was no mean task, I can tell you.'

Brawn, on the other hand, brought a calming presence to what had been a fraught technical department with messy lines of communication and hierarchy across two countries. Rob Smedley, who would join Ferrari in the subsequent decade and work at a Ferrari with and without Brawn at the helm, explained why he was such a vital cog: 'I didn't always agree with Ross, but I respected him as much as I've ever respected anyone. You just thought [to] yourself okay if he said that, there's a reason for saying it. You would never try and second guess him, even if you couldn't quite understand a decision through the lens of what you were looking through. People like Ross are so important for teams that want to go out and win World Championships, because you have that steady hand guiding everything, that calm leadership when everyone else's reaction might just be to panic. Especially at a team like Ferrari. Ross was never like that. He was very philosophical and he protected you from everything outside as well.'

The major arrivals of the 1990s gave Ferrari an obvious new feel – a German driver, a French team boss, a South African designer and an English technical director. 'Todt had a clear idea of who he wanted in every position,' said Luca Collajani, 'To him it didn't mean anything if you were Italian, French, Swedish, English, to him if you were functional to win, he didn't give a shit where you were from. The Todt I met when I arrived had one thing in mind – winning, no matter what. Doesn't matter if the cat is black or white, as long as it eats the mouse.'

Dyed in the wool Ferrari men like Colajanni are, perhaps understandably, still irked by the suggestion that the company's move away from Italian leaders had a direct impact on their on-track performances. 'I always remember Lauda once said a quote on the cliché that the Italians in Ferrari cannot win, that they cannot win alone. Which is not true. Lauda should have remembered he won two championships with the [Mauro] Forghieri team. It was the typical cliché.'

Coincidentally, Lauda had been brought back by di Montezemolo in a consultancy role in 1993, which he would keep until 2001, adding to the Foreign Legion feel of the team which was being assembled. But Maranello was also looking for home-grown talent.

'So many young people, so many young engineers were being employed at the time,' Binotto said of the mid to late 1990s. 'Certainly there was the top management, Jean, Ross, Paolo [Martinelli who ran the engine department] . . . But I think the effort Ferrari made at the time was really to employ very young engineers as the base of the future of the team. They were leading, they were the ones having the vision and the strategy in mind, but there were a lot of people, young engineers, who created the team below which was delivering on that vision.'

The evidence is easy to find. Aldo Costa, who went on to become Byrne's successor as lead designer, arrived in 1995, the same year as Binotto. By that point Stefano Domenicali, who had joined in 1991 and would eventually be named Todt's successor, had become head of personnel in Ferrari's sporting department. At the start of the 2000s, Andrea Stella would start at the team in an engineering role. All of those individuals would carve out significant careers of their own.

'I'm proud to see that the people who have worked with me, close to me, and have had my support, have gone on to occupy important positions,' di Montezemolo said. 'Todt was the FIA president, Ross was the number one director of Mercedes [in 2010] – if you want my opinion, he was behind the success of Mercedes in the beginning. Domenicali became team boss and then he became the head of Formula 1. Andrea Stella is now the number one at McLaren. And Binotto was a young boy coming from the engine, to the test team, to team boss. So it was a really good group.'

Di Montezemolo and Todt had, in the space of a few years, built a dream team, with the best driver in the world supported by a blend of experience, passion, leadership and youthful ambition. Ferrari's facilities were improving fast and Todt's organizational skills had put together a clear structure which helped the team navigate through the choking expectations which often came with the territory.

So now, with everything in place, and with Ferrari's facilities improving with every passing year, came the hard part: actually returning the team to glory and winning championships again.

4

SCHUMACHER

'For me he was the only driver who could make Ferrari World Champion again. It was the combination of great talent, total dedication and loyalty. And he was the reference – also for the technicians and engineers.'

Jean Todt

Michael Schumacher gives himself a moment to take it all in. The euphoric tones of the Italian national anthem, a song he loves as much as his own nation's, echo out around him.

Below is a sea of faces in red uniforms – happy faces, bellowing the words to Il Canto degli Italiani *– Brothers of Italy, Italy has risen. Today the words feel as appropriate as ever.*

He outstretches his hands as he always does, as if a conductor leading a great orchestra.

He's done it dozens of times before from the top step. But this one is different – the mixed sense of joy and relief is palpable. The journey to this moment has been long and arduous.

Memories come flooding back to him. The first win in Spain. His moment of madness in Jerez in 1997. Wondering if he was dying, his leg broken and his heartbeat slowing as he sat in his crashed car at Silverstone in 1999.

Breaking down in tears on TV at Monza a few weeks before this day, this wonderful realization of five years of hard work.

The questions. The criticism. The pressure. The doubters. The headlines in Italy. All of it worth it for this moment. A weight has been lifted. The words he heard as he crossed the line still ring in his ear: 'Michael, you are the World Champion!'

A World Champion with Ferrari. Part of a rare club.

As the anthem ends, a familiar figure moves onto the top step with him. It's his team boss, Jean Todt, his closest ally within the team, his biggest supporter through the good times and the bad, who has protected him from so much on the outside. Todt puts his arm around Schumacher and leans close to his ear. What he says is something neither man will ever forget.

'Michael . . . Our lives are never going to be the same again.'

It took Schumacher and Todt five long years to share their moment of triumph together. Ferrari had won the constructors' title a year earlier but the drivers' title of 2000, Schumacher's first for Ferrari and third overall, was finally the one which lifted the burden both men had been carrying. The worldwide congregation of *tifosi* celebrated. Italian newspaper *La Gazzetta dello Sport* summed up the relief on its front page the next day, its headline reading simply: '*Grazie Ferrari*'.

A cascade of success followed, but it did not always seem so inevitable. 'Before those achievements I thought many times: "Well, they were right, we'll never make it",' Todt admitted years later. He was not the only one who felt that way. Ferrari's dream team had gone through setbacks and missteps on the way and, were it not for the 2000 title, which culminated with the celebration on the Suzuka podium, things might have looked very different for the two men who shared in that moment of triumph. The road to get there had been arduous.

Finally Jerez...

After his three-win debut season, Schumacher and Ferrari had felt emboldened about the chance to win a championship in 1997. After 1996 Williams remained the team to beat and the challenge would come from Jacques Villeneuve, the son of Enzo's old favourite, Gilles. Although his career faded after 1997, in his first two seasons in Formula 1 Jacques had been a sensation. Arriving as winner of the Indy 500 and the prestigious CART championship, he was narrowly beaten to a debut F1 championship by team-mate Damon Hill in Suzuka that year. Hill had been ditched by Frank Williams and could only find a drive at the struggling Arrows team, making Villeneuve the defacto team leader for 1997. Alongside Villeneuve was the driver Williams thought to be a far superior driver to Hill, Heinz-Harald Frentzen, a team-mate of Schumacher's from his Mercedes sports car days.

Ferrari was a contender from the start. John Barnard's final contribution to Ferrari had been the F310 of 1996 and some major upgrades from Rory Byrne and Ross Brawn saw the car rechristened the F310B. The new-look version vaulted Ferrari into a title fight. Victories in Monaco, Canada, France and Belgium put Schumacher in the hunt before a victory at the penultimate Japanese Grand Prix earned him a one-point lead going into the season finale at Jerez in Spain, host of the European Grand Prix.

In a classic winner-takes-all showdown, a flashpoint occurred late in the race as Villeneuve reeled his rival in. Schumacher's mirrors showed the blue and white Rothmans Williams gaining. Then on Lap 47 of 69 came the decisive moment. Villeneuve caught Schumacher down the long back straight and made a perfect pass down the inside at the Turn 6 right-hander, his car nosing ahead as they hurtled towards the apex. It was a clean pass and the Canadian's corner. For the briefest fraction of a second, Schumacher's hands flicked his car to the left, as if to move away, before he turned fully right and into Villeneuve's car. Schumacher's car went into the gravel and stopped, but Villeneuve crawled around the corner and out of sight. 'That won't work Michael! You hit the wrong part of him my friend!' Martin Brundle (an ex-team-mate of Schumacher) exclaimed on the ITV commentary.

It was a moment of utter madness from Schumacher, revealing a tendency to show cracks in some of the highest-pressure situations, as he had done with Hill at Adelaide three years earlier. While on that occasion there had been at least vaguely plausible deniability on Schumacher's part, Jerez was cut and dried. Even to the biggest Ferrari or Schumacher die-hard, the intention was undeniable.

'He was the fiercest competitor because he didn't take any quarter,' Villeneuve said. 'There was no limit to what he was willing to do. His line was different than ours.'

Like Adelaide, Schumacher's car could not continue, but the Williams could – unlike Adelaide, where Hill had retired in the pit-lane. Now it was just a case of making it to the flag in one piece and, crucially, in the position Villeneuve needed to be champion. With third place now enough, the Canadian driver let the charging McLarens of Mika Häkkinen and David Coulthard past as he nursed his car to the line to become champion.

Later that evening, Villeneuve would be irked when celebrating at his hotel. Schumacher joined him in serving patrons from behind the bar, acting as though he had not just tried to screw him out of the World Championship a few hours earlier. It suggested Schumacher that evening did not understand the magnitude of what had happened. Pictures taken by Corinne Schumacher of her husband with an arm around Villeneuve made it to the German newspapers the following day, suggesting the two were chummy, which was not the case. Even though he won the title Villeneuve still holds a grudge about it to this day. Those who knew Schumacher best suggest it was in his nature to see incidents like Jerez 1997 differently to the rest of us.

Brawn himself noticed this. Speaking to *Motor Sport* magazine years later, he said: 'It was a mistake by Michael, he shouldn't have done it. Interestingly, when he came back into the pits, he had a completely different mental view of what had happened. It wasn't until he saw the TV that he realized what had really happened. He came back to the pits and he was telling us, "We have to get Villeneuve disqualified," and I said "Michael, you really need to look at the TV because it really doesn't look that way I'm afraid." He looked, and he went quiet and realized that things hadn't been quite the way he thought they were from the cockpit.'

'We are talking about an incredible man who won an incredible number of titles because of his skills, his characteristics, and his talent,' Stefano Domenicali said. 'That was his strength. Really pushing at the limit. Sometimes more than the limit. That was Michael. There are clear moments in his career, like all human beings, where you believe you are right. Then rationally you understand you made a mistake. He was not ashamed to recognize that . . . maybe he just recognized it a little bit later than most.'

At a press conference days later, Schumacher showed his mindset had shifted. 'I really thought that Jacques Villeneuve had not been in front of me and that I had the right to defend my position. But in the evening I was not so sure any more. I remember exactly that I was flabbergasted when our president, Luca di Montezemolo, said to me something like: "Man, what were you thinking?" – and I thought: "What? Why am I the idiot now?".' Schumacher added: 'I am a human being, sometimes I make mistakes too. Not very often, but this was a big one.'

To add insult to injury, Jody Sheckter, whose 1979 title hung over Schumacher and Ferrari like a giant shadow, labelled the move 'disgusting'. An FIA hearing would find Schumacher's move, 'was an instinctive reaction and although deliberate not made with malice or premeditation'. Yet he was disqualified from the championship and ordered to go on a road safety course. Many felt the punishment was not a punishment at all – although it was unprecedented for a driver to be thrown out of the final standings of a season, Schumacher had been allowed to keep his wins from the season. FIA president Max Mosley reasoned the disqualification was a clear precedent to any driver who would attempt to win a championship in future by driving their rival off the race track, but it still left many unhappy.

The Häkkinen Challenge

Jerez was significant for another reason in that Villeneuve's late survival drive had handed Mika Häkkinen his first Formula 1 victory. He went into the new season full of confidence as the McLaren team started 1998 with the first car designed by Adrian Newey – Häkkinen promptly won the first two races of the season. With Ron Dennis's team replacing the fading Williams team, it was soon obvious 1998 would be Schumacher vs Häkkinen and Byrne vs Newey. It would remain the state of play in Formula 1 for the next few years. The 1998 season went right to the wire, but is perhaps best remembered for a showdown between Schumacher and Häkkinen's team-mate, Scottish driver David Coulthard, in Belgium, the only race that year not won by Ferrari or McLaren.

The event is famous for two incidents: the crash at the start which wiped out nearly every car and forced a long red-flag stoppage, and the collision between Schumacher and Coulthard. The second was pivotal in the championship. Leading the race comfortably, with 20 laps left, *Der Regenmeister* came up to lap Coulthard. Steaming towards him as they approached Pouhon, Schumacher's Ferrari slammed into the back of the McLaren, sending his right tyre flying and tearing his front wing off the car. Schumacher and Ferrari would argue the Scot made little attempt to get off the racing line in awful conditions; Coulthard said the spray meant he had no idea Schumacher's Ferrari was coming. The truth is probably somewhere in the middle. Remarkably Schumacher managed to three-wheel his car half way round the circuit and back to the pit-lane ahead of Coulthard, who had to stop for his McLaren team to assess the damage.

With his Ferrari barely stationary in the pit box, Schumacher jumped out of his car, angrily ripping off his helmet and balaclava, a look of righteous anger on his face. Ferrari mechanics and Todt tried in vain to hold him back as Schumacher, still removing his earpiece, strode down the pit-lane towards the McLaren garage to find Coulthard. He was met with a wall of McLaren mechanics, with the Scot on the other side.

'He's shouting at me, "Were you trying to fucking kill me?" I was shouting back at him, "You ran into the back of me!".' It was a rare moment when real anger was on display in the pit-lane and summed up not only the rivalry between the two teams but the intense pressure there was for Ferrari to win. Coulthard finds it amusing now. 'What it has done is guaranteed me a place in the Schumacher documentary and it always gets brought up every time we go to Spa.' DC told the Red Flag podcast.

One of the best weekends for the Scuderia followed a few weeks later, as Coulthard's engine blew while leading from Häkkinen and Schumacher early in the Italian Grand Prix. As they passed the smokey McLaren, Schumacher weaved right and then left, passing Häkkinen at the Roggia chicane, to roars and blaring horns from the delighted *tifosi*. It seemed like the sort of moment which could help propel a driver to a World Championship, but the title showdown that followed at Suzuka was a damp squib, with Schumacher stalling his car as it sat on the grid ahead of the formation lap. With Schumacher starting at the back, Häkkinen took a straightforward victory to claim his first title. For the second straight year, Schumacher would have to settle for runner-up, although at least this time he got to keep the trophy.

The 1999 season was another round of the Ferrari vs McLaren duel, but it took a different turn than anyone could have expected. Irvine claimed a surprise win for Ferrari at the opening race of the year, where Schumacher stalled on the grid again and the McLarens failed to finish. Wins at Imola and Monaco had got Schumacher back on track and arriving at the British Grand Prix on 27 June he was eight points behind Häkkinen and six points ahead of Irvine, who was enjoying the strongest season of his career by a comfortable margin. A poor start saw Schumacher, who had started behind Häkkinen, lose a position to Coulthard and Irvine at Turn 1. Schumacher found himself behind his team-mate, who defended as they came through the Maggots and Beckets sequence. Down the Hangar Straight, in excess of 191 mph (307 km/h), Schumacher got back alongside and looked set for a routine pass on the inside of the approaching corner. But when the braking zone for Stowe corner arrived, Irvine's car slowed dramatically as normal, Schumacher's did not – with a puff of smoke from his rear wheels, he went straight on, skidded over the gravel trap and plunged into a barrier of tyres.

Schumacher threw his steering wheel out of the car and it was immediately obvious he was in intense pain. Ferrari later explained his rear brakes had failed, with his car locking up at 121 mph (195 km/h) and his car hitting the barrier at 67 mph (108 km/h). Schumacher was taken to hospital, where it was revealed he had broken his left leg. Sat in the car immediately after the accident, he experienced something he had never encountered before in his racing career. 'I was very calm and I could feel my heart beating,' he told German broadcaster ZDF. 'And suddenly I noticed that the heartbeat was increasingly weak until it disappeared altogether. The lights went out. And then I thought this was how someone feels when they know they're on their way to heaven. I don't know if it was only a faint or a shock, I just know that I felt my heart stopped beating. It was an interesting experience.'

For the fourth year since joining, and the third in which Ferrari felt it had a car to compete, Schumacher would not be champion. Irvine had gone on to finish second behind David Coulthard that day at Silverstone. The Ulsterman, famed as a playboy, had been a diligent team-mate since joining in 1996 but had never imagined himself in such a role: he now held Ferrari's hopes of ending the Scheckter drought in his hands. Wins at the next two races followed – Schumacher's replacement, Mika Salo, moved over for Irvine to win at the German Grand Prix, giving up what would have been his only F1 victory in the process.

The 1999 season took on a bizarre feel as the season drew on, with no driver or team looking like they really wanted to win it: Ferrari ruined Irvine's European Grand Prix with a botched pit-stop, before Häkkinen made an unforced error and spun out of the Italian Grand Prix while leading, famously finding a spot behind the trees to break down in tears. The season was so wide open, even Jordan's German driver Heinz-Harald Frentzen was in the hunt until late on. With Irvine's charge faltering, it was clear an extra something was needed.

Schumacher, the benchmark for driver fitness and health at the time, had made a quicker-than-expected recovery but had been targeting a return for the start of 2000. Ferrari needed that extra push and the Italian media started to demand Michael come back as early as possible to help Eddie win the championship. An intervention had to come from on high. Luca di Montezemolo rang Schumacher's home in Geneva and his daughter Gina Marie answered the phone. She told him that 'Daddy was getting out his football boots'. An angry di Montezemolo realized that if he was fit enough to play football, he was fit enough to drive and personally ordered him to compete in the last two races of the season.

Di Montezemolo was also not best pleased about rumours that Jean Todt was not wholeheartedly behind Irv becoming champion. 'I did my best to make sure Irvine had the best conditions he could have,' he told *The Times'* Kevin Eason, 'There were rumours about Irvine and Ferrari not helping him, but how can people think that? I would like to make it clear that the stories about a boycott of Irvine are a personal insult.' Irvine was already on his way to Jaguar next year and would have taken the No.1 with him. And di Montezemolo was aware of the alleged favouritism the team chief had shown towards Michael at the expense of Irvine. 'He is very much in love with Schumacher and I have told him he is wrong,' di Montezemolo said. 'I expect we will have two very strong drivers [next season] and I expect Todt to support both of them. Barrichello will stimulate Schumacher and I do not expect him to be a butler or servant to Schumacher.'

In his return at the Malaysian Grand Prix Schumacher quickly let Irvine past. The Northern Irishman went on to win, with Schumacher finishing just one second behind him as if to remind everyone watching he still had plenty left in reserve if he needed it. 'This guy is depressing,' Irvine joked after the race. 'He's the best number one driver in the world, we know that, but it turns out he's also the best number two driver as well!'

Drama was to follow that evening: a stunning announcement that both Ferraris had been disqualified from the race because the sidepods on both cars had been 'dimensionally non-compliant'. That would mean Häkkinen was World Champion and McLaren were Constructors' Champions for the second year in a row. Todt and Ferrari appealed and, perhaps unsurprisingly to anyone who followed Ferrari at that time, the appeal was successful – Max Mosley, the president of the FIA (cynically called 'Ferrari International Assistance' for much of the Schumacher era, largely because of incidents such as this one), stated the governing body's regulations around side pods were 'insufficiently clear'. The Ferrari drivers were reinstated back into the race and the title race was back on. Eyebrows were raised at the finale. Matt Bishop wrote in *Motor Sport*: 'Ferrari redesigned its cars' bargeboards for the season's showdown at Suzuka, which caused Coulthard to wonder aloud, with some justification it had to be said, how it was that they could have been legal in Malaysia if they now required re-profiling for Japan. Satisfactory answer came there none.' The result reinstated Irvine's win, and Schumacher finishing second, ahead of Häkkinen, meant Irvine would go into the final race four points ahead.

At Suzuka, Schumacher once again took pole, but Irvine laboured to fifth on the grid. A win would guarantee Häkkinen the title due to countback rules and the McLaren driver beat Schumacher on the run down to Turn 1 and scampered off into the distance. In a race which showed how unlikely it had always been that Irvine could have got the job done, Schumacher finished five seconds behind Häkkinen – Irvine was third, a minute and a half off the leader. Even if Schumacher had slowed dramatically and let Irvine through, it would have made no difference to the outcome. Häkkinen was World Champion. Ferrari had reason to celebrate – the result meant they had won the Constructors' Championship for the first time since 1983 thanks, in part, to the points they regained from Malaysia. McLaren lost out – they would not win that title again until December 2024.

It's Now or Never

Only one outcome was acceptable for the *tifosi* in 2000: the Drivers' Championship. Coming into the new millennium, pressure had reached near breaking point behind the scenes. While the team had been buoyed by the constructors' title, there was every reason to believe that Schumacher would have been champion without his Silverstone crash.

The stakes suddenly seemed higher for Schumacher than just ending the title drought. 'It is fair to say if 2000 would not have brought [the title] the risk would have been extremely high that everything breaks apart and maybe Ferrari moves on to another driver,' Sabine Kehm, Michael's press spokesman and subsequent manager, told me. 'The tension and pressure was extremely high. It was extremely intense.'

Schumacher won the first three races and was comfortably clear when he claimed his fourth victory of the season at the Nürburgring, establishing an early 18-point lead over Häkkinen. Then came trouble – across the next five races, Schumacher won once and retired four times, blowing the championship wide open. Häkkinen would win in Austria and Hungary before what could have been a morale-crushing defeat for Ferrari at the Belgian Grand Prix. At Spa, Häkkinen had pulled off one of the great F1 overtaking moves on the final lap of the race. While chasing Schumacher for the lead on the final tour, the pair approached the backmarking British American Racing car of Ricardo Zonta on the Kemmel Straight. While Schumacher went to the left to overtake, Häkkinen dived down the other side – giving him the inside line for the chicane that followed.

Arriving at the Italian Grand Prix, Häkkinen had the championship lead and the momentum behind him. Todt called the team together at Monza and made it clear what was expected of his staff and Ferrari's star driver for the remaining races. Recalling the tone of the meeting, Kehm said: 'It amounted to: "If you don't win these next four, we're fucked," kind of thing. Internally everybody was panicking.'

As has so often been the case with Ferrari at Monza, the Italian Grand Prix would come with a flood of emotions. Tragedy would overshadow the contest. A multi-car pileup on the opening lap claimed the life of trackside marshal Paolo Gislimberti, who was struck by a flying tyre. Schumacher would beat Häkkinen in the race, cutting the gap down to two points with three races to run. The championship was back on. After basking in the glory of Monza's unique podium, which sits over the start–finish straight, Schumacher went to the press conference for the top three finishers. What followed was a moment many who followed the German's career, especially those who had a view of him as a Teutonic man of limited empathetic range, would not forget.

As the customary back and forth between interviewer and driver started, the emotions that had been bubbling away inside Schumacher were suddenly exposed.

'Michael, many, many congratulations, it's your sixth win of the season, but you've not had a race win in six races, you've done it in front of your home fans, the *tifosi*, you must be delighted.'

'Yeah, I think delighted is the wrong word,' Schumacher said, shuffling in his seat and looking down at the microphone, before glancing back up again, his eyes already glazed over. 'I have no vocabulary for anything higher than that. I'm sorry but, I'm just happy. I'm just exhausted,' he continued, with a long exhale of breath.

The host then added: 'I'm not sure if you're aware but this is your 41st victory, which puts you joint-second all time with Ayrton Senna. Do those records mean a lot to you?'

'Yes,' he said, softly. 'It does mean a lot to me . . .'

He then paused, looked down, and exhaled loudly. 'Sorry,' he added, as he started to cry. Moments later, Schumacher was weeping uncontrollably. Brother Ralf Schumacher, who had finished third for Williams, quickly put his arm around his brother. Bizarrely the press conference continued on with questions to a very awkward Häkkinen, with Schumacher in tears next to him. 'Can we have a break?' Häkkinen asked. 'Go to Ralf. Ralf can continue.'

The truth was, a bottleneck of pressure that had been building up inside Schumacher had exploded open in that press conference room. Few drivers would ever experience the combination of feelings Schumacher did that day. Most obviously was the euphoric thrill of winning for Ferrari at Monza and the satisfaction of rising to the challenge set by Todt and knowing the title fight was back in his hands. But there were darker feelings pulling at him too. Going into the race weekend, Schumacher had learned that Willi Bergmeister, a Kerpen garage owner who had given him an apprenticeship which had helped to fund his early racing career, had suffered a heart attack. Schumacher, loyal to a fault to those closest to him, had struggled to internalize the news. Then came the race, and the death of the trackside marshal. Schumacher did not know Gislimberti at all, but once again he found himself in the odd situation of claiming a victory under the cloud of another man's death – he had done the same at the 1994 San Marino

Grand Prix after Senna's accident. Schumacher had never got to properly race Senna to a championship – the Brazilian had died that day convinced Schumacher was driving an illegal Benetton and they had never had a chance to go toe-to-toe for the title. The very mention of Senna's name, let alone the towering achievement of matching his career tally of wins, pushed him over the edge.

Sabine Kehm told me, 'Senna was one of his weak spots, his soft spots, because of Imola. So everything came together. I really remember that. I never understood how people could think that Michael had no emotion and was a robot. I always thought he had a lot of emotions but he didn't want to bring them to the outside as such because he saw it as a weakness.'

After Monza, there was no looking back. It was the highest the tensions would get that year. At Indianapolis the following month, Schumacher led away into Turn 1 but Häkkinen was second. The Finn was catching, catching, when suddenly . . . flames. Smoke started pouring from the back of the Finn's McLaren-Mercedes and he was forced to crawl around the circuit to retire from the race. Schumacher's win and Häkkinen's DNF gave him an eight-point lead going into the penultimate round at Japan's Suzuka circuit – another race victory would be enough to win the Drivers' Championship. After a long and tense race, Schumacher won again in Japan – slamming his hands into the steering wheel as he crossed the line. The dream team had finally done it.

'For me he was the only driver who could make Ferrari World Champion again,' Todt said. 'It was the combination of great talent, total dedication and loyalty. And he was the reference – also for the technicians and engineers.'

The first title also shone a light on Schumi's supporting cast that Todt had assembled in key areas. 'They are the ultimate partnership in contemporary Formula 1. Michael Schumacher, the lean, mean and supremely focused sporting technocrat, and Ross Brawn, the scholarly, owlish and bespectacled pit-wall strategist who has helped his colleague sprint to three World Championships in 10 years,' Alan Henry wrote in *Autoweek*. 'Yet Brawn is more, much more, than simply an accomplished engineer and man manager. He has pulled off probably the most remarkable trick of all: integrating himself within the notoriously nationalistic Ferrari F1 team, without prompting the groundswell of resentment which has in the past blighted the progress of non-Italians at Maranello. Make no mistake about it, Brawn is now a Ferrari insider.'

The Suzuka win would create five years of unrivalled success – the doubts which lingered over 2000 would be a distant memory for a little while afterwards.

'Several times I've been asked: "Ferrari without Todt? Ferrari without Michael? Ferrari without Ross . . .?" You cannot say there is one or two of those elements that is the only one that made it all happen,' long-serving press officer Luca Colajanni told me. 'To me it's all three elements. The secret of success to Ferrari was that combination and the strength of Montezemolo to protect the three of them from everything above. Unfortunately that was lost later on. I'm convinced the reason Ferrari is not succeeding now is that Ferrari lost the patience. The first to lose the patience was di Montezemolo. What happened from 2009, 2010 onwards, he started to lose patience and then we started to accumulate people who had to pay the price.'

Like Clockwork

After a year of tears, doubts and shredded nerves in 2000, the next two seasons were a cakewalk. The F2001 was the first in a line of incredible Byrne designs. Schumacher took two wins and a second place to kick off the season in 2001, although he failed to finish at Imola. A symbolic moment occurred at the Spanish Grand Prix, where Häkkinen led in the closing stages, looking for his first win of the season. As the McLaren driver started the final lap, his hydraulics failed and the car slowed. Schumacher swept by to claim the victory. A run of wins and second-place finishes followed, which helped Schumacher wrap the title up by the Hungarian Grand Prix at the end of August, with four races left.

Remarkably, 2002 would be even better. 'Evolution, not revolution' had always been the Byrne design philosophy (one echoed by Adrian Newey) and his F2002, a natural progression from Ferrari's previous two cars, would end up being his greatest, winning 15 out of 17 races and scoring as many points as all the other teams combined that year in the Constructors' Championship. While this era's team is so often viewed from the perspective of Schumacher–Todt–Brawn, Byrne was one of the key elements without whom much would not have been possible.

The F2002 relied on Ferrari's extensive relationship with Bridgestone in this era – while F1 today has a sole tyre supplier in the form of Pirelli, these were the days of tyre wars: Bridgestone vs Michelin. While Ferrari could prescribe the tyres they wanted from Bridgestone, its major rivals had to share Michelin's time and resources through a season.

'Was it a perfect design? As far as I'm concerned, it's certainly the best Ferrari I've been responsible for and the best car I ever designed for sure,' Byrne told *Automobilist* in 2020. 'There were a number of reasons for this. The first being we designed it specifically around the characteristics of the Bridgestone tyres. Their race tyres had a lot of grip but they didn't have the same length of life as the Michelin. So generally we would be much faster with a two-stop race, whereas the Michelins often did a one-stop race. Because we decided to commit to a two-stop race, we made the fuel tank smaller, so that you had to refuel twice, except at Monaco, and that gave us a number of advantages of the car in terms of where we positioned the fuel. We positioned the fuel in such a way that as the fuel level came down during a stint, the centre of gravity came forward, which counteracted the natural oversteering tendency as the tyres degraded. So it kept the balance through the race much more constant.'

Byrne's marvel car only failed to win twice in 2002 – in Malaysia, where Schumacher lost his front wing at Turn 1 and had to fight back through the field, and Monaco, where McLaren locked out the front row on a circuit where overtaking is difficult if not impossible. Years later, *Motor Sport* magazine deemed the F2002 the fastest Formula 1 car ever built. Schumacher alone won 11 races, a then-record which surpassed his own tallies from the previous two seasons, with Barrichello finishing as runner-up in the championship for the second successive season.

That year Ferrari had also avoided losing its guiding force at the top of the organizational chart. Often linked with a career in politics, di Montezemolo turned down an offer from Italian president Silvio Berlusconi to serve in his cabinet. There is a story that the day he arrived at Maranello after the news item broke he was presented with a petition signed by 1,000 employees begging him not to take the job.

Other moments in 2002 were not so heart-warming. Todt's obsession with making sure Michael won backfired at the Austrian Grand Prix that year when they invoked team orders. Schumacher had won four of the opening five races and was clearly cruising to another championship. He arrived in Austria already 21 points (in 2002, that was more than two race wins) ahead of Williams driver Juan Pablo Montoya. Team-mate Barrichello led Schumacher for much of the contest until the final metres of the race, when the Brazilian driver slowed and allowed Schumacher through as they approached the chequered flag. Fans were outraged at such a brazen team order given Ferrari's already clear advantage. Schumacher later reasoned 'The team is investing a lot of money for one target and imagine if in the end it wouldn't be enough by this amount of points, how stupid would we look?'

Most did not buy that explanation. Fans booed as the German and Italian anthems played on the podium after the race and an awkward Schumacher pulled Barrichello to the top step with him, earning Ferrari a $1 million fine for contravening the podium protocol. Although no rules had been broken, a series of meetings in the aftermath saw the FIA decree that team orders would be banned from the 2003 season onwards. Schumacher finished first or second at every remaining event and had the title wrapped up at the French Grand Prix in July with six races to spare. Schumacher's 2002 title moved him level with Fangio's five and he was in no mood to slow down.

'We won the title in Magny-Cours, in 2002, in the middle of July,' Mattia Binotto said. 'We celebrated in France on the Sunday. The Tuesday we had a test in Mugello. We thought – "Okay, he's World Champion, he'll rest, Luca Badoer will do the test and we can rest a bit." No. 8 a.m. he was there with a list of tasks, checking everything we had to do, like always. It was now about winning the next race, the next title. So that's why he was demanding. But demanding is the wrong word for Michael. He was also very generous to people and a great leader.'

Chris Dyer, who started working with Schumacher in a race engineer role from 2002 onwards, saw the German's qualities first hand. 'Michael was a good leader because people wanted to follow him, not because he wanted to lead. He was driven like no-one else. It was like winning did nothing to him except push him on to win again. Us mere mortals can't fathom it!'

The End of the Roman Empire

As the winning became routine, a different feeling grew around the Prancing Horse. This was no longer Enzo's boom or bust Ferrari, the flawed team which always seem to tread a tightrope between joy and despair or triumph and tragedy. The Ferrari of the new millennium had become something much different: a well-oiled, meticulously assembled machine, an F1 victory factory designed to deliver perfection race after race, year after year.

After years as the plucky underdogs, to some Ferrari had been recast as the Evil Empire.

Schumacher would beat McLaren's Kimi Räikkönen at the season finale in 2003, but that is slightly misleading – in a bid to stop one-sided seasons, the FIA had tweaked the way it handed out points. Ten–six–four for the top three finishers became ten–eight–six, meaning race victories became less important than consistency. That year Schumacher won six times and Räikkönen only once, but the Finn had made far more visits to the podium. Schumacher clinched the title with a rather dramatic drive to eighth position at Suzuka, enough for the single point he needed to be champion. Normality resumed in 2004, as Schumacher won 12 of the first 13 races in a year where he shattered his own records from a few years earlier. The F2004 won all but two races it contested that season.

By the end of 2004, Schumacher had amassed five straight titles. The following year Sauber's long-time sponsor had bought the failing Jaguar squad with the intention of injecting some much-needed fun into the sport and breaking the red monolith. Red Bull Racing was seen by cynics as a peculiarly expensive marketing gimmick of the Austrian energy drinks company. Red Bull's first team boss, Christian Horner, built it into one of the sport's great competitive forces. But when he and the upstart team first arrived, Ferrari was the only game in town.

'When I came in, they had been on an incredibly successful run,' Horner said. 'They had the best tyres from Bridgestone. They've got their own test track. They've got the best driver in the world. They've got the best sponsors. They've got the best budget. They always got the best deal out of Bernie. I remember when we came to do the Concorde Agreement, Bernie would tell me, "Ferrari are the Rolling Stones and I'll pay a premium for the Rolling Stones. The rest of you are a warm-up act." He said, "I quite like you guys, you guys bring a bit of fun and energy to it. But you are all a warm-up act." So that was Ferrari.'

In a bid to make the sport more exciting and improve overtaking, rule changes were on the horizon. In 2005, routine tyre changes were banned. Drivers would have to start and finish on the same set. Michelin tyres had always been more durable, while Bridgestones were faster but degraded. The rule was dubbed 'anti-Ferrari' by di Montezemolo. The change had the desired effect: the red team won just once in 2005, as the next generation emerged in title contenders Fernando Alonso at Renault and Kimi Räikkönen at McLaren.

'It felt a bit like the end of the Roman Empire,' said Guenther Steiner, who had moved to a management role at Red Bull. 'All good things have to come to an end eventually and that's what it felt like around that time.'

That season did give one of the best examples of Ferrari's political power and willingness to do whatever was felt to be in the best interest of the team above all else. After years of dominance Ferrari did not win a race in the first half of the year, with its car simply not able to lean on the tyres across a full race. Then came the trip to the Indianapolis Motor Speedway for the United States Grand Prix. In Friday practice, Schumacher's brother Ralf had crashed his Toyota through Turn 13, the banked final corner. Michelin teams started to notice a worrying trend – their cars were coming back to the pits with large cuts in the sidewalls of the tyres. Meetings at Michelin's Clermont-Ferrand headquarters did not yield any encouraging updates and the teams running the French tyre suggested a solution for safety – a chicane at Turn 13. Despite precedent from the 1994 Spanish Grand Prix, Ferrari dug their heels in, saying the solution had not been tested. Multiple options were discussed, with the Michelin runners even assessing an option which would see them come through the pit-lane every lap, with the Bridgestone teams (Ferrari, Minardi and Jordan) allowed to race as normal through Turn 13 and down the main straight. As meetings intensified in the build-up to race day, Ferrari still refused to budge on the safety change.

'The most frustrating thing was that at the time Ferrari and the FIA would not accept that we change the course, even though we would give them all the points,' Jacques Villeneuve, by then a Sauber driver, told *Autosport* in 2015. 'They didn't want to play the game and think about the good of the sport.'

FIA chief Max Mosley had no sympathy for Michelin – it was a problem of their own making. At the end of the formation lap, with no chicane or other solution in place, the Michelin runners peeled into the pit-lane at the end of the formation lap. That left the Ferraris at the front of the grid, with a giant gap to the back, where the four other Bridgestone runners, the yellow Jordans and black Minardis, now found themselves in an unlikely and completely farcical battle for the final spot on the podium.

'Todt ran Ferrari very much with an iron grip,' Horner said. 'Jean just wouldn't compromise for the good of the sport to put in a chicane. He was resolute with Ferrari in every scenario, totally uncompromising.'

Schumacher's bizarre (and, arguably, fairly meaningless) win in the States would be Ferrari's only victory in 2005 and did nothing to disturb the scrap between the young contenders, Alonso and Räikkönen.

Alonso eventually won out, with McLaren's poor reliability record through the year helping the Spaniard to his first Drivers' Championship, while Renault also won the constructors' title. The streak of unprecedented success for the red team was over.

Fernando or Kimi?

The tyre change rule was scrapped in 2006, giving Schumacher what would be one final shot at an eighth title. Barrichello had finally grown tired of life in Schumacher's shadow and moved on to Honda, giving Ferrari a chance to promote long-time academy driver Felipe Massa into the main race seat after his time at Honda. The season quickly developed into a gripping duel between Schumacher and Alonso, who shared victories at 11 of the opening 12 races. The darker side of Schumacher's overarching will to win revealed itself again at the Monaco Grand Prix.

Qualifying between the two title protagonists was tight. In Q3, the final segment of qualifying, Schumacher was on provisional pole thanks to the first time he set. At the end of the session, he attempted his second timed lap, but it was slower than his original effort. On track, he was ahead of Alonso, who was doing a timed lap further back. Schumacher had no way of knowing if Alonso was on course for pole position or not but would have known a crash on the tight and narrow Monte Carlo circuit would end the session prematurely and cement his P1. As he rounded the Rascasse corner, he stopped, gently nudging into the barrier and prompting yellow flags which forced all drivers, including Alonso, to slow.

Many immediately cried foul and Schumacher's move was investigated by the stewards, who deemed it had been a deliberate stoppage. The German was stripped of pole position and ordered to start from the back.

'Michael had occasional aberrations, things that you could never give a logical explanation for,' Brawn said in a 2020 Sky Sports documentary, *The Race to Perfection*. 'He had this incredible competitiveness that drove him. And sometimes it would short-circuit.' Most frustratingly of all for Ferrari, Brawn believed they had a race-winning strategy where P2 would have served just as well.

As with Jerez, Schumacher appeared to realize the error of his ways after the fact. 'I can't believe he did it,' Massa said in the same documentary. 'He did it. And then the only thing is he was not able to say that he did it. It took one year for him to tell me that he did it on purpose. One year. It shows that everybody makes mistake in life and this was, definitely, [a mistake].

While there was no greater penalty as in 1997, Schumacher's punishment would ultimately cost him the championship. Alonso went on to win the race and gained six points on his title rival, who managed an extraordinary fightback to fifth position. Alonso won the next three races, before Schumacher answered the challenge with three in a row. Neither scored well in Hungary before Massa claimed the first win of his career at the Turkish Grand Prix – Alonso was second, Schumacher third.

Four races from the end, there was drama at Monza. An irate Alonso was given a grid penalty for apparently blocking Massa during qualifying and, while trying to fight his way back into a battle with the Ferraris, his engine failed on the main straight. Schumacher won the race to move within four points of the Spanish driver. Moments after the euphoria of the Monza podium, Schumacher announced in the press conference he would retire from racing at the end of the season. The seven-time World Champion had been non-committal about a new contract – his neck issues were growing bothersome and he was unsure whether he had another stint in Formula 1 in him. Jean Todt had already signed McLaren driver Kimi Räikkönen, who had emerged as one of the grid's most exciting talents, albeit without being certain who the Finnish driver would be replacing. While Räikkönen and Alonso seemed like obvious contenders, the latter had fallen out of favour with Todt at a much earlier stage of his career.

'When it was clear Michael was going to retire soon, we wanted to have Kimi or Fernando,' Luca Colajanni said. 'Todt and Fernando had a difficult relationship since the very beginning. In 2000, we were already thinking to recruit new, young drivers and we were evaluating a number of profiles. One of the most attractive was Fernando. And actually Todt reached some sort of verbal agreement for a development programme. But then he found out that at the same time Fernando was talking with Briatore [then the boss of Renault] and this didn't go down well with Todt. When he found out he'd made an agreement with Briatore . . . if there is something you cannot do with Todt, it's play this game.

'So at the end of 2004 we started to work on the option of hiring Kimi. We actually hired Kimi in summer 2005 for the 2007 season. At that time we had two options. Kimi and Michael, if Michael would have decided to stay longer. Or Kimi and someone else, probably Felipe.'

Schumacher had made Ferrari's decision for them. By the end of the Sunday of the Italian Grand Prix, the news had been confirmed that Räikkönen would replace Schumacher in 2007. Ferrari without him seemed unthinkable – like Manchester United without Sir Alex Ferguson, or even Ferrari itself without Enzo in 1988. He had become woven into the fabric of the team. He had three races left to clinch a farewell championship.

With the wind in his sails, he then moved level with Alonso's 116 points thanks to victory at the Chinese Grand Prix, the 91st of his illustrious career. Felipe Massa beat Schumacher to pole at the penultimate round in Japan but the German driver was quickly let by at the circuit which had started the remarkable run of titles all those years earlier. It felt like another of those inevitable victories was coming until Lap 37, when there was a bang from the engine and a puff of smoke. For a career that had become so associated with crushing inevitability and predictability, this was an untimely anomaly – it was the first time the engine inside one of Schumacher's cars had failed since before he ended the Ferrari Drivers' Championship drought, during the 2000 French Grand Prix.' 'That one still haunts me,' Schumacher's former race engineer Dyer said.

At the final race, Interlagos, Schumacher was 10 points down in the days when a victory earned a driver 10 points. Schumacher needed to win and Alonso not to score. While the red-hot Massa took pole position on his home track, Schumacher could only qualify tenth after an issue in qualifying. A storming start saw him rise to sixth before the race was neutralized by a safety car – at the restart, the front wing of Giancarlo Fisichella's Renault clipped Schumacher's left rear tyre, giving the Ferrari a puncture. After a pit-stop far earlier than intended, the conditions were in place for a storming drive through the field, as Schumacher turned in overtake after overtake to rise back up the order. He saved the best till last, reeling in fourth-placed Kimi Räikkönen. Four laps from the finish he struck, diving for the inside at Turn 1 and squeezing into the narrow gap between the Finn and the Interlagos pit-wall. The two went wheel-to-wheel into the corner and Schumacher emerged in front. It would be his final overtake in a Ferrari. Schumacher finished fourth, behind Alonso, who claimed the championship. 'We couldn't win the title but in the circumstances it was a great way to end it,' said Chris Dyer, who was set to become race engineer for Räikkönen in 2007. 'That last overtake on Kimi too, it just seemed like a fitting end for him.'

5

MARANELLO

'Each day his entrance into the factory would be witnessed by the faithful who had travelled to Maranello to catch a glimpse of the great man. Doctors, politicians and self-assured tycoons stood on the kerbs of the Abetone road like Canterbury pilgrims, palms sweating, eyes bulging with anticipation, in the hope of sighting a man who – to the naïve and the gullible – had reached the level of a quasi-deity. He would pass by, seated beside his driver, and reward them with a regal wave, his face unsmiling and inert behind his opaque sunglasses. For the supplicants, this was a gift from the heavens.'

Brock Yates, *Enzo Ferrari: The Man and the Machine*

Maranello, the spiritual home of Ferrari, feels like a contradiction. It's a modest Italian village of about 17,000 residents, unremarkable at first glance. Strip away Ferrari, and Maranello could be just an anonymous dot on the map of Emilia-Romagna. But add the Prancing Horse, and the transformation is profound. It becomes hallowed ground – a Mecca for petrolheads.

Enzo Ferrari may no longer walk its streets, but the sense of reverence Brock Yates described has lived on. The pilgrims still come in droves but they are usually clutching smartphones as they pose for selfies in front of the main gates, the same gates where once the great man himself passed through, unsmiling, enigmatic. Beyond them lies the famous factory, its inner courtyard untouched by time.

Like Buckingham Palace, the allure lies in what you can't see. Visitors peer through to catch glimpses of the sacred – perhaps a flash of a test car, a delivery truck, or a Ferrari employee blessed with access to the hallowed inner sanctum.

'If I look at the history of Ferrari . . . Ferrari is a small company,' Luca Colajanni said. 'A small company, in a small village, in the middle of nowhere. Humid weather in the summer. It's not the place where you say, "I'm going to spend one week of my holidays in Maranello". But for someone like Enzo Ferrari to create such a myth from a place like there is incredible.'

There is the famous Ristorante Cavallino across the road where Enzo would talk with his test drivers and engineers between work hours. Also beyond the gates lies the house of Enzo Ferrari himself. Only a select few have been given access to this sacred part of the town, the small house which sits on one side of the Fiorano test track. Red Bull's Christian Horner remembers the thrill of going into that much-revered office. 'We went to several meetings in Maranello and Bernie took me into Enzo Ferrari's office, showed me the back room where all the bottles of alcohol are. Everything untouched.'

'There are a lot of fairy tales about Ferrari and how it feels to drive a red car. In the end I can only confirm these fairy tales,' Sebastian Vettel told F1 cameras after his first laps in a Ferrari in December 2014. 'It's not just a story, it's a true legend that exists and it feels really special to become part of that, and to be inside the car, to see the people coming, running to the track and trying to climb the walls to see the car.

'I was here a long time ago as a little child, driving through Maranello and trying to look over the fence and trying to see a glimpse of Michael [Schumacher] lapping on the track. Well, today I was the one running and saw the *tifosi* around.'

There are two restaurants of note at Maranello. There is Enzo's favourite, Cavallino, right across the street from the factory. The other is Michael Schumacher's favourite, the Montana.

In his autobiography, *To Hell and Back*, Niki Lauda described a contract negotiation with Enzo Ferrari at the Cavallino. The Old Man was a shrewd tactician who would usually negotiate his driver contracts late in the season when their options for the following year were limited. Believing Lauda to be on course for his second successive World Championship in 1976 (after nine races Lauda was on 61 points and second-place James Hunt was on 26), Enzo broke a habit of a lifetime and decided to get Lauda's signature for 1977 early. He convened a meeting in a back room at his favourite lunchspot. Although Niki's Italian was passable, Piero Lardi came along to translate the finer points.

They start off the discussion with Lauda saying he would like to keep Clay Regazzoni as a team-mate. 'Suddenly, Ferrari brings up the subject of money. How much am I asking? I give him an amount in schillings, so-and-so-many million. He says nothing, stands up, goes over to the telephone, calls his accountant, Della Casa, and asks him how much that is in lire. He waits for a reply, replaces the receiver, walks back across the room and sits down facing me. Then he screams at me – "I've never heard anything like it in my life. You insolent pig, how dare you? Are you crazy? We have nothing more to say to each other. We are parting company this minute!"

'He pauses for breath as Piero rapidly translates the last in a string of obscenities (it is handy having an interpreter in this kind of negotiation, his interposition somehow makes the expletives a shade more abstract).'

Lauda replied that yes, they would be parting company and he is flying home immediately. Piero hurriedly persuades him to stay and the talking continues, although Enzo refuses to make a counter-offer. Then Lauda informs him that current team boss Daniele Audetto has already offered him more than the figure Enzo started with. *Il Commendatore* summons

Audetto from the factory, the team boss crosses to the restaurant and has to admit that Lauda is correct. 'Well, if one of my employees is mad enough to offer that kind of money, I guess I'll have to go along with it,' Enzo replies. Audetto is sent out of the room. Ferrari will talk to him later.

It's still not the figure that Lauda believes he should be getting as the reigning World Champion, Ferrari's first since 1964, so he turns to Piero and says, 'Tell him that Ferrari would never have been World Champion (in 1975) without me.' Piero refuses. 'Go on, don't be a coward, tell him now.'

'Piero braces himself. He is blushing. He translates. Ferrari starts his bellowing again. We go at it for another hour or so until he finally asks again, "How much do you want?".' Lauda drops another four per cent and they strike a deal. 'The next moment he is pleasant and friendly again. A charming old man, the most delightful company anyone could imagine.'

The Montana restaurant is on the drive out of town, just after the overpass from which you can glimpse a view of the Fiorano race track. It has a tangled Ferrari history. Enzo fell out with the original Swiss family owners who gave the place its mountain chalet feel and prompted his switch of allegiance to Cavallino down the road. Then the Giannini family purchased it and cordial relations returned.

Inside, at any hour of the day, you will find Rossella Giannini, affectionately known as Mama Rossella. The restaurant's walls are a shrine to Ferrari history, adorned with photos of legends like Schumacher, Alonso, Vettel and Charles Leclerc; even a young Lance Stroll and Sergio Perez adorn the walls from their days in the junior academy. The walls feature race helmets from many who made the pilgrimage, such as Nelson Piquet, despite never racing in red himself. Littered all around are letters and pictures from a roll call of sporting greats and celebrities – Cristiano Ronaldo, Erling Haaland, Keanu Reeves, Hugh Grant, Tom Cruise – but for Rossella, only one name truly matters.

'Schumacher,' she says, her voice filled with admiration. 'The rest ... they are equal, because they are all second to him.' Rossella recalls a date she'll never forget: 14 February 1996 – the day Schumacher first walked into her restaurant, just before his official unveiling as a Ferrari driver. It was the beginning of a special bond. Schumacher, famous for his obsessive testing schedule at Fiorano, would rely on her cooking whenever he was in town.

The meticulous attention to detail can even be seen in his food choices: 'At 11 a.m a salad; at 3 p.m. a pasta; in the evening he came for dinner', she remembers, her face beaming with pride at her service to Ferrari's winning machine. Dinner would be a range of pastas, or a quattro formaggio, while he would occasionally allow himself a bacardi and coke.

Giannini's restaurant is a family affair – silver-haired husband Maurizio mans the bar in the corner, while son Alberto and daughter-in-law Francesca are each several decades into their tenure. The connection to Schumacher also feels like family. In 2000, Rosella went to the Monaco Grand Prix, where he took pole position – in the press conference afterwards, he dedicated it to her. 'Suddenly I had all of the journalists around me, asking for a quote,' she laughs, admitting that she felt out of place as the centre of attention.

She enjoys recalling Rubens Barrichello doing donuts in the car park, or Schumacher pranking his Brazilian team-mate during one of the boozier sessions (presumably out of season) by calling Luca di Montezemolo and saying 'Rubens said he wants to buy one of your cars'. To Rosella, this was the golden era.

As we scan a photograph of Charles Leclerc, a clear pang of regret follows. 'They don't come so much any more,' she says. Schumacher's era allowed endless testing and the huge budget Ferrari had amassed by the late 1990s and 2000s allowed them almost unlimited track time, which is why he would see Rossella so often.

'Mick used to run around here,' she tells me about Michael's son, the former Haas driver, looking around the room as the memory plays out in front of her eyes, holding her hand out to her side to show how tall he was. 'When his dad was testing he used to help make me food in the kitchen, always standing on his tiptoes.' Today teams are limited to the pre-season testing schedule and the odd filming day. Rosella's devotion to Schumacher is a reminder of an era of Formula 1 now consigned to the history books.

'It is not the same as it was,' she says. 'We are still busy, but I miss those days.'

Ferrari designer Rory Byrne captured it best when recalling the scenes after Schumacher's 2000 championship win. 'I live five kilometres [about three miles] from the factory. It took me an hour to get there! It was simply unbelievable,' Byrne told *Car* magazine, 'There were something like 60,000 fans at Maranello. I don't know about the exact figure, but there were people singing; every car and every pedestrian had Ferrari flags; there were fans hanging over balconies. Everywhere you looked, it was Ferrari! Ferrari! Ferrari! I thought I would enjoy a bit of the moment by bringing the Ferrari Modena to work. Big mistake!

'When I got stuck in the traffic, there must have been at least 50 people, real fanatics, coming up and offering congratulations. They were kneeling down and kissing the Ferrari badge on the front of the car. I keep a fairly low profile, but one or two of them knew who I was. So, once the word was out, they had to shake me by the hand. Then more and more people came over and, eventually, my car was completely surrounded. I had to get the police to escort me to work. I just couldn't get in! I don't believe you'll find anything like this with any other race team, because Ferrari is part of the local community. In fact, on days like that, you really believe it is the community.'

That celebratory energy feels overdue for a return. While tourists still crowd the streets, driving rented Ferraris up and down Maranello's roads, the mood is quieter now and the test track does not resonate to the sound of screaming V10s or V12s. The glory days of unlimited testing and unrelenting triumphs have given way to fleeting moments of hope – Monza victories and occasional pre-season hype – but the sense of inevitability is missing. One day, though, Maranello's streets will erupt again. Whether on the floor of the Montana or at the gates of the old factory, another great Ferrari triumph is surely only a question of time.

6

THE ICEMAN COMETH

'I knew that Kimi was an incredible talent, an incredible person – totally different from Michael! You recognize characteristics of the Nordic drivers very clearly.'

Stefano Domenicali

Gary Monteith looks again at the wad of papers on the desk next to him.

The logo at the top is one he recognizes instantly. Against a deep yellow backdrop, the outline of a prancing horse stands majestically on its hind legs.

Gary, a clerk at a photocopy shop in Surrey, is a devoted Formula 1 fan. Always has been.

This might be McLaren country but he's always been a proud Ferrari supporter.

That might be why he felt so suspicious the moment he saw these documents.

The woman had given her name as 'Trudy Coughlan'. She said her husband works in Formula 1.

Seeing some of the technical jargon on the first pages he had rifled through, curiosity had got the better of him.

Gary googled 'Coughlan' and 'Formula 1', but the answer he got surprised him.

'Mike Coughlan – chief designer, McLaren Formula 1 team'.

As he dug more, his suspicions grew.

And that's why he was now here, staring at the unsent email on his computer screen.

The title reads simply: 'Industrial espionage'. The recipient? Ferrari sporting director Stefano Domenicali.

Monteith exhales loudly and then hits send.

Without Michael Schumacher, Formula 1 had a completely fresh feel. Unpredictable was one way of putting it – the year would turn into one of the most remarkable Formula 1 has ever seen. Ferrari and McLaren would be at the centre of the on-track and off-track drama, and McLaren would end up fighting for their existence as an F1 racing team. Kimi Räikkönen had replaced Schumacher at Ferrari as Felipe Massa's team-mate, while reigning two-time world champion Fernando Alonso had moved across to McLaren, where he would partner rookie sensation Lewis Hamilton.

In his five years at McLaren, Räikkönen had built a fearsome reputation. An old motor racing adage – especially true in rallying – was, 'If you want to win, hire a Finn' and as Häkkinen's successor he fitted the bill perfectly as the sport's next Scandinavian star. He had also developed a cult following – endearing stories about him were plentiful. Thirty minutes before his debut in 2001, Sauber mechanics had found him asleep underneath a table. After retiring from the 2006 Monaco Grand Prix, he had walked straight to his yacht to have a beer rather than to the paddock for what Ron Dennis would consider essential duties, like team debriefs and media interviews. Replacing the eloquent and logical Schumacher, Räikkönen was known for his deadpan, monosyllabic answers. He gave off the impression of a man who only cared about racing cars as fast as they could go – they called him 'The Iceman'.

'It was a need for the team to reset,' Stefano Domenicali told me. 'I knew that Kimi was an incredible talent, an incredible person – totally different from Michael! You recognize characteristics of the Nordic drivers very clearly.'

While their personalities were a complete contrast, Räikkönen and Schumacher had similar high-energy driving styles. Kimi always liked a strong front-end of the car, one which could slip and slide around in the corners. As was the case with Schumacher, he would use this to rotate the car through corners, a skill that was hard to replicate and required a car set-up to be right on the limit. Although Räikkönen would struggle later in his career, this generation of Formula 1 cars was perfect for the way he raced. 'Kimi in the car was absolutely a machine,' Domenicali said. 'Kimi was a guy who was pushing whatever he had. He was following instructions. No discussion. It was a totally different relationship [to Schumacher].'

Massa, who had recorded two race wins in his first season at Ferrari, was still seen as an unpolished driver. After years of Schumacher pushing, driving the team forward, it was a big shift in vibe. 'I love Michael,' said Mattia Binotto, who was one of Schumacher's top engineers, 'but I enjoyed so much working with Felipe. Felipe is like a little brother to me. And Kimi as well, an incredible driver. He was just happy to drive. Kimi was one of the fastest I ever saw at Ferrari. He has very little words but he's direct, he's fair, reliable. But developing a team – maybe that's another matter.'

The Brazilian national media felt sure what Räikkönen's arrival meant for Felipe. 'Massa's side of the story is often overlooked,' Brazilian journalist Julianne Cerasoli told me. 'But this is a guy who played the game when Michael was around only to see Kimi hired as the number one driver.' Ensuring Massa raised his game to Räikkönen's level was essential. 'The key in that second year was to get the consistency,' his former race engineer Rob Smedley explained. 'We knew how quick he was, it was just getting him to be that quick over a consistent period and assert himself as the main guy.' Räikkönen had other ideas, announcing himself in the only language the *tifosi* recognizes: victory. At Melbourne's Australian Grand Prix Räikkönen took a dominant pole, beating Alonso's McLaren by 0.4s. At the start Räikkönen's F2007 outdragged everyone to Turn 1 and controlled the race from that point onwards, beating Alonso and Mclaren team-mate Lewis Hamilton to set the tone for the season which followed. Räikkönen was the first driver to win on his Ferrari debut since Nigel Mansell in 1989. Massa could only manage sixth place and the die looked cast.

After the race there followed a seemingly banal Formula 1 story. The FIA had looked at Ferrari's car floor and deemed the design to be illegal because of how it flexed. The design was banned – Ferrari kept the win, but any time a team has a piece of kit banned it represents a setback because of the resources and time that have gone into developing it. No-one could have known it then, but the story behind how the FIA investigated the Ferrari car would be the tip of an iceberg which was about to cause a scandal of titanic proportions.

Espionage!

The unlikely hero of Ferrari's 2007 season was not a Maranello employee. Gary Monteith worked at a photocopying shop in Walton-on-Thames, in Surrey, a short drive away from McLaren's headquarters in Woking. In June of that year he helped unravel the biggest (in ultimate financial terms) scandal Formula 1 had ever seen. Without his intervention the truth may never have come out.

Two men were central in the scandal: Ferrari's Nigel Stepney was the instigator with McLaren's Mike Coughlan the recipient of precious Ferrari intellectual property. 'One of the biggest stories ever in Formula 1,' said journalist Andrew Benson in a BBC podcast on Spygate, released in 2022. 'It will haunt the people involved for as long as they live.' And one of them only lived seven years longer.

The two friends had crossed paths at Lotus in the 1980s, working with a young Ayrton Senna, before Stepney joined John Barnard in the second iteration of Ferrari's Italy–UK set-up. Originally a mechanic, Stepney stayed with the Scuderia after Barnard left and became an important part of the team, organizing the race team structure and helping make the cars reliable.

When Ross Brawn left the team in 2006, Stepney thought it would pave the way for a career advancement for him. But the technical director role went to Mario Almondo, an engineer who had been with the Scuderia for a decade and a half. Some within the team saw Stepney as a glorified mechanic with ideas above his station. 'When Nigel arrived in Ferrari it was 1993, it was before Ross, he was key to managing the whole group of the mechanics at that time,' former press officer Luca Colajanni told me. 'He grew up and was in charge of managing all the assembly department, he did a very good job. He didn't have the capability or the talent to be the technical director, or the capability or the talent to be Ross's replacement. But there are people who overestimate themselves in every profession.'

For Stepney, Ferrari's decision to bypass him for another candidate felt like a snub. Aldo Costa, a rising star in the technical department – only compounded the internal discord. 'Everyone thought Costa should have been the natural successor,' said Colajanni. 'Having Almondo is what prompted the spy story. It started because of that. Nigel didn't accept it.'

Resentment and frustration prompted drastic action. Ahead of the Australian Grand Prix Stepney emailed Coughlan alerting him to technical questions about Ferrari. This prompted McLaren to seek clarification about whether they would be allowed to race with a floor design similar to Ferrari's, which has always been a clever way for one team to get the FIA to have a look at what is going on. McLaren would later claim this was separate from the espionage but it was the first meaningful contact between the two over the matter. Everything escalated from there.

McLaren claimed it then asked Coughlan to stop talking to Stepney and even installed a firewall on his computer to stop his emails from arriving, but still the contact kept coming. In late April, Coughlan and Stepney met in Barcelona after a test event. As FIA president Max Mosley would later say in the first hearing on the matter, 'Going to Barcelona is much more consistent with going to pick up 700 pages of documents than to ceasing communications.'

Weeks later, Stepney wound up in trouble in Italy. During a routine test of the Ferrari cars which were about to be shipped off to Monte Carlo for the Monaco Grand Prix, a white powdery substance was found inside the fuel tank. Livery aficionados will point out that race was significant for another reason – it was the first time that year Ferrari swapped back to the darker shade of Rosso Corsa after years of the slightly lighter Marlboro red.

An Italian judge later deemed it to be protein powder, although some still insist it was washing detergent. Ferrari soon zoned in on Stepney as the culprit – it quickly became apparent that he was the only person who could have put the substance into the car. Ferrari later said they had CCTV of him lurking around the car around the time it must have been placed inside, although that was never made public. While it cannot be known what the intention was by whoever placed it there, any alien object or substance placed on or inside a race car creates an unknown danger factor – it had to be regarded as an attempt at sabotage. Stepney was immediately suspended. 'It was like a bomb had gone off in the team,' Colajanni recalled.

Fast forward a couple more weeks to late June and the most baffling moment of the whole saga, a moment which still beggars belief. Coughlan, keen to digitize the information he possessed, sent his wife Trudy to their local copy shop with the 780-page dossier to get it copied onto discs. Here is where she met Ferrari fan Monteith. What she walked in with was a treasure trove of information – car design information, technical details, budget spreadsheets, salary information, strategic plans, you name it, it was in this bundle of documents. One piece of paper even accurately predicted what lap Räikkönen was going to pit at in one of the races that season, with added information on the guiding principles behind Ferrari's strategy at the time. The bundle of papers might as well have had a cover page titled 'The How to Beat Ferrari Handbook'.

You can imagine Ferrari's reaction when they received Monteith's email. Stefano Domenicali maintains he almost didn't open it, given the number of random communications he gets in the average working day. There in England was a McLaren employee with a dossier of Ferrari's deepest secrets, while here in Italy was a team member they had caught trying to sabotage the car. You did not need to be Hercule Poirot to put two and two together. What followed next was like a scene from a movie, as Ferrari hired a UK investigator to look into Monteith's claim, expecting him to be grilled on documents he had seen but no longer held.

Speaking to the BBC *Spygate* podcast, former lawyer Duncan Aldred said: 'Gary was a little bit a fish out of water in an office in the city. He brought his rucksack with him. When we were sat there having coffee I was thinking, "Is this guy the real deal or is it an act?" He described his dealings with Mike Coughlan's wife and what he'd done to get these documents scanned. I was still thinking this is all too good to be true and wanted to push him further. I said, "Thank you very much for coming in but please, I really need a lot more detail, what more can you tell me about these documents?" Then the chap turned round, picked up his rucksack, took out 780 pages of copies and said, "Well I did make a set for myself . . ."'

Armed with the dossier, on 3 July 2007, Aldred and another investigator turned up at the Coughlan household just as Mike was leaving for work. The couple immediately spilled the beans and would later sign affidavits saying the Ferrari dossier had been from Stepney. Later that day Ferrari put out a statement: 'Ferrari announces it has recently presented a case against Nigel Stepney and an engineer from the Vodafone McLaren–Mercedes team with the Modena Tribunal, concerning the theft of technical information. Furthermore, legal action has been instigated in England and a search warrant has been issued concerning the engineer. This produced a positive outcome'. Stepney was dismissed from Ferrari the same day.

McLaren then announced an unnamed engineer had been suspended, although Coughlan's identity was quickly reported. This bombshell dropped on the eve of the British Grand Prix. The timing overshadowed McLaren boss Ron Dennis's grand unveiling of the team's new three-storey, black-tinted glass hospitality unit, the Brand Centre (quickly dubbed 'the Death Star' by rivals). Embarrassingly for Dennis, he quickly realized the Brand Centre's fridges had been filled to the brim with wine from team founder Bruce McLaren's native New Zealand – made by a company called Spy Valley. It was hurriedly removed.

On 12 July, an FIA hearing started in Paris at its headquarters on Place de la Concorde. The spot where King Louis XVI and Marie Antoinette had met their end during the French Revolution was a short walk away – McLaren was now there to face the guillotine, accused of violating the governing body's World Council code on fairness and conduct. Ferrari alleged the information from Stepney's dossier filtered around the team beyond Coughlan; McLaren countered that Coughlan was 'becoming increasingly emotional and acerbic' at a perceived erosion of his own authority at work and had acted as a rogue agent. Otherwise, why would Coughlan go to an external copy shop, when he could have scanned the files in-house . . .

The team also argued that the FIA should consider the tip-off Stepney originally passed to Coughlan about Ferrari's now-illegal floor should be considered as a different strand of the information. Stepney had simply been a whistleblower and that tip-off had come long before the dossier had been passed over in Spain. The hearings, transcripts of which can still be found online, quickly turned into a showdown between Ron Dennis and Max Mosley, who loathed each other.

There was no doubting the depth of the dossier's information. Sports barrister Graham Stoker, at the time the UK representative on the FIA's World Council, told the BBC: 'From what we could see in terms of the information it was incredibly valuable and incredibly important. If you think about the consequences if one team knows everything about perhaps their main competitor's car, one could understand the significance of it. It's also important to remember that we were not only thinking about the 2007 car and its operations, because the dossier explained that, but this was also a critical time where you were designing the 2008 car as well.'

On 27 July the FIA found McLaren had been in breach of Article 151c of the sporting code because they were in possession of the information, but said evidence Ferrari's dossier had been used on their own car was insufficient. Ferrari were livid, as you might expect – given that Coughlan had been employed as McLaren's chief designer – and labelled the verdict 'incomprehensible'. But it seemed as though McLaren was in the clear and that might have been how it stayed – were it not for Alonso and the controversial Hungarian Grand Prix.

This is where the on-track drama came back into it. Alonso had gone to McLaren that year as a reigning two-time champion and, though it was not written into the contract, expected preferential treatment over his rookie team-mate. That had not happened. Lewis Hamilton finished on the podium at his first ten races (winning two of them, in Canada and the USA). Due to a series of poorly managed on-track incidents and some unclear statements by Dennis which Alonso completely misunderstood, he was convinced the team was giving Hamilton preferential treatment. This feeling deepened in Hungary, when Hamilton ignored the team's rotation procedure and went out for his qualifying run first, which gave him a significant advantage due to draconian and incredibly dull fuel burning rules which were in operation at the time.

Ahead of the final runs in Q3, Hamilton was on provisional pole but Alonso was in front of him on track. With tyres fitted to his car, Alonso waited in the box for just over ten seconds after McLaren signalled him to go, before driving off. Hamilton had his tyres changed and was sent out but did not get back around in time to set another lap. Alonso just squeaked in and managed to set a time good enough for pole position. Bizarrely, Alonso would get a grid penalty for what was entirely an intra-team squabble. Alonso was livid, annoyed he had been punished when Hamilton had broken team rules and got away with pole position.

On race day, Alonso and his manager went to see Dennis and demanded McLaren ensure Hamilton's car would run out of fuel during the grand prix. Should Dennis say no, Alonso told him he was in possession of incriminating emails which showed McLaren personnel (other than Coughlan) discussing the leaked Ferrari information. Dennis called in McLaren Chief Operating Officer (COO) Martin Whitmarsh and asked Alonso to repeat what he had just said – Alonso obliged. He quickly regretted the blackmail – with the race about to start, Alonso's manager went to Dennis and said he was sorry for the threat. After the race, Alonso repeated the apology to Dennis in person.

But it was too late. Dennis might not have been the most popular man in the paddock but he prided himself on what he felt was an unimpeachable sense of integrity – he had already notified the FIA about Alonso's threat and informed them that there might be emails he had previously been unaware of. Dennis also assured Mosley there was nothing incriminating in them, which of course turned out to be false.

A month later, the FIA confirmed it was in possession of the emails, which had already been shown to Mosley by F1 boss Bernie Ecclestone. 'Yes, he spoke to me about them and told me they were compromising,' Mosley was quoted in *La Gazzetta dello Sport* at the time. 'I don't know who gave them to him, but I have a suspicion.' This was ambiguous and typical Mosley. In Max's 2015 autobiography he wrote that Flavio Briatore had passed them to Bernie.

After the lengthy first hearings, the incriminating emails were a slam-dunk. With this new information proving the information had been shared around at least some team members, McLaren was fined $100 million and kicked out of the Constructors' Championship, while their 2008 car was subject to a rigorous investigation. Hamilton and Alonso were allowed to keep their points in the Drivers' Championship, keeping that title fight alive. At the end of the year, McLaren COO Whitmarsh wrote to the FIA to acknowledge 'a number of McLaren employees' had access to Ferrari's information and apologized it had taken two investigations for it to come to light. Italian legal proceedings were dropped but Coughlan, who was sacked by McLaren, had to pay €180,000, while McLaren employees Paddy Lowe, Jonathan Neale and Rob Taylor had to pay smaller fines.

As for Stepney, he could never shake Spygate. After being sentenced to 18 months in prison for 'sabotage, industrial espionage, sporting fraud and attempted serious injury', he entered a plea bargain and avoided jail time. Stepney never worked in Formula 1 again. In May 2014, he was killed on the M20 motorway in Kent; he had parked his car up on the side of the road and walked into the path of an oncoming articulated goods vehicle. A coroner's inquest returned an open verdict.

The Final Countdown

As the Formula 1 world found itself captivated by Spygate, the on-track battle between Ferrari and McLaren swung back and forth. The scandal meant Ferrari had an easy run to the constructors' title that year but the Drivers' Championship was tight. While many focused on the internal McLaren battle, Ferrari had their own battle going on too, and it had gone differently to how many expected earlier in the year. After Räikkönen's win in Australia, Alonso had won Malaysia, before Massa recorded back-to-back victories in Bahrain and Spain.

As the protagonists lined up ahead of the Italian Grand Prix, Hamilton led the title race on 84 points, with Alonso on 79, Massa on 69 and Räikkönen on 68. Massa might have been closer to the McLarens were it not for a disqualification in Canada. Räikkönen had arrived at Ferrari with the billing as Schumacher's replacement but he had not emerged as the clear number one and so neither could get the team's full backing. Coming to Monza he was behind Massa, who had five pole positions across the season to the Finn's two and appeared to have momentum going into the final European races of the year. Räikkönen's performance floor appeared to be higher, but Massa's more erratic edges of the previous season had started to disappear.

'I can remember a change in the dynamic of the team and a change in stature of Felipe in 2007,' Rob Smedley told me. 'That was a psychological shift, but it was also a physical shift in how well he was driving. We got to the point where his consistency in the races was incredible. He was super fast in qualifying, we'd often qualify with a ton of fuel in the car, he'd put it on pole with much more fuel than Kimi had, and that had a negative [effect] on Kimi. While Felipe was gaining in confidence, the opposite was true for Kimi. He's come in, he's the established star but "[Massa's] a crasher, he's not going to beat me" right? All of a sudden Felipe starts to beat him and it became a problem for Kimi. The dynamic between the two drivers ebbed and flowed all of that season. But then we got to Monza.'

Monza would be a body blow to Massa's title ambitions. Having again out-qualified Räikkönen, he was running behind the McLaren drivers in third when his suspension failed in a season-defining moment. Alonso won ahead of Hamilton and Räikkönen, who then beat Massa to victory at the Belgian Grand Prix, a track where the Finn always performed well. 'That's where it all just seemed to click into place for Kimi,' his former race engineer Chris Dyer told me. 'Once those results happened it was like there was no looking back for him. We felt like outsiders in the title fight and that was the ideal spot to be.'

The Iceman then took third position at a soaking Japanese Grand Prix at Fuji, which had briefly replaced Suzuka in hosting the famous race, while Massa finished a lowly sixth. That result eliminated Massa from contention going into the penultimate round in China. Hamilton's Japan win had made him the firm favourite, with a 12-point lead over Alonso and 17-point lead over Räikkönen with a maximum of 20 at play.

'The good thing was the pressure had very much fallen on to McLaren by that point and we were just maximizing our results every weekend and thinking maybe this thing will keep falling our way,' Dyer recalled. That pressure showed itself in China, a race run in changing conditions. Hamilton had been in control at the start but the decision to stay out on tyres far too old would blow the championship wide open – entering the pits on severely worn tyres, he went wide and got beached in the gravel. Hamilton had only needed third place to be champion and yet McLaren had gambled on what some considered to be a risky, aggressive tyre strategy.

With Hamilton out of the race, Räikkönen beat Alonso to victory in Shanghai. Räikkönen now had an outside chance of securing the title, although he would have to do it at the Brazilian Grand Prix, Massa's home race, where Felipe had won a year earlier and always looked strong. To win the title, Ferrari might need to call in a favour from the other side of the garage. Jean Todt intervened ahead of the Shanghai celebrations. 'I remember after that race, Jean told me to go up onto the podium, because Felipe should have been in this race too,' Smedley said. 'I don't know if it was a political statement or a goodwill gesture or what, as I was Felipe's race engineer. Everyone in the paddock asked me "Why were you on the podium?".'

Hamilton still had the points advantage going into the Interlagos showdown, but it was now 107 points to Alonso's 103 and Räikkönen's 100. Sure enough, Massa took pole ahead of Hamilton, Räikkönen and Alonso. Räikkönen passed the championship leader at Turn 1 before Alonso got past him at Turn 3, before Hamilton ran wide and rejoined eighth. Hamilton was up to sixth by the fifth lap when his McLaren suddenly suffered a strange gearbox issue, slowing his car dramatically. Retirement beckoned, and then suddenly the gearbox glitch went away. Hamilton got going again but the issue had dropped him to the back of the field.

Alonso got no higher than third, Massa duly relinquished the lead to Räikkönen through careful choreography of the pit-stops and Ferrari finished the year with a one–two. And the World Championship. As Kimi crossed the line, Dyer told him on the radio: 'It's all over, Hamilton's seventh. By my calculations we win the championship by one point.' Dyer's calculations were correct. Räikkönen won the title with 110 points, while both McLaren drivers would be tied on 109. Räikkönen and Ferrari had snatched the Drivers' Championship away from the McLaren drivers in the most dramatic of circumstances.

'We were not in the strongest position at some points of the season but we always believed we could recover and do a better job than the others,' Räikkönen said after the race. 'Even in the hard times we stuck together and we didn't give up. Even from a long way behind we didn't give up. We worked very hard and Felipe helped too. The team has been very close together.'

After such a strange season, Ferrari had emerged with both championships. 'I am proud that we won the title in the first year without Michael,' Luca di Montezemolo told me. 'Of course, Michael is Michael, but it proves that behind him there was a good group, a good team.' It would be the last race Jean Todt watched from the pit-wall as team boss.

At Ferrari's end-of-season media event, di Montezemolo took a moment to thank Monteith, who by now had been promised a hero's welcome in

Italy as a thank-you for his act of duty to the Prancing Horse. 'If it had not been for that photocopy man we would not have known anything about this story,' di Montezemolo told the assembled media. 'That's why we have invited him to the Mugello race track and will invite him to our factory.'

For Räikkönen, it was a crowning moment in a year which for so long had looked like it would not end with a championship. The Finn summed up what it was like being World Champion with a classically Räikkönen-esque understatement in an appearance on the *Beyond the Grid* podcast with Tom Clarkson: 'It's something I always wanted to do. I achieved it – and also with Ferrari, it was nice to win with them definitely. But it looks better on the paper than it makes a difference in your life.'

If you visit the Maranello factory today there is a room full of Ferrari's title-winning cars, including Räikkönen's F2007, in the slightly darker shade of red to all of Schumacher's cars which came before. A montage on screen shows the championship cars in action and Räikkönen's winning moment, along with Dyer's radio message which finishes the loop. 'At the end of that year we had a team party,' Dyer told me. 'At one point, the lights went down and a short video played. I could hear that radio message playing . . . it was pretty emotional. That actually meant a whole lot to me.'

The emotions for Dyer would be whole lot different three years down the road.

7

FELIPE, BABY, STAY COOL!

'I think we would have got a lot more out of those key races if Ross had still been with us. I think that calmness as overall technical leader and his ability not to get caught up in the long game was absolutely imperative. Maybe not winning those races, but certainly getting eight points or six points. Without him I didn't feel calm. I don't think any of us did.'

Rob Smedley

Felipe Massa emerges out onto the podium stage and into the glare of the deep beaming Interlagos floodlights.

Instead of stepping out onto the top step, he walks down the stage, towards the sea of faces in front of him.

The crowd roars with delight as their national hero comes nearer.

He can still remember crossing the line, the fleeting seconds he thought he was World Champion.

He can still hear Rob Smedley's voice telling him he was not.

He outstretches his arm, then beats his heart once, twice, again and again, right where the Prancing Horse proudly sits.

Even in this weirdly contrasting moment – winner of his home race, but runner-up in the title fight – he feels pride surging through his body.

Crashgate

After Kimi Räikkönen snatched the title from McLaren in 2007, the sporting gods deemed that McLaren should snatch the title away from Räikkönen's team-mate in 2008. Felipe Massa's 2008 was a painful year, remembered for the heartbreaking way he lost the drivers' title at the end, but there were missteps along the way which left vital points on the table.

After winning two of the first four races, reigning champion Kimi Räikkönen held an early championship lead, but his title defence faltered from there. The Finn would not win again in 2008 and as his form dropped off, Massa quickly picked up the flag in Ferrari's title challenge. Räikkönen never quite looked the same after becoming champion – you could even argue he was never as good after leaving McLaren, where he first earned the Iceman label. Former race engineer Chris Dyer had a theory for why. 'I think Kimi was extremely motivated to win one World Championship,' he told me. 'I don't think he was motivated to win three or four or five. Michael, it was like each championship spurred him on to win the next one. It really spurred him on every year. With Kimi you never felt that. He was still quick after that championship. I don't think he ever stopped caring, that's not the right way to say it, but did the intensity go down? I think it would be fair to suggest that.'

The perception of who was Ferrari's lead driver quickly shifted. Massa won Bahrain, Turkey and France, and he might have won Monaco, where Ferrari lined up in P1 and P2 on the grid, but numerous safety cars, a wet race and a trip down the St. Dévote escape road for Felipe contrived to lose him the race. Then came Hungary, where Massa's engine failed three laps from the finish. 'That was a conrod failure,' Mattia Binotto told me. 'It was from hitting too hard the kerbs, generating vibrations, dynamics on the wheel and vibrations to the engine, over-revving. That was a lesson learned for us later on, but very unlucky for him that day.'

To make matters worse, the failure occurred on a brand new engine. Here, Smedley suggested, was a glaring example of how much Ferrari were missing one of their most important figures. 'In Hungary we were too greedy with the engine. I remember before that race in Budapest we were testing new engine components. Back in Ross's day, that engine would have never made it to the track. I think we all managed to coerce the engine guy to bring it to Budapest, because it was another half a tenth, or a tenth, whatever, which seemed really important in the fight with McLaren. But Ross would have said, 'until it's completely ready, it's not going'. Ross had such a presence and overarching view on things, he would say yes or no on every technical aspect and you just listened and followed everything he said'. Hamilton finished fifth – the late engine failure meant a seven-point gain on the McLaren driver turned into a four-point loss.

Massa won back-to-back races in Valencia and then Spa, where a controversial late penalty cost Hamilton the win following a thrilling duel with Räikkönen in the rain. A new F1 superstar emerged in similar conditions at Monza, where Sebastian Vettel took his Ferrari-powered Toro Rosso to their first victory (Red Bull's junior team clinching a win before the Renault-powered senior team). Then came Singapore, where Hamilton arrived protecting a one-point lead.

The title protagonists lined up alongside each other on the front row of the grid, but Massa controlled the early stages from pole position with Hamilton behind him. The race was thrown into disarray when Nelson Piquet Jr. crashed on Lap 14. F1's rules at the time dictated that the pit-lane could not open under a safety car until the field had bunched up. In the days of prolonged stops for refuelling, this could be massively damaging for strategy, if the safety car emerged just as a car needed to refuel.

'He was ahead at a canter,' Smedley recalls. 'He was on pole comfortably, six tenths to Lewis, nearly a second on Kimi, and pulling away at a similar amount. His race to lose. Then Nelson Jr. crashes. Safety car out, pit-lane closes. We had been right on the verge of pitting – so we were trying to eke out the fuel. If you go back there's lots of decisions we could have made retrospectively – one of them is, just come in and take the penalty, because we'd still have guaranteed ourselves good points (indeed, Nico Rosberg, who was effectively out of fuel in his Williams and had to make a pit-stop, took a 10-second stop/go penalty and still finished second). It would have been difficult in that scenario to finish ahead of the McLaren but that doesn't matter because actually, you know, the trick here is to collect points. But we didn't. We were just, like, all in.'

Massa's pit-stop would become a notorious part of F1 history. Smedley can still recall it vividly. 'We were in such a panic at that point, you're trying to get the car back out and again, not really thinking about all the scenarios. What happened, basically, was that we were trying to get the car out in front of the McLaren, and we pressed the green light on the pit gantry while the fuel [hose] was still in . . . And the worst mistake you could ever make in Formula 1 is starting to concentrate on what other people are doing, rather than what you're doing.'

With the green light activated, Massa drove away, dragging the fuel hose along with it. He did not stop until he had reached the end of the pit-lane. An agonizing wait followed for Ferrari's mechanics to sprint to his car, before three of them pulled the hose free from his car. Massa got going again but the damage was done – he would finish 13th, way out of the points. Hamilton finished third.

'I want to continue to lay the foundations to my theory,' Smedley added. 'Singapore, 100 per cent, Budapest, 100 per cent, and probably a big percentage in Monaco. I think we would have got a lot more out of those key races if Ross had still been with us. I think that calmness as overall technical leader and his ability not to get caught up in the long game was absolutely imperative. Maybe not winning those races, but certainly getting eight points or six points. Without him I didn't feel calm. I don't think any of us did. And that showed in results like that'.

After squandering numerous opportunities, Ferrari went into the Brazil finale as underdogs. Hamilton needed just a fifth-place finish to be champion. Interlagos had become Massa's domain and he took pole and led away comfortably at the beginning, letting the pressure of the situation shift back to a McLaren team still suffering from the scars of losing the championship the previous year.

As is so often the case in F1 at Interlagos, rain turned the encounter on its head in the closing stages. Hamilton had been protecting fourth position, but this became fifth when he pitted and Toyota's Timo Glock stayed out on dry tyres in a strategic gamble to get to the end. Glock's decision would set up one of the all-time great championship finishes. Four laps from the finish, Hamilton made a mistake, running wide at the top of the hill, letting Vettel swing by to snatch fifth away. Suddenly he was out of the position he needed and Massa was on course to be World Champion.

Had it been down to Glock, the dramatic finish would never have happened. 'I told the team, 'I need to come in because it's already raining in the last corner", Glock told me for an ESPN feature in 2018. 'They told me I couldn't as the pits were already closed because there were people already preparing the area for Felipe and the top three to park their cars. People were walking around the pit-lane so I wasn't allowed to come in, the team said, 'now you need to stay out'.'

Smedley recalls the drama, watching the rain increase. Suddenly the championship was all on whether Hamilton could catch Glock in the remaining laps. 'It became very, very difficult not to be concentrated on Lewis from that point,' Smedley said. 'At this point what I was watching the whole time was how wet it was getting in the pit-lane. I was thinking shit, and just saying to myself over and over again 'please just stop raining', because it was getting heavier and heavier and obviously I knew what that meant.'

Suddenly the Ferrari pit-wall saw it – Glock's lap times dropped off a cliff. 'I could barely keep the car pointing forwards,' Glock recalled. 'I was just trying to focus on myself, keep the car on track. I was slipping and sliding around and really couldn't do anything, but hope I made it to the finish.'

As Glock tiptoed home, Massa finished the race. 'The whole place erupted,' Smedley told me. Massa later said that he 'could really feel the place shaking', even from inside the car. The explosion of noise outside was impossible to ignore. The thick, nervous energy which had been so palpable within the Ferrari garage all race was now fizzing and cracking into joy. One mechanic excitedly grabbed another, who in turn grabbed another – the unbearable hushed silence which had hung in the air seconds before was replaced by shouting, screaming, jumping and laughing. In what seemed like a flash, everyone – including Massa's family – were celebrating like Italy (or Brazil) had just won the World Cup.

But the race was not finished. Vettel in the Ferrari-powered Toro Rosso was doing his best to hold Hamilton in sixth place on the final lap. 'Can Hamilton do anything – can he run it up the inside of Vettel?' asked commentator James Allen as the TV cameras followed the end of Hamilton's race on the world feed. 'Only a few corners to go now and desperation starts to creep in for Lewis Hamilton. Räikkönen's third – and . . .' Martin Brundle suddenly cut in: 'Is that, is that Glock going slowly? That's Glock!' Hamilton was back up to fifth. As he crossed the line, the timing screens confirmed it. The conditions had been so bad, neither Glock or Hamilton were sure what had happened. 'I didn't know I had passed Glock,' Hamilton told ESPN for the same feature. 'I knew there was some commotion, a bunch of cars, I thought they were backmarkers. I came up that hill [not knowing]. It was the worst feeling I can remember having . . . then I was shouting, 'Do I have it, do I have it?' and then as I went into Turn 1 they told me. I was ecstatic. I'll never forget that moment.'

Massa was waiting for confirmation. 'I was just waiting for a message – it took forever to come,' he said after the race. 'Unfortunately the message that came was a little bit different from the one I was hoping for, or expecting to hear.' The bitter reality quickly dawned on team boss Stefano Domenicali, who immediately realized the Massa family was probably caught up in celebrations behind him. 'As you can imagine, it was painful,' he said. 'Very painful. I went immediately onto the radio, because behind me the team was already cheering . . . someone had to tell Felipe's family they had lost the championship.'

Smedley struggled to find the right words in the moment. In his radio message, he told Massa: 'What I can only say is . . . very, very good job, I'm very proud of you.' A tearful Massa replied: 'I'm so proud of you anyway . . .' As Massa pulled his car to a stop in parc ferme, he took a moment before getting out of the car. He opened the visor of his race helmet and held his hands to his eyes.

When he got to the media pen, Glock found himself surrounded by angry Italian journalists, 'pointing fingers at me and saying I had done this on purpose, 'how much did Mercedes [McLaren's engine supplier] and Lewis pay you?' It was a situation I never thought I would be in.' During the course of our interview, di Montezemolo said Massa would have been champion '. . . had it not been for Mr Glock', although the suggestion the German driver somehow conspired with Mercedes, McLaren, the Interlagos pit-lane officials and the weather has never quite been believable. Di Montezemolo and Massa have both made references to this in the past, although both have publicly admitted they do not think anything untoward happened.

On the day, despite the heartbreak, Massa still kept his dignity. Formula 1's regulations around trophy presentations are bizarre – as is still the case today, the World Champion does not receive the trophy until the annual

FIA Gala several weeks after the final race. Every race conducts a normal podium for the top three finishers of that individual race. On that day in 2008 it created a bizarre spectacle – as Hamilton, McLaren celebrated in the paddock, Massa went to the podium to receive a trophy as the winner of the race. In that moment, the quirk in the rules seemed unreasonably cruel.

As he walked out on the stage Massa, his teary eyes glittering under the beams of floodlights starting to light up around the circuit, roared and thumped his chest. The throng of Brazilians standing beneath the podium, themselves still digesting what had happened, responded in kind, screaming their approval.

'I was proud,' Massa said afterwards. 'Winning the Brazilian race is the most important thing a Brazilian driver can achieve. I was looking at the people – my people, the Brazilian people – under the podium and just wanted to show them that I was proud to be there and that we always fight until the end. This was my feeling.'

To many, Massa's moment on the podium is the image they recall when they think of Massa's career. 'That podium ceremony stands out,' Brundle recalled in my ESPN feature. 'Felipe was very magnanimous. I thought it was an incredible sporting moment, sadly not an incredible moment for him. But he took it with great professional style and a certain amount of humility in a moment of immense pain. To win the World Championship a few kilometres from where he was born, in a Ferrari for goodness sake . . . he felt that for a short moment. Talking about it now I still feel pain for him.'

Rob Smedley was surprised at his driver's reaction. 'What's funny is . . . in 2007, I can remember having to comfort him for a long time. He was sat in his room and he was visibly upset. He just felt the injustice, you know? Having to give up the win to Kimi, effectively, in front of his home crowd. He was so disappointed. I probably consoled him for an hour after the race. But in 2008, it was like it flipped completely. He was totally philosophical about it and it was me who was all over the place. He had to console me after the race because I was a mess. We were fastest in first practice, second practice, third practice. We were fastest in qualifying. We had done a lot of work before we got there to ensure all of that was going to happen. And the race was a nightmare to manage. Once I got over that emotion, I think the resounding memory was that it's the most perfect weekend I ever had the pleasure of being involved in from a performance point of view.'

Massa would later say in an F1 feature: 'If the rain had worsened one minute later, I would have won the title. But it had to be that way. I believe things happen for a reason. Maybe one day I will find out why.'

Anyone who worked at Ferrari at the time felt the same way. 'Of all the drivers I worked with, Felipe has been the most unlucky,' Mattia Binotto said. 'Sometimes between hero and zero is just a matter of tiny details.' Domenicali agreed: 'I say this with a lot of respect for Lewis because he is a fantastic champion but Felipe deserved the title that season. He had been the better driver. But nothing was in Felipe's hands because of everything that happened before then.' A fair argument could be that Ferrari won a title McLaren should have won in 2007 and McLaren won a title Ferrari should have won in 2008.

Massa will definitely agree with the latter. A year later, when Renault attempted to fire Nelson Piquet Jr., the Brazilian driver informed the FIA that team boss Flavio Briatore and technical director Pat Symonds had instructed him to crash in order for Alonso to win the race. Dubbed 'Crashgate', Ferrari had been on the wrong end of Formula 1's second major scandal in 12 months. Curiously Alonso, who was talking to Ferrari about a 2010 move, found himself in the middle of both, but was absolved of any blame. Massa has alleged that the FIA and F1's management knew of the race fix before the end of the 2008 season, meaning they could have expunged the result of the race. Given that Hamilton won the championship by a single point that would have been enough to give Massa the championship. As of publication, Massa is still seeking compensation – the Associated Press reported $80 million – in lost earnings and sponsorship opportunities he could have collected had he been World Champion.

Double Diffuser Blues

After being a contender in 2008, Ferrari found itself out of step with the rule change in 2009. 'The car was really quite bad,' Domenicali told me. 'We knew immediately we had a tough year ahead of us.'

A familiar name emerged in the competitive order – Brawn GP. Ferrari's old technical boss had rescued the former Honda team from collapse and remarkably, they had become the lead team, one of the great sporting fairy tales of all time, up there with Leicester City winning the Premier League. Jenson Button dominated the early part of the season.

Ferrari's problems were deep. A moment of levity came during a rain delay during the Malaysian Grand Prix, highlighting the contrasting characters of both of Ferrari's drivers. As the grid clung to the hope of a restart, cameras showed Räikkönen, out of his race overalls, grabbing an ice cream from the fridge. In the other car, a flustered Massa was barking requests back to his team.

Smedley's radio message back became one of the first viral F1 team radio clips: 'Felipe, Baby, stay cool!' This was in the days long before Peter Bonnington's 'Okay, Lewis, it's Hammer Time' or Gianpiero Lambiase's terse exchanges with Max Verstappen at Red Bull. Smedley laughed at the reminder of his iconic message. 'Nowadays there's a whole industry around radio messages to drivers, but it wasn't like that then. You didn't really think about what you were saying because it never got broadcast – never. You'd be . . . less guarded, shall we say. So the "Felipe, Baby, stay cool" . . . that was just a way of saying, like if you've got a colleague in your office who's freaking out about something, it's like, "Shut up, I've got 99 problems, I don't need your shit one, right!".'

It was a light moment in what would be a difficult year for Ferrari. Off track, new regulation changes, a proposed budget cap and the double diffuser innovated by Brawn GP were all making political waves. Luca di Montezemolo, apart from overseeing a team that had struggled to interpret the new rules to good advantage was spearheading a mass revolt by the teams. The Formula One Teams Association (FOTA) were taking on the FIA and Bernie Ecclestone, who controlled the commercial rights, the equivalent of today's Liberty Media. Ferrari did not want a budget cap and, unhappy with the FIA's governance, threatened to lead a breakaway series – cooler heads eventually prevailed.

Away from the politics an incident in qualifying at the Hungarian Grand Prix sent shockwaves through the sport and put it all in proportion. At first it had looked like an innocuous crash – cameras showing Massa's car in the wall at the top of the hill at the Hungaroring. The fair assumption was he had just locked up and gone straight on. But as time elapsed, it quickly became evident something different had taken place.

'Back then, we'd watch the speed traces – you'd have a one-in-twenty chance of being on TV, so you tended just to watch the data on the screens,' said Rob Smedley, monitoring from the pit-wall. 'We saw he had just stopped on track. I thought, "Oh, what's happened, is there a failure somewhere?" as there was nothing on the screens. Asked the guys . . . waiting for Felipe to report on the radio. Hydraulics, okay. Engine, okay. Gearbox, okay. I opened the radio and asked, "What happened?" No response. "You there?" No response. Then they show it on TV, his car in the wall. And it actually doesn't shed any more light to what's happened. They show a replay – he's going up the hill, you can't see anything, and it's like he just drove into the wall. Then I realized he had both pedals pressed down – so he's demanding three-quarter power but has three-quarter brake pressure applied too. He's driving the car against the brakes, in the car. I thought, "What on earth has he done that for?"'

Head injuries will force one of two responses, depending on what part of the brain is injured – contraction or expansion of limbs. 'He had gone into extension mode,' Smedley said. 'We can see on the onboard replays they show his hands are on the steering wheel, and he just drives straight on. Why doesn't he just turn into the corner? Bear in mind this realization is all happening in a 90-second period. Obviously afterwards we understand it better.'

Then something happened which startled the entire Ferrari garage. 'He's opened the radio and there's this . . . like, almost death throe murmuring. It was just awful. I can't explain it. Thankfully I had on my panel a way to turn him off. But I don't know what the fuck is going on at this point. I'm panicking and freaking out. My first thought is, has he had a heart attack or something? He's clearly opened up the radio by mistake but from the sound he made it's clearly someone in a huge amount of pain. Clearly something serious had happened to this person.'

An unlikely visitor came to the Ferrari pit-wall – Renault boss Flavio Briatore, with a printed picture in his hand. He showed Smedley and Stefano Domenicali. 'He said, "I think he's hit a bird". It was a screenshot they'd taken we'd missed altogether, our heads down in the data. We're all over the place and obviously they could see it more objectively. But on the screen is this little black thing. We started playing the onboard in super-slow-mo, you see the spring. It's almost taken his head off. Just horrendous.'

The replays quickly revealed what had happened. A coil spring from Rubens Barrichello's Brawn car had come loose, bouncing down the track as Massa arrived at the same piece of road. The impact happened while his Ferrari was traveling at around around 160mph (260 km/h).

He was rushed to the medical centre in critical condition. 'I'm very grateful that it was my day, thank God,' Massa told *Motorsport Brasil*. 'A lot of people say it was unlucky, but I think that, if you look at what happened . . . on the one hand, I was unlucky, because the spring ended up right in my head. But I was also very lucky, because today I'm here living my life, in great health, and I'm happy to have my family.'

Another stroke of good fortune for Massa was that he was able to be taken to the Hungarian Armed Forces Health Centre in Budapest. 'I think that's part of what saved his life,' Smedley said. 'It's one of the best cranial trauma units in the world and had some of the world's best specialists – I guess for if you get shot in the head or whatever. So they knew exactly what to do with him. They put him in a coma. That basically saved his life. But it was a horrible 48 hours.'

While it put sporting events into perspective, the business of F1 continued. In the weeks that followed, rumours swirled of a sensational return for Michael Schumacher to fill Massa's seat. It was all but confirmed, pending a test at Mugello, only for the seven-time world champion to back out. 'Unfortunately, we did not manage to get a grip on the pain in the neck which occurred after the private F1-day in Mugello', Schumacher announced in a statement. He had provoked an old neck injury in a bike crash earlier that year. It had already been a source of irritation in his original F1 stint. 'My neck cannot stand the extreme stresses caused by F1 yet,' Schumacher continued.

'Maybe he would not have wanted to come back anyway,' di Montezemolo confided. Ferrari's car had been bad all season. The team had not won a race all year. Massa's replacement Luca Badoer, a long-time test driver, had an awful time in Massa's seat, failing to score points in his two appearances with the team. Parts of the motorsport press soon nicknamed him Look-How-Bad-You-Are.

Kimi Räikkönen would take a morale-boosting win in Belgium, holding off Force India's Italian driver Giancarlo Fisichella. That drive led to a dream deal for the Italian, putting him in Massa's car for the Italian Grand Prix. Giancarlo finished ninth in front of his home crowd but, like Badoer, Fisichella failed to register a single point in the remaining races.

Massa would return to full fitness for 2010. Joining him would be a new team-mate – Fernando Alonso, the man who had been involved in both Spygate and Crashgate but absolved by the FIA of any blame in either.

And Now, Fernando...

Drivers returning from serious injury will always be posed the key question: 'Are you as fast as you used to be?' This has been true of drivers from Stirling Moss in the 1960s to Robert Kubica in recent times. Felipe Massa seemed to have conclusively answered that question one afternoon at Hockenheim in 2010. Exactly one year on from his Hungary crash, Massa found himself with a chance to win his first race since Brazil, 2008. Leading the German Grand Prix, he seemed to be cruising to a beautiful victory. Massa was leading his new team-mate Fernando Alonso and Red Bull driver Sebastian Vettel in the closing laps when Smedley delivered another iconic radio message – albeit, one remembered for different reasons than Malaysia.

'Fernando . . . is . . . faster . . . than . . . you. Can you confirm you understood this message?'

Explicit team orders had been banned after Ferrari's decision to have Rubens Barrichello move over for Schumacher in Austria eight years earlier, but it was quickly interpreted that this was a veiled instruction. Alonso, who had emulated Kimi Räikkönen by winning on his Ferrari debut, was let through by Massa. David Tremayne wrote in *The Independent* that the message, 'revived bad old ways from Ferrari'. Many could not fathom the decision – either way, Ferrari would leave with the maximum 43 points, but it was a clear indication of the new pecking order at the team. 'Lots of people said Felipe wasn't the same after his accident. Nonsense. Fucking nonsense,' Smedley insisted. 'He hadn't lost a step. Germany was the moment that killed his confidence. He never seemed quite the same after that.'

Coming a year after the Budapest crash just added to the pain. 'That was the saddest day of my life,' Massa told *Motorsport Brasil* in 2024. Brazilian journalist Julianne Cerasoli told me: 'Massa's side of the story so often gets overlooked, but this is a guy who played the team game when Michael was around, only to see Kimi Räikkönen hired as the number one driver. Felipe then out-performed him in 2008 and was ahead in 2009 before his accident. During his recovery, he sees Fernando Alonso hired and he comes back to a new dynamic. Alonso made sure the team was working towards his own goals. It's hard enough to be Fernando's team-mate given his ability to extract the maximum from the car.'

A few races earlier, Massa had been overtaken by Alonso at the pit entry during the Chinese Grand Prix, a moment which infuriated him. 'Massa's plea to Domenicali for intervention was met with silence,' Cerasoli added. The Germany moment just hammered home the point that it was not Massa's team any more.

As the season progressed, Ferrari would feel vindicated by the call. Squabbling Red Bull drivers Vettel and Mark Webber, McLaren team-mates Hamilton and Button would join Alonso in a thrilling battle for the championship, all five exchanging wins in the year. Three races from the end, Alonso appeared to be on the brink. Webber had crashed out of the inaugural Korean Grand prix in the early stages, before Vettel's engine had conked out a few laps from the finish. Alonso's 25-point gain on his two rivals that day appeared to be monumental at the time.

Chris Dyer, who by then had been promoted to head of trackside engineering, stood with him on the podium that day. 'We never ever assumed a championship was done, even when Michael was around. But that day it did feel like there was a really big light at the end of the tunnel and we could almost touch it.'

Alonso and Dyer did not know it then, but the championship was about to slip agonizingly through their grasp. But unlike with Massa and what had happened in Brazil, this was not going to be down to the weather – it was going to be a defeat snatched from the jaws of victory by Ferrari themselves.

8

ABU DHABI 2010: DEBACLE IN THE DESERT

'That mistake was, in terms of magnitude, huge, and it produced devastating effects.'

Stefano Domenicali

Fernando Alonso is stuck. He can't believe he's in this situation. This was supposed to be his night, the night he became a Formula 1 World Champion for Ferrari at the first attempt.

Everything had been going fine until the team had called him in for his pit-stop. It's been a living nightmare since.

He needs to be fourth, but instead he's seventh and the laps are ticking away. Worst of all, he's been looking at the rear wing of the Renault in front of him for what seems like an eternity. If he can't get past Vitaly Petrov and the next two cars up the road, he will not be the 2010 World Champion.

As valuable time slips away, a reassuring voice rings in Alonso's ear.

'Use the most of your talent, we know how big it is,' says his race engineer Andrea Stella, speaking to him from the Ferrari pit-wall. Stella's calm voice conceals the sense of panic and dread he and his colleagues are feeling.

Alonso, talented as he is, needs all the help he can get. Red Bull's Sebastian Vettel has not led the championship at any time this year and is about to snatch the title away from him and Ferrari. Alonso's old rival and McLaren teammate Lewis Hamilton is second. Maybe Lewis can get past Vettel and make his life easier?

'Is there a chance Hamilton will win the race?' Alonso asks breathlessly, somehow thinking of a million different scenarios and outcomes while driving his car at breakneck speed.

If Hamilton can get past Vettel, then seventh for Alonso would be enough . . . It's a desperate thought, but this is a desperate situation. The reply he gets back brings the reality of the situation into sharp focus.

'No, no,' Stella replies.

'Vettel will win.'

***

Some defeats haunt a sports team and a fanbase for a generation. Losing on a big occasion is never a nice feeling but getting beaten fair and square by a better opponent on the day can be easier to absorb with the passage of time. The defeats that leave the deepest wounds are the ones that somehow came about through unforced errors, the days when defeat was snatched from the jaws of victory, leaving that awful question to rattle around the brain for years afterwards: 'How did we let that happen?'

There are examples across all sports. Liverpool captain Steven Gerrard slipping over against Chelsea and blowing his best chance of winning a Premier League title, the Atlanta Falcons blowing a 28–3 third quarter Super Bowl lead over Tom Brady and the New England Patriots. The Ferrari strategy call that cost Fernando Alonso the championship in 2010, leaving him stuck behind the Renault of Petrov at a circuit with limited overtaking opportunities and handing Sebastian Vettel the title on a silver plate, has to be up there with the biggest sporting chokes of all time.

Ferrari fans of this era might point to the two decisive moments in 2008 as more egregious or painful. There was Felipe Massa's disastrous pit-stop in Singapore and his agonizing defeat in Brazil a month later. While both were undoubtedly significant in that year's championship and an equally infamous part of Ferrari's story, there are some differences to the 2010 climax.

The mistake by the pit-crew in Singapore, releasing Massa before the fuel rig was detached, happened in a flash, while Hamilton catching and passing Timo Glock so late at Interlagos was pure theatre – Ferrari had done little wrong that day, the sporting gods were just on a different side. Abu Dhabi 2010 was also a major moment in a title fight, but unlike Singapore, they had enough time to analyze the situation and get it right. 'That was pure Ferrari. Abu Dhabi was all Ferrari,' remembered Spanish journalist Carlos Miguel, a long-time follower of Alonso's career.

F1 fans know the venue well. It has hosted three title showdowns since – the most recent, in 2021, the most notorious. On that night the crucial factor was the incorrect decision made by FIA race director Michael Masi, who ignored the rulebook he was supposed to uphold in order to force a one-lap shootout which helped Max Verstappen pass Hamilton and win it all. In 2010 there was no controversy at the outcome, only disbelief. That night, the first time a Red Bull driver celebrated winning his first championship under the Yas Marina lights, the mistakes were made exclusively by those wearing the red of Ferrari. For those involved, the scars still linger – thinking back to that night still takes them to a dark place. It was noticeable while interviewing those who were there. The events of that night still elicit a common feeling: agony.

'I am still sick to the stomach [about it]' then-president Luca di Montezemolo said when I brought up Abu Dhabi. Sitting back in his chair and letting his face crunch up as the memories came flooding back. 'It was more easy to win than to lose.'

Mattia Binotto paused for an uncomfortably long time on the subject when asked: 'Details. Sometimes, between hero and zero, it's just little details.'

'That probably could have changed the outcome of many things, and the history behind a few things,' Alonso said of 2010 years later, reflecting on his failure to win a title for Ferrari. Another near-miss would follow for him in 2012, but in Abu Dhabi he arrived with the championship lead and left without the title. Today, the Spanish driver is racing in his early forties, having committed to Aston Martin through to 2026, still chasing the third World Championship which should have been his that night.

One man is haunted by the spectre of Abu Dhabi more than anyone else. Aussie Chris Dyer, former race engineer for Michael Schumacher and Kimi Räikkönen, who a year earlier had become head of race engineering and therefore the point-person for all things strategy. It was his plans in Abu Dhabi and his calls from the pit-wall that would ultimately doom Alonso – the race would ultimately cost him his job. Arguably they set a new normal which all fans understood about the post-Dream Team Ferrari, whether fairly or not: in the big moments, the Scuderia just could not get it right on strategy.

'It's still very painful. It's still something that sometimes I think about and mostly it involves shaking the head and "what the hell were we doing?" I think it's absolutely the worst moment of my career. What was extremely painful was that it was instantly recognizable that we'd made a mistake. The moment he drove out of pit-lane I was like, "Oh . . . what did we do?" It was about 30 seconds from thinking we'd made the right decision to realizing it was absolutely the wrong decision.'

Doing the Math

To understand that climactic race in Abu Dhabi, plus the moments and decisions that affected the outcome, the context is required. Arriving at Abu Dhabi, the championship standings had Alonso on 246 points, Red Bull pair Mark Webber and Sebastian Vettel on 238 and 231 respectively, while Lewis Hamilton had a slim mathematical chance of winning the title on 222. Alonso's win in South Korea and the internal division at Red Bull that season had made life easier for Ferrari. Vettel and Webber had collided at the Turkish Grand Prix earlier in the season and the relationship between the drivers had disintegrated from that point.

At the penultimate race in Brazil, the event after Korea, Vettel had led Webber home in a one–two finish ahead of Alonso in third. Webber had felt the situation warranted the use of team orders to switch positions to bolster his chances of beating Alonso at the last race. Red Bull resisted the temptation to make that call, reasoning that it was better to have two drivers in with a shout of winning the championship than having all their eggs in one basket. It was still very much Advantage Alonso in Abu Dhabi, but Red Bull's decision not to swap its drivers at Interlagos would prove to be crucial to how the decider unfolded. Had Red Bull swapped its drivers a race earlier, Webber would have been one point adrift, but Vettel would have been left in a similar position to Hamilton in needing a miracle to be champion. Crucially, the Brazil race meant F1 arrived at the climactic race with both Red Bull drivers well placed to threaten Alonso.

F1's points scoring system had been changed for 2010, extended from the top eight to the top ten and handed out as 25–18–15–12–10–8–6–4–2–1, (the bonus point for fastest lap was not added until 2021) meaning various permutations existed. The simplest was that a top-two finish guaranteed Alonso the title, regardless of who finished elsewhere. If Webber won, Alonso could not afford to be third or lower, but if Vettel won he could be fourth. If Vettel was second and Alonso finished ahead of Webber, he could finish as low as eighth and claim the title. Hamilton needed to win and hope Alonso did not score a point to have a chance.

The bookies had Alonso as the overwhelming favourite. Since his controversial team orders victory in Germany, the Spaniard's run of results had been Second, DNF, First, First, Third, First, Third. While Vettel was carrying momentum, most of the focus from the media was on Alonso and Webber. Thriving with their underdog status, Vettel took a convincing pole position on Saturday evening ahead of Hamilton. Alonso was third fastest, ahead of McLaren's Jenson Button and Webber. Alonso's team-mate Massa, who Ferrari had hoped could be used as a buffer to the other Red Bull, was sixth. That qualifying session had featured one of the three moments Dyer later felt were key in setting Ferrari up for the strategy blunder which would define the race.

'It's not one thing that goes wrong. It's like the story about the slices of Swiss cheese – on that day all the holes lined up,' Dyer said, looking back. Ferrari had left it late with Massa's last lap in Q3 but he was on course to just make it across the finish line, which is where a new lap started, before the clock ran out of time. A driver can cross with one second left in a session and still complete that lap. Massa made it across the line, which sits just after the exit of the final corner, in the nick of time. But in a moment of confusion behind the wheel, the Brazilian driver eased off the throttle, noticing as he approached the start line a little further down the straight that the clock had now hit zero. Massa did apply the throttle quickly afterwards, realizing his mistake, but by then his car had slowed down too much to improve on his previous best. It all happened in the blink of an eye but by backing off, Massa lost any chance he had of getting ahead of Webber on the grid with a quicker final attempt.

'I reached the exit of the final corner, I saw the red light and, instinctively, I thought I had not got there in time to do the flying lap,' Massa said that evening. 'It's a real shame because I could definitely have done better and started further up the grid.'

Moments two and three would happen on the opening lap. 'It has been such a magnificent season that it would come as a desperate anti-climax if the front three merely held their positions,' Paul Weaver wrote in the *Guardian* ahead of the race. Alonso obliged with a bad start, getting bogged down off the line. He lost a position to Button on the short run to Turn 1. This immediately ramped up the pressure on an already jittery Ferrari pit-wall – rather than being tucked up safely behind another car, Webber was now looming large in Alonso's mirrors. One mistake and the whole thing could unravel. 'Had we not lost that place at the start we would have been much less worried about Mark,' Dyer said.

A few corners later came another flashpoint. After a clash with Mercedes team-mate Nico Rosberg, Michael Schumacher, who Dyer had worked with for so long, spun around while coming through the Turn 3/4 chicane. Vitantonio Liuzzi was unable to stop in time and ended up on top of Schumacher's Mercedes dangerously close to hitting the seven-time World Champion's famous red crash helmet. The safety car came out and the pre-race tyre strategy went out of the window. Most of the grid had started on the softer of Bridgestone's two compounds – some teams thought they could go to the end of the race on the other set. A group of drivers, including Petrov, pitted. Even to some of them, it seemed early. 'Are you sure, box this lap, yes?' Petrov asked his team on the radio. 'We're looking at doing the whole race on these tyres, let's see how it goes,' was the reply from Renault. Fans of modern F1 might not be used to such steadfast optimism that tyres could last for 54 laps, but this was a different era.

'Those tyres were more stones than Bridgestones. You probably could have taken one set all the way to Dubai,' joked former press officer Colajanni. He now works in a similar role for Pirelli, who today are the sole tyre supplier for F1 and have designed their tyres around the demand for overtaking and different strategies (with varying degrees of success). Bridgestone's tyres were of a different era – there was more tyre testing and therefore the tyres were more sophisticated. But the fundamentals were still the same: there was still a 'soft' tyre that degraded quicker but offered more performance, and a 'medium' which lasted longer but had a lower ceiling in terms of outright pace. There was also a quirky characteristic of those tyres which would prove to be decisive. They would start to degrade as the current Pirellis do, which is marked by a loss in pace, but would then enter what was called a 'cleaning' phase – drivers often found, after a brief lull in pace, performance could return to the earlier lap times if that phase had been managed correctly and the tyres had been nursed well.

On Lap 8, while being chased by Massa, Webber brushed the barrier at the penultimate corner. 'Losing the rear tyres mate, losing the rear tyres,' he told Red Bull. Four laps later, with Webber struggling to find performance in his tyres and with his team worried he was going to drop completely out of contention, he pitted for a new set. He emerged seven seconds behind Petrov. Now Ferrari's attention turned to whether Massa could pit and get out in front of Webber – known today as the over-cut, effectively going slightly longer on one set of tyres and leapfrogging another car.

'If you can pass him in one lap, you bring him in!' Alonso said over the radio, his voice rising as he did so. Ferrari followed Alonso's thought process and called Massa in on Lap 13. 'We need a perfect stop and we'll beat Webber,' Massa's race engineer Rob Smedley said, but Massa emerged further behind the Australian than he had been a couple of laps earlier. Ferrari was now at a crossroads. Alonso was going well on his first set of tyres and was lapping quicker than anyone else. But there was no knowing what Webber could do with his new set of tyres – if he was able to carve through the field and pass the cars in front of him, Alonso could be vulnerable himself.

'We were looking at a few options and I remember at that stage none of the options looked good,' Dyer said. 'We felt at the time we were choosing between the lesser of two evils kind of decision. In hindsight, there were a couple of options . . . we did a lot of work after that race which involved rolling the clock back to 30 seconds before that decision and seeing if there was a better path forward. When we looked at it, there was a better path forward and that was staying out, going long, playing the long game. But we missed that one.'

Going long certainly made sense when you listen to the message Alonso heard shortly before being told to pit. 'Okay, you are the fastest car on the track,' Andrea Stella told him. While he was lapping well relative to the rest, Alonso and the three cars in front of him were all seeing a similar thing: the pace from the first ten laps was gone and the lap times were dropping. Was this the 'cleaning' phase, or were these tyres toast? Dyer and the Ferrari pit-wall did not have long to decide. Around a minute later, the call was made: 'Box, box!' Ferrari had, in effect, decided to cover Webber and not Vettel, who stayed out. The charge levelled at the team after the race was that they had been so blinded by Webber they forgot about Vettel, but Dyer said that was not the case.

'It wasn't that we didn't see Seb as a threat, quite the opposite' Dyer said. 'We understood what the points were and what we needed to do against both the cars. That was all pretty clear to us. There's been a lot written about that race and a lot of people have made the comment that we were overly focused on Mark, and not on Seb. We were very focused on Mark once the race got underway and as things panned out. But we weren't focused on Mark because we thought he was going to beat us to the championship, we were focused on Mark because we thought he could be the one who could push us down far enough for Seb to win. There was no "We can forget about Seb, we just need to beat Mark". We got to a point where it was like, "If we don't beat Mark, we won't beat Seb". So we were absolutely certain at that point that we were racing Seb for the championship, not Mark. So yes, as the race panned out and where it evolved at the, shall we say, fateful moment, we were focused on Mark, but not because we had forgotten about Seb.'

Alonso came in at the end of Lap 14. It was a smooth stop and he rejoined the race track in the gap between Petrov and Webber. Ferrari's relief at getting out in front of the Red Bull quickly disappeared. Dyer had been slightly misled by the data screens running along the team's pit gantry. While F1 teams today have an incredible amount of information at their fingertips, in 2010 many of the teams were trying to play catch-up with technology which was consistently improving.

'The tools let us down that day,' Massa's engineer Rob Smedley, sat further down the pit-wall from Dyer, recalled. 'I remember we pitted Felipe and then two laps later we pitted Fernando. But what the tool was showing us was that if we did that, Fernando would go on to win the championship. What it hadn't taken into account was the overtaking difficulty, it just had him breezing past everybody. What we'd missed was the nuance of that and it thinking he would easily pass, which was bollocks obviously. He wasn't going to pass, easily or otherwise. I remember when he came out, I saw on the screen he was out behind Petrov and I thought "Oh, I didn't realize that".

Dyer's call had sacrificed good position on track at a time when Alonso's pace had still looked good relative to the others. The Renault cars had been quick down the straight all weekend and suddenly a horrible thought crossed Dyer's mind: 'What if we can't get past Petrov for the rest of this bloody race?'

As soon as Alonso joined the track behind Petrov the magnitude of what had just happened became clear. TV cameras started to show the faces of the men sat in red along the pit-wall as commentators started to second guess the feeling of the call which had just been made, but they had no way of picking up what was being said between them. As Alonso entered the first sequence of corners behind Petrov but ahead of Webber, Stella turned to Dyer next to him looking for reassurance.

'We're alright aren't we?' Stella asked. 'We're okay?'

Dyer, who now had the severity of the situation they had just dropped Alonso into crystallizing in front of his eyes, dropped his head. 'No,' he replied. 'We're fucked.'

Aftermath

Alonso would spend the next 41 laps of the race in seventh, stuck behind Petrov. The drop in pace Alonso, Button, Hamilton and Vettel had been seeing shortly before his stop had spooked Ferrari – a lap or two later, the three cars who were still out on track found the soft tyre come back to life. Soon the three lead cars on old soft tyres were lapping quicker than the cars on brand new mediums. 'I do remember it was really uncanny that the performance of the tyres almost switched the moment we pitted. Not just for us, but for everyone else,' Dyer said. Had Alonso stayed out for just one more lap, Ferrari might have noticed this themselves and corrected which plan they wanted to follow. Ultimately, it was too late to do anything about that. With the soft tyres now effectively having a second wind, the three lead cars were able to pull a gap to the pack of cars which had pitted, the same cluster Alonso and Webber now found themselves in.

It was immediately clear to Ferrari they did not have the straight-line speed to contend with the Renault, which had roots in what had happened 12 months earlier, when Giancarlo Fisichella and Kimi Räikkönen had struggled at the inaugural Abu Dhabi Grand Prix and failed to finish in the points. 'They tried to do a very conservative car set-up, no speed on the straights,' Carlos Miguel said. 'I remember in 2009 they had a problem with the tyres and didn't finish in the points. I think that was important, they believed the tyres would degrade a lot. But nothing happened.'

Alonso could not find a way past – and it was not for lack of trying. He nearly went over the back of the Renault on Lap 23, trying a late-breaking move at the inside of the long back straight. They nearly came to blows on two other occasions as Alonso became increasingly desperate. There was an added human factor at play too: Petrov had not yet signed a contract for the following season. He knew his chances of a Renault extension were 50/50 going into the season (he would eventually get it). This was massively significant – most drivers, facing a desperate championship leader in a title showdown and with no skin in the game themselves would have left the door wide open, to avoid writing their name in the history books for accidentally altering the outcome. But not Petrov – he slammed the door in Alonso's face every time. Alonso later complained Petrov had driven like it was he who was in line to win the championship if they held positions.

Ultimately, once the call had been made Renault's superior straight-line speed was fatal for Alonso's title ambitions. When the lead drivers pitted on Lap 23 and 24, Hamilton would encounter similar – Petrov's team-mate Robert Kubica had stayed out longer than anyone, but even with fresh tyres Hamilton had immediately found the Renault to be a road block in his way. 'I'm stuck, I'm frickin' stuck,' he complained over the radio. While catching and passing Vettel always looked like a long shot, the additional time Hamilton lost in those laps all but confirmed the German driver would win the grand prix.

Had it not been for the dramatic way the championship was unfolding, the 2010 Abu Dhabi Grand Prix, would not have lived long in the memory. It was a largely uneventful affair after Alonso's stop. Much of the broadcast centred on Alonso chasing Petrov, in vain, as the laps ticked away. This was the last race before the Drag Reduction System (DRS) was introduced in 2011 and the perfect example of why it was needed to inject some action into races. It became an increasingly hopeless situation, with Alonso and Ferrari knowing he still needed to pass another two cars to be champion. The race was supposed to have been a Ferrari coronation but it was turning into a televized nightmare.

'I felt very sorry for Fernando that night because they had all their sponsors there, they had all the board, they'd arranged a massive party for him,' Horner said. 'Santander were all there. They were going to paint a stadium back home in red and all this kind of thing. And we nicked it, last race of the year, bang.'

As the race ended, even Vettel was not sure he was champion. His race engineer waited until Alonso had crossed the line to tell him. 'You just wait, sunshine,' he told him, refusing to tempt fate until Alonso and Webber had both crossed the line without the points they needed. After

ABU DHABI 2010: DEBACLE IN THE DESERT

finishing, Alonso drove alongside Petrov, pinched his two fingers together and waggled them at the Russian driver – perhaps the most stereotypically Italian gestures of them all. Vettel screamed and wept as he was told he was World Champion. In one of the more remarkable statistics of that season, the end of that race was the first time he had ever led the F1 World Championship.

As the fireworks exploded above the circuit, Dyer wanted the desert beneath him to swallow him whole, his brain was already thinking about where he could go to avoid the inevitable bludgeoning that was about to follow from the journalists and Ferrari executives at the circuit.

'The moment the chequered flag fell I just wanted to disappear,' Dyer said. 'As soon as it finished, I remember jumping down from the pit-wall, walking across the pit-lane, through the garage, out into the offices and upstairs, because I thought the one place I knew I could hide was Stefano Domenicali's office. Because I knew he was going to be quite busy and it would be empty. Di Montezemolo was always quite superstitious. He almost never came to the track on a day where the championship was on the line. Thinking back to the early years with Michael, he would kind of magically appear at some point after the championship had been won, or you would hear that he was on his way. He hadn't been at Abu Dhabi that day. So I went upstairs and I went into Stefano's office.

'I remember it was dark because all of the blinds were drawn. There was a television on, which I think had Seb on it going berserk on the radio . . . . And there hidden in the dark room was Montezemolo and Piero Ferrari. So I had run to hide from seeing anyone but run straight into Montezemolo and Piero. Montezemolo was furious and had a few choice words to say to me.'

Dyer did not want to go into the specifics of their conversation, but he laughed at the suggestion the vibe after the race had been 'we win together and we lose together', as others have said in their recollection. Di Montezemolo's temper was famous – most point out that he was capable of a biblical blow up at someone one moment and then a calm conversation with the same person 15 minutes later. Very Enzo. Dyer never got the luxury of the second part of the usual di Montezemolo emotional swing that evening.

'A lot was said. Di Montezemolo said his piece and then he disappeared. Then it was myself and Piero left behind in this dark room. Then after that it got a bit blurry. I remember spending a lot of time out the back on the balcony hoping nobody would come near me. Then many hours later when Fernando turned up it was a bit of a difficult moment as well. Not one of the highlights of my motor racing story. I guess it makes a half-good story now.'

When I asked di Montezemolo about the Dyer interaction, the former president paused for a long time and then said, 'I called the team together after the race. Some of them had tears streaming down their faces. I said we had done the best job we could and that we should all be very proud to have taken the fight to the last race.'

As Red Bull celebrated further down the paddock, the dark mood at Ferrari deepened. There were indeed tears. Dyer said he cried on the balcony and then intermittently over the next few days, mostly in private. Domenicali had a similar moment – the ex-team boss once claimed he did not sleep for three straight days after the race. Dyer and Alonso had always had a tense relationship due, primarily, to a clash in personalities, but the bitterly disappointed driver did not single Dyer out in the aftermath – in his media interviews afterwards, he refused to blame the strategy. He struck a similar tone when he saw Dyer later that evening.

'There was no blaming from Fernando. I was grateful for that. I think we were both just gutted that it had slipped away. I got all the words from di Montezemolo! I didn't need any from Fernando too.'

Di Montezemolo was not the only one who struggled to contain his frustration after the race. A story swirled in Italy the following day.

An outraged Roberto Calderoni, a minister in Silvio Berlusconi's cabinet, felt Ferrari's president should shoulder all the blame for what had taken place. In an extraordinary statement to the press he said: 'Ferrari has managed to lose a championship already won. We are ashamed of this insane strategy and di Montezemolo is guilty. He should get out of Maranello immediately so he does no further harm to Ferrari. By the evening, we expect his resignation.'

Calderoni got an answer by the evening, although not the one he hoped. Di Montezemolo told the press in reply: 'When the statesman has achieved in his life one percent of what Ferrari has done for this country in terms of industry and sports, then he'll deserve an answer.' Fiat president Sergio Marchionne, who four years later would oust di Montezemolo from his position, said: 'It's true we lacked something in the final sprint but I am convinced that everyone at Ferrari, from its president to the last mechanic, did a great job. These sarcastic comments, mostly from the political world, seem thoughtless and offensive.'

The following day Stefano Domenicali offered his resignation, but it was rejected by di Montezemolo. To him, there was only one person who should shoulder the blame: Dyer. It would be a slow and torturous death rather than a quick one.

'When I came back to Italy, I kind of tiptoed back into the office kind of expecting to be summarily executed. And that didn't happen,' Dyer said. 'We just kind of got on with planning for the next year. It was very much, "Let's look forward, let's understand really what went wrong, why we made the wrong decision", all that stuff. I went all the way up to Christmas and by that stage, it was like "well, perhaps I am going to survive". Then I went into work between Christmas and New Year, a pretty quiet time, and that's when the call came. And that was it. Literally walked into work one day, got that call, then walked out the building and never went back.'

Today, Dyer is technical director of McLaren's Formula E team. The affable Australian clearly still carries a lot of emotional baggage from that night. His dismissal was a knee-jerk reaction and one which di Montezemolo felt had to be made, but robbed Ferrari of a man who had been an important cog in the championship years of Schumacher and Räikkönen.

'Dyer was a very nice guy, it was sad what happened to him,' Carlos Miguel remembers. 'Very specific, very mathematic, analytical. A lot of talent. It was a bad decision at the end. They shouldn't have fired Chris, he could have been a value to other parts of the team. He'd worked with Michael, with Kimi. A lot of experience. Okay, the strategy was a mistake, but otherwise the work of Dyer was very good. They would have been better off keeping him there.'

The legacy of Abu Dhabi 2010, both for Ferrari and Formula 1, is monumental. While the drama had been incredible, as a spectacle the race had been an awful procession around a rather soulless desert track. For F1, the sight of Alonso's Ferrari being stuck behind Petrov's Renault would be the exclamation point on an initiative which had been gaining momentum for years. While Ferrari's strategy stole the main headlines, the issue of 'dirty air' had reached a nadir – it was difficult for the sport to explain to the wider public how one car, driven by one of the most talented drivers of all time, simply could not get past another. For the 2011 season, it became mandatory for F1 cars to feature the Drag Reduction System on the rear wing. The DRS is a flap that opens and gives cars a speed increase down the straight by reducing drag. Some say it has made overtaking a little routine in the years since, but it has been carefully fine-tuned over the years.

'I wish I had DRS here last year,' Alonso said on his return to Abu Dhabi in 2011, before adding what has to be considered a bit of revisionist history into the mix. 'But we were not competitive. We were not good enough all weekend. We were not competitive and there were people more competitive than us.'

ABOVE: Enzo Ferrari (right) with his roadcar designer, Battista 'Pinin' Farina, at a Monza test in 1964.

BELOW: Enzo Ferrari's house close to the Fiorano test circuit in Maranello.

ABOVE: Luca di Montezemolo talks to former Ferrari driver Carlos Reutemann in the pit-lane at Monza in 1981.

BELOW: Nigel Mansell rounds the Fairmont Hairpin at Monaco in 1989 driving the John Barnard-designed Ferrari 640.

ABOVE: Ferrari team principal Jean Todt (left) and technical director John Barnard in the paddock before the 1994 Canadian GP.

BELOW: Michael Schumacher with Ross Brawn on the podium at Suzuka in 2004. Already World Champion, Schumacher won from pole.

LEFT: Michael Schumacher, Luca di Montezemolo and Piero Ferrari (right) at Monza in 2006.

RIGHT: Engineer Rob Smedley with Felipe Massa on the podium at Valencia in 2008.

BELOW: (From L-R) Designer Aldo Costa, Massa, Kimi Räikkönen, technical director Mario Almondo, team principal Stefano Domenicali and engine director Gilles Simon at the F2008 launch.

ABOVE: The season finale at Abu Dhabi in 2010 proved to be a strategic nightmare for Fernando Alonso, engineer Andrea Stella and head of trackside engineering Chris Dyer.

BELOW: Two years later it was more heartbreak for Alonso at the final race in Interlagos. Here Sebastian Vettel shadows Fernando's F2012.

RIGHT: Maurizio Arrivabene (left) walking through the Austrian GP paddock with Fiat and Ferrari boss Sergio Marchionne.

(BIG TEAM PHOTO ON LH PAGE) BELOW: A team photo from 2019 with drivers Vettel and Charles Leclerc, Mattia Binotto (tallest in centre) standing next to Piero Ferrari.

BELOW: A promotional photo for long-time sponsor Shell arranged on a restored section of the Monza banking in 2015 with Maurizio Arrivabene (centre) and Vettel and Räikkönen.

BOTTOM: Vettel moves across on Max Verstappen at the start of the 2017 Singapore Grand Prix, pushing the Red Bull into team-mate Räikkönen and taking out all three cars.

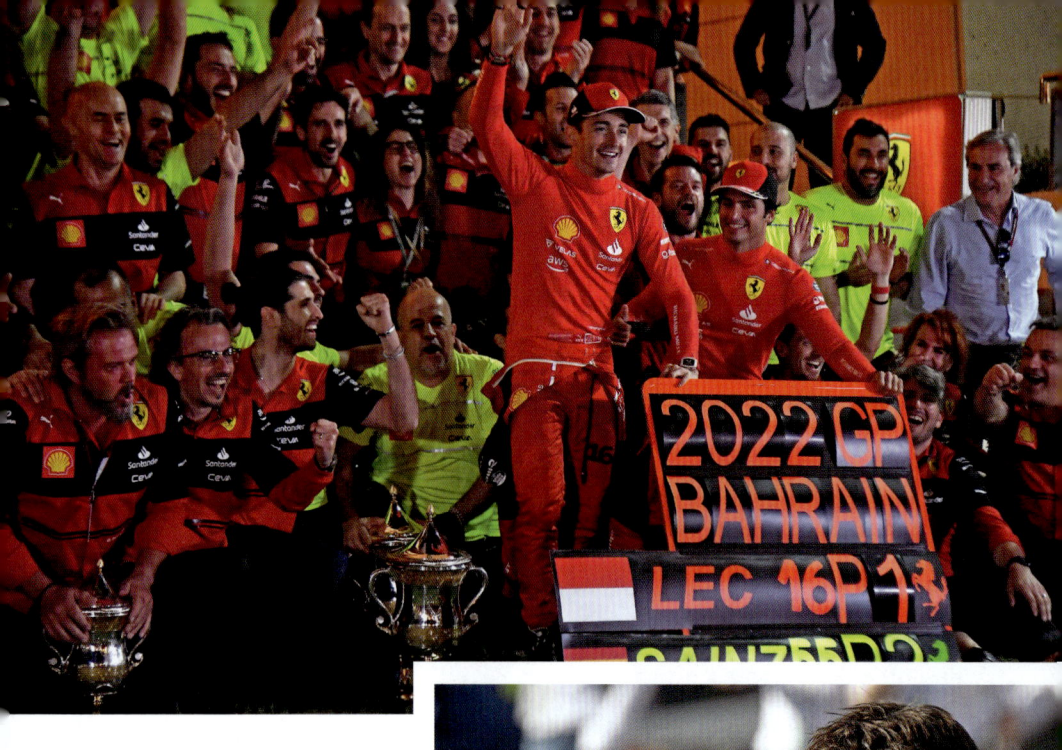

ABOVE: Ferrari celebrates a 1-2 finish at Bahrain in 2022, Leclerc beating Carlos Sainz Jr., raising hopes for the season.

RIGHT: Lewis Hamilton with Charles Leclerc having narrowly beaten him at the 2021 British GP.

LEFT: Lewis Hamilton poses outside Enzo Ferrari's house in January 2025 with his favourite supercar, the Ferrari F40.

That narrative has gained traction in recent years, that somehow Ferrari's car was not up to the job. Dyer is convinced that without his strategy error, Alonso would have been celebrating in Vettel's place. 'We absolutely should have won the championship that day,' Dyer said. 'I don't agree with the idea we somehow weren't fast enough that weekend. I don't think anybody was beating Seb in the race but we had a car more than capable of finishing fourth. We just let it get away from us.'

While every team has made a woeful strategy call since 2010, the idea of strategic ineptitude sticks to Ferrari most of all. The roots of the 'same old Ferrari' adage, which can be understood by lifelong F1 fans and those who entered the sport through *Drive to Survive*, has roots in Abu Dhabi 2010. Today some F1 social media influencers make a good living through overblown and borderline infantile reactions to Ferrari mistakes. If Alonso's heartbreaking evening had taken place in the era of TikTok videos and Twitch streams, they would have had a field day.

While that is the legacy of Abu Dhabi, in a broader sense the ramifications beyond the immediate heartache were less obvious. As Dyer had experienced in that dimly lit room with an irate di Montezemolo and Piero Ferrari, there was a fundamental mood shift taking place among the most important people at the company. As former press officer Colajanni remembered: 'I think in 2008, it was so close, everyone knew it was just unlucky. Then 2009, we had a terrible car. But 2010 . . . the way we lost it, I think that's when the patience of di Montezemolo started to go. It never came back again.'

That patience from the president during the near misses of the late 1990s had been so crucial in building what followed in the 2000s, but now di Montezemolo was growing agitated. He had always said he could stomach losing a championship if Ferrari was in contention at the end of the season, but three straight years without a title – after such a long spell of winning before that – was starting to chisel away at his belief in the team.

Worst of all, Alonso's bad luck in title deciders was only going to continue. As if the heartaches of 2008 and now 2010 weren't enough, another agonizing last race defeat was waiting for Ferrari just around the corner.

9

GLORY DAYS...

'What I know is that people who see me in the streets hug me and call me gladiator or samurai. What matters to me are the 1,200 people in the Ferrari family, who gave me a standing ovation at a dinner.'

Fernando Alonso

No-one leaving Yas Marina in 2010 would have believed that Fernando Alonso had just one more serious chance to win a World Championship. It would come in a season that would bolster his legacy as one of the finest racing drivers of all time, but would also sit either side of two chastening seasons which would push his patience and love of Ferrari to breaking point.

With Chris Dyer cast out after Abu Dhabi and the memory of Alonso's 2010 heartbreak still stinging for the *tifosi*, Ferrari came into the new season with the normal expectations of being a contender. Those hopes would quickly dissipate. Ferrari unveiled the 2011 car with a nod to the past – the F150, named as a celebration of 150 years since the unification of Italy by Garibaldi in 1861, but the title quickly prompted a bizarre news story ahead of winter testing. In February 2011 Ford announced its intention to sue Ferrari over the use of the name, with the American company owning the rights to the trademark for its classic, four-door pickup truck. Ferrari's race car was promptly renamed the Ferrari 150º Italia – with the middle part pronounced as *centocinquantesimo* – and Ford withdrew the legal challenge. Ferrari put out a sassy press release after making the change.

'In order to avoid the slightest risk of anyone confusing a Formula 1 car with a pick-up truck, for their part, the men from Maranello have decided that the car will lose the F that precedes the number 150 and which stands for Ferrari, as it has done on numerous occasions when it has come to giving a car a code name, be it for the race track or the road. It appears that this could have caused so much confusion in the minds of the consumer across the Pond . . . Therefore the name will now read as the Ferrari 150º Italia, which should make it clear even to the thickest of people that the name of the car is a tribute to the anniversary of the unification of our country. Let's hope the matter is now definitely closed and that we can concentrate on more serious matters, namely ensuring that our car that already seems to be pretty good out of the box, becomes a real winner.' Sadly, despite the press attention and the great name, it was immediately clear the Ferrari 150º Italia was not one.

Before the season came a blow to Ferrari's longer-term plans. During pre-season, concerning news filtered back from a rally in Andorra. Highly respected driver Robert Kubica, who had won for BMW at the 2008 Canadian Grand Prix and was considered a future World Champion if given the right car, had crashed heavily, a metal barrier had penetrated the car's cabin and almost severed his arm. Kubica's name had been linked with Ferrari for much of the previous season and there was speculation he had signed a deal for 2012, in classic Luca di Montezemolo style of getting a contract sorted way ahead of time. The crash left Kubica with severe arm and hand injuries which restricted his career afterwards. In 2018, speaking on the *Beyond the Grid* podcast, host Tom Clarkson asked Kubica if he had signed to be Alonso's team-mate for 2012, to which he replied simply: 'Yes'. It would have been a mouth-watering team-mate partnership, Alonso and

Kubica were also great friends, but Kubica's setback ultimately extended Massa's career at Ferrari for another two seasons.

The opener in Australia was a shocker with Alonso 1.4 seconds off Sebastian Vettel's Red Bull and Massa a further 0.6s slower, huge margins in the context of a modern Formula 1 qualifying lap. Vettel won six of the first eight races in the team's Adrian Newey-designed RB7, which featured an evolution of the previous year's innovative blown diffuser. Since the 2009 rule change, the attention of F1 car designers had shifted more towards the back end of the car, especially around the hot exhaust gases cars would emit and how these could be used for improved downforce generation. Brawn GP's iconic double diffuser in 2009 nearly caused the Formula 1 world to implode with the fallout from rival team protests. In 2010, Adrian Newey's RB6 had pioneered the blown diffuser, with the exhaust outlet positioned low above the floor, an extremely beneficial design in terms of maximizing airflow. Although that concept was banned for 2011, Newey and McLaren found some loopholes, rolling out with what became known as the exhaust blown diffuser. It would help keep Red Bull above the rest of the pack for the majority of the season.

Despite the poor start on track Alonso gave the team reason for optimism by signing a contract extension until 2016 – it was a deal he would not end up seeing to its conclusion. 'We are laying the groundwork for an unbeatable structure,' Domenicali told *La Repubblica* newspaper after the announcement. 'Alonso believes in it. He is in the heart of his career and has signed with us to 2016, which is not something a winner would do if he was not convinced.'

It was hard to see any progress on track. After leading the opening stages of the Spanish Grand Prix in Barcelona Alonso faded. Formula 1 had switched single tyre supplier from Bridgestone to Pirelli for the 2011 season and Ferrari found the change tricky. Humiliatingly, at his home race Alonso would finish the grand prix in fifth, having been lapped by the four cars in front of him. Just months after Dyer had been made the scapegoat for Abu Dhabi, technical director Aldo Costa, who many people felt was the long-term future of the department, was removed from his job. His departure from Ferrari was confirmed two months later. Costa had been one of the important pieces of the dream team, below the management level, and had been essential in transitioning the UK elements of the team back to Maranello after John Barnard's departure in 1996. He would go on to become a 'key pillar' in Toto Wolff's Mercedes team.

'We sacked Aldo Costa and sent him to Mercedes,' Rob Smedley remembers. 'It was like, "Are you serious?" I know the car isn't where we need it to be. But you've sacked literally, objectively, one of the best mechanical designers in Formula 1. And what did we achieve from that? We went backwards. I would like anyone to counter the argument that sacking Aldo was a mistake. That was one of the more public versions of what was going on at that point, but it acts as a microcosm for the team just not being united on multiple levels. We weren't doing anything fundamentally wrong in aerodynamics. We weren't doing anything fundamentally wrong with mechanical design of the car. It just didn't feel united. It felt like, in 2010 and 2011, [the attitude was] let's almost blow the whole thing up and let's start again.'

Ferrari's problems were bigger than a single person or group of people. At the heart of the issue was the 2009 rule change that massively limited in-season testing, aimed primarily at cost saving. Unlimited testing at Fiorano had helped Ferrari turn its advantage into absolute domination at the start of the 2000s, but it had lost a major strength of the past. 'The current Formula 1 is still too dependent on aerodynamics and cutting out testing during the season has put too much emphasis on simulation work,' di Montezemolo complained in a press conference later that year. 'At the mid-point of the last decade, there was definitely too much testing, but now we have gone in the completely opposite direction.' He was right – the ingredients needed to make a successful team in F1 were different. With testing now limited, Ferrari's flaws in the area he now understood to be the most important were being brutally exposed.

'Sport is all about cycles,' former press officer Luca Colajanni believes. 'After the Michael, Todt, Ross era, we needed a new cycle. In 2007 and 2008 we benefitted from the long-term effect of that team. But then it started to slow down. There were technical reasons we were not at the top. First, we did not invest in a new wind tunnel in 2006. Fiat said we couldn't invest. We also did not invest enough in simulation. For a long time our car development model had been based on testing on track. But testing was now less and less important. So we were falling behind. The crucial time we did not invest properly was from 2006 onwards. In the last two, three, four years, Ferrari has got back at the top with the others. But it took a generation.'

Without Costa, the technical department was restructured. Former McLaren man Pat Fry became director for chassis, Corrado Lanzone headed up production, while Luca Marmorini continued to head up engine and electronics. The structure of that department would chop and change over the next few years. A brief distraction from the situation off track came at the British Grand Prix. F1 arrived at Silverstone with a row brewing over exhaust blown diffusers and the rules around that area were tightened temporarily, which Red Bull complained hurt them most of all.

Alonso would emerge victorious, capitalizing on a slow final pit-stop for Vettel to get out in front. In clear air he was able to scamper clear. Many felt as though the result was evidence enough that Ferrari had simply not innovated in that area like its rivals. Alonso's victory was four days shy of the 60th anniversary of Ferrari's first win at the same circuit, by José Froilán González and was a momentary pause of the doom and gloom which was growing around the team. It would be the high point of the season. The rules around blown diffusers were relaxed again after the race and Alonso did not win again, although he consistently appeared on the podium. He finished fourth in the standings, behind Vettel, McLaren's Jenson Button and Red Bull's Mark Webber. Massa finished sixth in a year remembered for his numerous collisions with 2008 title rival Lewis Hamilton. Massa scored less than a third of Ferrari's points but, with Kubica out of the picture, there were no desirable and available candidates to be recruited.

With F1 banning the blown diffuser concepts for 2012, and Ferrari's one win of 2011 coming at the race those rules had been tightened up, some felt it was the year for the red team to return to the front.

Groundhog Day

New fans to Formula 1 might occasionally wonder why there is such reverence around Alonso beyond his record as the driver to start the most Formula 1 grands prix. Anyone wanting a crash-course in the Spaniard's brilliance should grab some popcorn, fire up YouTube and dig out a review of the 2012 season.

The prospect of another lame Prancing Horse was the major talking point coming into the year. The Australian Grand Prix highlighted just how bad things were. Alonso and Massa spent a lot of the race wrestling with the F2012 around the atypical Albert Park circuit, which cruelly exposed its weakness through slower corners. Alonso qualified 12th and Massa 16th – both cars were behind the Ferrari-powered Toro Rossos of Daniel Ricciardo and Jean-Éric Vergne.

Alonso managed to drag the car to fifth position, while Massa was a DNF after tangling with Bruno Senna. 'The car at the moment is slow in a straight line and has poor traction and slow corner performance,' team boss Stefano Domenicali said, giving a pretty bleak assessment about how things looked.

Focus shifted to the European leg of races which traditionally follow the handful of flyaway races that open the season. 'It's clear that the unfavourable picture painted by winter testing was all-too-accurate and that the F2012 is currently one wayward piece of kit,' Mark Hughes wrote for *Sky Sports F1* after the opening race. 'That's the bad news for Ferrari fans. The good is that the team is confident it has understood why the car is so bad and that a major update, hopefully in time for the European season, should see a correspondingly major improvement. Alonso is extremely adept at driving around problems, Massa is not – and the way the car is currently configured will only exaggerate the natural performance difference between them.'

At the second race of the year, the Malaysian Grand Prix, some Alonso magic would boost the team. Rain, the great leveller, would help Alonso flip the early narrative on its head and claim an unlikely win. As the weather changed at mid-race, Alonso found himself thrust into a surprising lead, with Sauber driver and Ferrari academy graduate Sergio Perez chasing him down in the final laps. True to form, Alonso made no mistake out in front; it was the young Mexican driver who did, running wide when he was in striking distance. Alonso clung on for the victory. 'This was the most, most beautiful,' race engineer Andrea Stella told Alonso on the radio at the finish.

'This is an unbelievable result, a great job from the team,' Alonso said after the race. 'We maximized the potential in our hands, keeping calm in some strange conditions at the beginning with inters and the switching to dry tyres. The team deserve this win. It's a tough time for us at the moment, but this is a Sunday we will remember.'

It was the start of a thrilling championship season, with the incredible statistic of seven different winners at the first seven races. Button had won in Australia before Alonso's brilliance in Malaysia, Nico Rosberg claimed his first F1 victory in China, before Vettel got his season on track with a win in Bahrain. Williams driver Pastor Maldonado beat Alonso to a shock first

F1 win in Spain, a race that had the worrying distraction of the Williams garage going up in flames as the team celebrated. Then it was Mark Webber who won in Monaco and Hamilton who took Canada. By the time Alonso broke the streak as the first driver to claim multiple victories that year, with a brilliant drive at Valencia's European Grand Prix, he held a 20-point lead over Webber in the championship, with Vettel a further six points back. Second at Silverstone, another win in Germany and fifth place in Hungary meant he had extended that lead over Webber to 40 points (and 42 over Vettel) going into the summer break. While the car had made small gains as the season had developed, the consensus in the paddock was that Alonso's consistency and ability to get the most out of whatever he was driving was the key factor in the wide-open title race. Not everyone bought the idea the F2012 was a terrible car being driven to amazing results. Red Bull racing advisor Helmut Marko told *Bild* (a German newspaper) in November of that season. 'Maybe Fernando has not always had the fastest car, but he has certainly had a very good one throughout the season. If he says he is fighting with blunt weapons, then I think he really is whining on a very high level.' Marko's quote did not age well – Germany would be Alonso's third and final win of the year, although he kept the title fight alive by finishing on the podium at seven of the last ten events.

The summer marked a turning point for Red Bull, which, as so often in this era, progressed under Adrian Newey's watchful eye as the year went on. Ferrari struggled to make big steps forward. Back at Maranello, the team had noticed correlation issues between its wind tunnel tests and the on-track the performance of its race car and this was a blow to Alonso's chances of staying ahead until the end of the season.

There was another key factor outside of their lead driver's control. 'Alonso only lost the title because of two instances of bad luck,' wrote the BBC's Andrew Benson in 2018, when Alonso left the sport in what turned out to be a two-year sabbatical. The first happened at the Belgian

Grand Prix – although it could easily be framed as good luck, given that he walked away unhurt. At the start of the race, the wild Romain Grosjean (once characterized by Mark Webber as 'that first lap nut-job Grosjean') tangled with Lewis Hamilton's McLaren at the short run down to Turn 1. Grosjean's Lotus, out of control and off the ground, did a pirouette over Alonso's car as he turned right at La Source hairpin, narrowly missing Fernando's head in the process. Alonso, Hamilton, Grosjean and Perez all retired from the multi-car collision. 'I am not angry,' Alonso said afterwards. 'No-one does this on purpose. They were fighting, two aggressive drivers on the start – Lewis and Romain – and this time it was us in the wrong place and the wrong moment.' Grosjean was given a one-race ban for the crash. The second slice of bad luck came at the Japanese Grand Prix three races later, when Alonso picked up a puncture from the front wing of Kimi Räikkönen's Lotus, sending him spinning across the track at the start and ending his race early. 'I don't understand why Kimi didn't lift off or anything, because there was no room,' Alonso said afterwards. 'I don't know what Kimi's idea was for the first corner. But this is the way it is and this time it was bad luck for us.'

Across those two races, Vettel scored an unanswered 43 points, finishing second in Belgium and winning in Japan. As Andrew Benson summarized: 'Had only one of those incidents not happened, Alonso would have been champion.'

The Japan victory was Vettel's second of a run of four straight wins – victory in South Korea moved him into the lead of the championship, before he won again in India, although Alonso finished second at both to minimize the damage. Kimi Räikkönen managed to win for Lotus in Abu Dhabi – where he uttered his famous, 'Leave me alone, I know what to do' radio message to his race engineer – ahead of Alonso and Vettel, leaving the gap at ten points in the German's favour with two races to go. At the first U.S. Grand Prix in Austin, Texas, Lewis Hamilton would win for

McLaren, with Vettel finishing ahead of Alonso to round out the podium to give himself another three points advantage.

For the third time in six years, Alonso came into the final race of the year in contention for the championship. As in 2007, it was Brazil, and as in 2010, it was against Vettel, although unlike their Abu Dhabi showdown two years earlier he did not have the points advantage. Thirteen points was the margin and, because of Vettel's superior number of victories that year, Alonso had to finish ahead of the Red Bull driver on points to be champion. Vettel would guarantee himself the title with fourth place, making him the overwhelming favourite. For Alonso to get it done, the racing gods would surely have to intervene.

Vettel and Alonso lined up fourth and seventh on the grid, with Hamilton taking pole position in his last race for McLaren before making what many assumed was career suicide: his move to Mercedes. Light rain ten minutes before the start heightened the tension and Vettel got away poorly, being squeezed close to the wall by his own team-mate Mark Webber at the start and dropping behind Alonso. Then came the big moment – at Turn 4, a rattled Vettel made contact with Bruno Senna, spinning his Red Bull around into the path of oncoming traffic. Amazingly, he avoided a race-ending crash, continuing with damage to the sidepod. He was in 22nd place. At the start of the next lap, Alonso passed Ferrari team-mate Massa and Webber into Turn 1, moving him into third place, which at the time was enough for the title. However, it was a long race. After photos of the damaged RB8 were analyzed on the pit-wall and back at Milton Keynes, Red Bull were satisfied Vettel's damage was not terminal and he set about carving back through the field.

A safety car came out on Lap 22, which bunched the field together, as Vettel started to climb back through the order. Nico Hulkenberg briefly led for Force India before colliding with Hamilton, handing the lead to Button. Alonso, who had dropped behind during the pit-stop phase, passed Massa again in the closing stages for second but by then Vettel had recovered back to seventh – enough for the title if Alonso did not win – before he easily got past Michael Schumacher, in the final race of his second F1 stint, whose final act on a race track appeared to be giving his fellow countryman a charitable donation of points.

A big Paul di Resta crash in the final laps stopped the drama, meaning Vettel took his third World Championship as the pack followed the safety car. Paul Weaver wrote in the *Guardian*: 'Alonso started the season with a dog of a car and although that dog is now good enough for Crufts it is still conspicuously slower than the Red Bulls and the McLarens. Yet such is the determined skill of the Spaniard, and such is the unrivalled reliability of the Ferrari, that even Vettel and Adrian Newey's famous drawing board were not enough to shake him off. Until Sunday.'

Speaking at a post-season event in Valencia, Alonso basked in his near miss. 'Before, the people had a more or less good opinion of me, but now I notice a whole different level of respect. And then, to be one of the greats of Formula 1, it's not enough to win titles, you must also tackle seasons like the one just ended . . . I'm not that interested in what the opinion is of me in Germany or elsewhere. What I know is that people who see me in the streets hug me and call me gladiator or samurai. What matters to me are the 1,200 people in the Ferrari family, who gave me a standing ovation at a dinner.' At the end of that interview, when asked what he wanted in 2013, he replied, 'three or four more points'.

For all of Alonso's heroics, Ferrari had been hurt by the constant media criticism of the car. By the end of the year a decision had been taken about the huge Renzo Piano-designed wind tunnel facility in Maranello. One of the reasons the F2012 had failed to get close to the RB8 was the inconsistency of data emerging from its wind tunnel. This led to a drastic decision. Ferrari confirmed it would shut down its existing facility for vital upgrades, moving temporarily to Toyota's state-of-the-art facility in

Germany. 'The ideal situation would be to have the wind tunnel right here [in Maranello] and I cannot say that using a wind tunnel in Cologne is the perfect solution,' chief designer Nikolas Tombazis said of the situation ahead of the launch of the following year's car. 'But weighing up the medium- and long-term advantages of having an upgrade on our wind tunnel or carrying on as it was, we concluded that our current strategy was the best.' With Ferrari's car already a step behind, the news did not bode well.

The 'Bad Fernando'

In season two of HBO's hit series *Succession*, the perpetually scheming Kendall Roy is described thus: 'He knows all the shots, he just doesn't know when to play them.' This seems to be an apt way of describing Alonso's manoeuvring through various Formula 1 teams over his career. By 2013, Fernando's patience was fading fast. He had chosen Ferrari over Red Bull several years earlier but had seen the Austrian team win three consecutive championships coming into 2013.

Alonso has rejected suggestions he can be a negative influence but the cracks in his Ferrari optimism were on display for all to see in 2013. Behind the scenes he could range between being a mope or a political menace. In the media, he had become outwardly pessimistic about Ferrari's chances. Beyond the obvious frustration of having two titles slip through his fingers, he realized his long-held view of Ferrari had been wrong. Years earlier, at the 2009 Singapore Grand Prix, while fending off the fallout of the previous year's Crashgate incident, Alonso had made a cryptic comment about his future team. 'Winning for Ferrari is easier than becoming champion against them,' he said, just several weeks before his 2010 switch was announced. What did he mean? One of the ex-Ferrari figures interviewed for this project agreed to offer a theory, providing their name was not put alongside the quote.

'He was very much convinced we had power, a political power, that we could fix something if necessary,' they revealed. 'Of course we had power, but not as much as he was thinking, and when he realized that wasn't the case.... Things were changing in that respect anyway. Monza 2006, the battle of Renault against Ferrari – we made a protest because he had impeded Felipe in qualifying. I have to say, Felipe was far away! When the grid penalty was confirmed he was mad... in the morning Fernando and Briatore called a press conference. Spitting mad. Then, 2007, there was the spy story. So he was thinking – "I'll go to Ferrari. Ferrari is Big Brother. They can do what they want."' Having entered Formula 1 during the era of the 'Ferrari International Assistance' moniker for the governing body, the FIA (actually the Fédération Internationale de l'Automobile), it was perhaps not an unreasonable view for Alonso or any other driver to have held.

Reporters who followed Alonso closely during this time believe a level of resentment began to grow at the path his career had taken. It was not uncommon in this era for Alonso to flippantly dismiss the achievements of Vettel, who he often claimed would not be winning championships had he not been blessed with a succession of world-beating Red Bulls. The comments always suggested Alonso felt like the Red Bull driver was carving out a legacy that should have been his own. At one stage, it had looked as though he would dominate the post-Schumacher landscape in the way Vettel was at that time.

Two early Alonso wins in 2013 would be the high point of that year. He beat Vettel in China, the third race on the calendar, but finished eighth in Bahrain. Then came the Spanish Grand Prix, where Alonso qualified fifth. After passing Hamilton and Räikkönen at Turn 1 Fernando managed to pull off an audacious four-stop strategy to beat Ferrari's last World Champion to victory. He would not win again for a decade. The scale of Alonso's frustration with the team in 2013 was never more apparent than at the Hungarian Grand Prix. He arrived at the race after weeks of reports he was once again talking to the Red Bull team, and according to a BBC report he had arrived in Budapest angry and agitated that a contract had not been forthcoming from Christian Horner's outfit. Alonso would qualify and finish fifth, 30 seconds behind Hamilton, who scored his first victory for Mercedes.

After the race, Alonso had his very own pithy Alain Prost moment, although the ramifications were not quite so severe. With his birthday falling a day later, a journalist had asked him what present he would like to get. Alonso replied, *'la machine deli altri'*, which translates as 'someone else's car'. It wasn't quite so egregious as Prost comparing his Ferrari to a truck, but Luca di Montezemolo took a dim view. 'There is a need to close ranks, without giving in to rash outbursts that, while understandable in the immediate aftermath of a bad result, are no use to anyone,' were the comments that leaked out into the Italian press. Ferrari went a step further, sending out a remarkable press release that noted di Montezemolo had phoned Alonso and wished him a happy 32nd birthday but had also 'tweaked his ear' for the comments made after the race. The statement added, 'All the great champions who have driven for Ferrari have always been asked to put the interests of the team above their own'. The Italian squad had never been one to air its dirty laundry in public.

This incident perhaps summed up best of all why Alonso was never going to be a longer term fit for Ferrari. Through sheer force of will he had taken Ferrari close to the title in 2010 and 2012 but his inability to put the Prancing Horse before his own interests is what ultimately set him apart from Schumacher. Räikkönen's strength had been that he was so unfazed by the media and such a no-nonsense kind of guy that he never caused the team unnecessary pressure. The fiery passion which made Alonso such a great racing driver too often would spill over into something a lot nastier. 'He started to lose faith in our technical capabilities, our staff capabilities, our political capabilities,' Colajanni said. 'And once that happened he became the bad Fernando, when he started to become a destabilizing factor.'

In 2018, after he had stepped down as president, di Montezemolo revealed: 'For sure, the biggest difference between Michael Schumacher and Alonso is that Michael in the best and in the worst moments was always very, very close to the team. Fernando is a guy that in comparison with Michael is more concentrated on himself than on the atmosphere of the team. This doesn't mean he is not good for the team. But I was obliged to work a lot with him on his mind, on his attitude. Because for him it was more easy to make criticisms. Not outside, but inside the team sometimes.'

It would be wrong to lay the blame for the problems behind the scenes solely at Alonso's feet. The years that followed Abu Dhabi and Ferrari's failure to adapt had changed di Montezemolo's mindset. For much of the remainder of the 2010s, it would be said that fear hung in the corridors of Maranello – the Abu Dhabi effect – with staff tiptoeing around management and afraid to make mistakes. Luca Colajanni is in no doubt who promoted it: 'Unfortunately the first person to apply this culture of fear was di Montezemolo,' revealed the former press officer, who left his role at the end of 2012. 'He lost the patience. In 2010 we fucked up in Abu Dhabi, Chris Dyer – gone. Four months later we realized the 2011 car was shit, Aldo Costa – gone. It happened to me as well. Because Fernando was not happy with me in 2012 – Colajanni's gone. Head of sponsorship – gone. In the end it would backfire on [di Montezemolo] too'.

With Alonso's future an open question, di Montezemolo had kept faith in his usual policy of signing a driver a season ahead of time. Former Ferrari champion Räikkönen had penned a deal in 2012 for a return in the 2014 season, but for a long time it was unclear to the team whether he would be Alonso or Massa's team-mate. A final meeting between Alonso and Red Bull after the Belgian Grand Prix had come to nothing and the

Spaniard's strong options were limited, meaning he opted to stay for the following season.

'By that point Felipe needed a change,' Rob Smedley said. 'It was clear for a while the direction the team wanted to go.' Massa and Smedley signed with Williams for 2014, which was a season pundits were finding increasingly difficult to call in advance. A change was on the horizon. In a bid to become more sustainable and relevant in the modern world, the sport had agreed a switch from V8 engines to V6 hybrids for the 2014 season. It was an extensive project for teams to focus on and it would require a complete refocus of energy and budget. It presented the chance for a reset in the pecking order after four straight Red Bull championships. Many worried it would be a cumbersome and expensive reset. But Ferrari was a company founded on the principle that the engine was the central piece of the puzzle, that what lay underneath the Rosso Corsa-painted bodywork should always be the envy of its rivals – this would surely be the chance to prove Enzo Ferrari's famous maxim . . .

10

2014: FATALLY FLAWED

'Aerodynamics are for people who can't build engines'
Enzo Ferrari

The engine is to Ferrari what the monarchy is to the United Kingdom or what the Constitution is to the United States of America. Enzo Ferrari saw the machine inside his cars as the fundamental singular thing around which everything else was built, perhaps even more important than the drivers he paid to push the pedals. Enzo's first love had been 12 cylinders – he once commented that he had married the V12 engine and never divorced – and his original race engine sits proudly in the Modena museum, which has converted the buildings in the company' original factory into a shrine to the company's early racing success.

Formula 1 has changed significantly since Enzo's death in 1988. Ferrari's 1995 car had been the last to run a V12. V10s had then become the norm until 2006 when teams switched to V8s. Even in years when Ferrari had not won a championship, the team's engine had always been competitive enough to leave the team in the mix. Part of the mythology around the team has always been what lay beneath the bodywork – every Italian Grand Prix would be met with excitement at the imminent arrival of Ferrari's latest 'Monza engine'. It was so intrinsic to the company's DNA it was hard to imagine Ferrari ever getting it wrong.

Then came 2014 and the switch from V8s to V6 turbo hybrids. Formula 1 has always moved in cycles of regulation changes, both in terms of aerodynamics and engines. Part of that is to act as a reset button to prevent long spells of domination, but the shift over several decades towards hybrid engine technology came from a mix of factors: environmental concerns, technological advancements, cost control, sustainability, road relevance and a desire to attract new manufacturers to compete in the sport. With that shift, the unthinkable came true: Ferrari built itself an uncompetitive engine. For a company so intertwined with the idea of a powerful engine that its rivals envied, this would quickly become a difficult reality to swallow.

It would become the headline of the year. Ferrari had not simply been beaten to a championship by Mercedes, they had failed to compete at all. The lacklustre engine the team built that year led to Ferrari's first winless F1 season since 1993, with only two visits to the podium. The magnitude of that failure would have huge ramifications. The season was one of the most turbulent Ferrari has experienced in the modern era – similar examples of a team being reshaped from top to bottom in such a short space of time are hard to find.

By the end of 2014, Luca di Montezemolo had been pushed aside after 23 years as Ferrari president, the F1 team had cycled through three different team principals, swapped one superstar driver in Fernando Alonso for another in Sebastian Vettel, axed both its chief car designer and the head of its engine division, while also overhauling most of its technical department. Most tragically, away from the staff moves and the petty politics, an avoidable accident in the pouring rain at the Japanese Grand Prix would cost Ferrari one of F1's brightest young talents, a driver who many thought would be the future of the race team – Jules Bianchi.

The end-of-year summary of Sergio Marchionne did not dress it up: '2014 for Ferrari was a huge disaster.' Marchionne was the ruthless and ambitious Chrysler executive who ousted di Montezemolo from his role mid-way through the season. It was a landmark year and a symbolic one, too: if you wanted to find a clear and unmistakable break between the glory days and what we might recognize as the modern Ferrari of 2024, this was it. Nothing would ever quite be the same again.

Power Struggle

Luca di Montezemolo can still remember the moment when he realized Ferrari was in big trouble.

'That was one of the worst days of Ferrari. The first test of that new engine the year before [2013], the first driver was Felipe. At the end of the day he called me and said, "Mr President, we have no power". I thought, "What do you mean, no power?" And remember, you were not able to do anything to the engine. So I said to myself, "Okay, first day, maybe they didn't adjust the engine properly." Second day, Fernando called me, he said, "Disaster. The car has no power." So I was really in the shit because I understood then our engine was not good enough. And I knew we were not able to change anything.'

By pre-season testing in 2014 Massa had made way for the returning Kimi Räikkönen, but the vibe remained the same. It quickly dawned on F1 media that year how much of a mess Ferrari and Renault were in relative to Mercedes. It was my first season covering the sport for ESPN and it was shocking to realize just how wrong both had got it when there had been so much time to prepare. F1 had outlined the new regulations in 2011, effectively giving the sport's three manufacturers (Ferrari, Mercedes and Renault) a three-year head start. Di Montezemolo, who had pioneered Ferrari's first hybrid road car, LaFerrari, had not wanted to block the regulation change despite reservations about it.

'I didn't want people to think Ferrari objected to change because we were not strong enough. I did not want to make the condition "No, no, no, leave everything as it is". No, we had to look ahead. Ferrari always looked ahead in terms of new technology. Don't forget, LaFerrari is still the only hybrid Ferrari. We were the first to introduce the Formula 1 gearbox to the road cars. So I didn't want to say "No" to the new rules, because maybe people would think, "Oh, Ferrari cannot make this car".'

But the idea Ferrari had simply not been up to the challenge of the new rules quickly grew. The F14T was an odd-looking beast, thanks mainly to the aerodynamic portion of the rule changes that year. That new era became notorious for the ugly nose designs on cars up and down the grid. Ferrari's looked awful, with the front end of the chassis sloping dramatically into the nose like a halfpipe down towards a small inlet at the front. Lotus went for a nose design that resembled walrus tusks, Sauber's was quickly compared to an anteater, while the tiny Caterham team went for something that looked downright phallic. From an aesthetic viewpoint it has to be one of the worst years for watching F1 on TV, especially when cars were racing head on towards the camera.

But, as Massa and Alonso had initially reported to the president, most worrisome of all about the F14T was the hybrid engine unit. While everyone quickly came to realize how unpopular the new engines were, only one manufacturer had embraced how complicated the project would be. Mercedes had returned to F1 by purchasing Brawn GP in 2010 but quickly traded in short-term gains for the big rules changes on the horizon. In those preceding years, the company worked at integrating the work of their aerodynamic factory at Brackley and engine department at Brixworth, situated some 30 miles (48 km) apart. They hired the best minds and invested in the right technology.

The comprehensive plan Mercedes had laid out for the 2014 engine change was so impressive that di Montezemolo's old favourite Niki Lauda, by then working in an executive role for the German manufacturer, used it as a pitch to convince Lewis Hamilton to leave McLaren one year before the new rules came into force. It seemed like a crazy move at the time but is now viewed as the best team switch any driver has ever made.

Worst of all, the quirks of the new rules meant the team which started with the best package would likely remain ahead for the foreseeable future. Mattia Binotto, who would emerge from the wreckage of 2014 as the head of Ferrari's engine department, summed it up simply. 'What happened was Mercedes doubled the budget, raised the level, and we never really were in the game,' he said. 'For us it was difficult to accept and difficult to understand. I think by 2014 we realized what had happened but by then it was too late.'

Di Montezemolo felt that Ferrari had lost out due to quirks in the European automotive industry. 'In Germany the car manufacturers had far more experience in hybrid cars than in Italy. So it was difficult for me even when I understood that our organization was not strong enough for this new engine, to find people in Italy, so expert like in Germany. Because Germany is not just Mercedes – it is BMW, Porsche, Audi. Even the universities. So we underestimated this.'

Whatever the reasons, Mercedes started the year in explosive fashion compared to Ferrari – it was clear their V6 turbo power unit was the class of the field. Many were shocked to see how far ahead the Silver Arrows cars – and the teams Mercedes sold engines to – were in early 2014. Nico Rosberg and Hamilton took a win apiece in Australia and Malaysia. In contrast to the Mercedes W04, the Ferrari F14T was overweight and underpowered. The Ferrari engine also gave a harsh delivery of power to the car, making it difficult to drive out of corners. Alonso had shown his class by dragging it to a pair of unlikely fourth-place finishes from those opening rounds, but huge disappointment followed at the Bahrain Grand Prix. Alonso and Räikkönen could only finish ninth and tenth in a race remembered for

Hamilton and Rosberg's thrilling battle for the win following a late safety car restart, but the result itself highlighted how stark the gap between the three engine manufacturers was. Seven of the top eight finishing positions were Mercedes-powered cars, broken only by Sebastian Vettel's Red Bull-Renault in seventh. Alonso and Räikkönen were the only Ferrari-powered cars in the top ten.

After Bahrain, something had to give. Di Montezemolo needed to make a change. The week after the race Ferrari announced Domenicali would be leaving the team. In the announcement of his departure, Domenicali's exit quote was tinged with regret: 'There are special moments that come along in everyone's professional life, when one needs courage to take difficult and very agonizing decisions. As the boss, I take responsibility, as I have always done, for our current situation. This decision has been taken with the aim of doing something to shake things up and for the good of this group of people that I feel very close to. I hope that very soon, Ferrari will be back where it deserves to be . . . I only regret that we have been unable to harvest what we worked so hard to sow in recent years.'

A Ferrari man to the very core of his being, Domenicali had joined Ferrari in June 1991, moving up to the race team in July 1993. He had climbed through just about every department until he replaced Jean Todt at the head of the team. He was given a hero's departure – he estimates that after the news went public, he walked around the Maranello factory and shook the hands of more than 1,000 employees. His legacy at F1 was an unfulfilled one – he had been a cog in the Schumacher years and risen to the position of team principal in November 2007 just as Kimi Räikkönen's name was engraved on the drivers' trophy. Although Domenicali's Ferrari won the 2008 Constructors' Championship, he never managed to get a driver over the line. His time at the top of the race team culminated in three agonizing defeats at the final race: with Massa in 2008 and with Alonso in 2010 and 2012.

Di Montezemolo was determined to promote from within, as he had done with Domenicali himself, but found no-one in the race team ready to step up. He turned to a man completely unknown in the world of F1, but a rising star within the wider Ferrari family. Marco Mattiacci, who had been hugely successful as the CEO of Ferrari North America, almost doubling brand sales in those markets, was the man chosen to take the job despite almost no motor racing experience. It was a quick turnaround – on the Monday of that week, he had woken to a call at 5.58 a.m. from di Montezemolo. He flew to Maranello to accept the job and then to Shanghai for the next round of the calendar – he memorably arrived wearing sunglasses, having barely slept.

'We do not give up,' he said in his first press conference. 'The world title must remain the goal.'

But the reality behind the scenes was very different. Ferrari was completely hamstrung by its engine and power unit and there seemed little to no chance of being competitive that year. Binotto remembers the situation well. 'When you are down hundreds of horsepower to your competitors, you are slow in the straights, there's nothing you can do really. I remember how much Fernando was unhappy with the performance.'

Formula 1's rules did not help in that regard either. The sport's three manufacturers were limited to a 'token' system, where they were literally given a certain number of tokens as currency – each upgrade cost a certain number, limiting the improvements that could actually be made through the year. As Mercedes had the same tokens as Ferrari and Renault, it was very difficult for anyone to make substantial gains on the class-leading team.

Christian Horner, whose Red Bull team had been held back by a significantly underpowered Renault power unit, became outspoken very quickly. 'Sometimes you have to put your hand up and say we got it wrong. I think with the engine regulations, the people involved got it wrong. Not only have we got an enormously expensive engine, we've got an engine that we have got very limited development on, so all you are going to do is freeze in the advantage that we currently see.'

In June, di Montezemolo made headlines in a *Wall Street Journal* interview in which he stated, 'F1 isn't working', which came with a thinly veiled threat that Ferrari might walk away if the sport persisted with the new formula. Though di Montezemolo had not wanted to block the engine change for fear of it looking like sour grapes, his response, now Ferrari was actually significantly behind Mercedes, looked to be exactly that. It was a misguided interview and looked like one final throw of the dice from someone who was now clinging on to his power and relevancy in the company. Unfortunately for him, Fiat boss Sergio Marchionne quickly decided it was di Montezemolo who was in fact not working. The ambitious Canadian–Italian had wanted control of the company for a while. Shots started to be fired in the press.

'The heart of Ferrari is winning in F1,' Marchionne said later that year. 'I don't want to see our drivers in 7th and 12th place. To see the Reds in this state, having the best drivers, exceptional facilities, engineers who are really good, to see all that and then to consider that we have not won since 2008. The important thing for Ferrari is not just the financial results, but also it is winning and we have been struggling for six years.'

He later added: 'Sports results are absolutely fundamental for Ferrari and Luca knows that as much as I do. Winning is part of the company's DNA and that must continue.'

Shortly afterwards, di Montezemolo announced he would leave the company in October, when Marchionne would take over. The pair announced the news together at an excruciatingly awkward press conference at an automotive show in Paris. Andrew Frankel of *Autocar* wrote: 'If all you did was read a transcript, you'd think the last press conference held by Luca Cordero di Montezemolo in his capacity as president of Ferrari was a rather dull affair. It was one of those occasions when you really did have to be in the room, because the body language between him and Sergio Marchionne, who will replace him on October 13, told a rather different story. Di Montezemolo sat alone in the middle of the room at the Paris motor show, arms open and gesturing as he spoke. Marchionne sat to one side at a table, arms folded or with one hand under his chin. At one time in di Montezemolo's farewell speech to the company for which he became almost as synonymous as its founder, Marchionne found time to flick through some fabric swatches. There were, of course, kind and I am sure sincere words for di Montezemolo from Signor Marchionne but when the time came to ask questions I took the microphone and said simply to di Montezemolo, "Why are you leaving?" More simply still and while staring straight at me, di Montezemolo pointed straight at Marchionne before going on to explain in PR-friendly terms about how he'd reached the end of his natural time there.'

After a string of near-misses and the team's least competitive season in 20 years, coupled with the grim realization they might be behind for a few more years, di Montezemolo had simply lost the leverage he had always had within the company. His bravado had always been a key part of his charm, appeal and success, but without on-track results for the team there was nowhere he could hide from the inevitable conclusion.

The BBC's Andrew Benson summed it up neatly: 'Luca di Montezemolo is an iconic figure in motorsport and Italian public life, for his many great achievements, for his charisma, and for the theatre with which he conducted himself. His problem was that in recent years the play was not very good and the acting had gone stale.'

It was a seismic moment. Since the early 1990s the team had seen different drivers, team bosses, engineers, press officers, and even different shades of red on its race cars, but di Montezemolo had been the face of it all. He had saved Enzo Ferrari's great company from the doldrums and created success worthy of the company's name and stature, turning it for a spell into the greatest F1 team ever seen to that point. Although it had drifted away from the lofty heights of the previous decade, for most of his time in charge, Ferrari had been the benchmark most other teams had measured themselves against. His unceremonious departure did not match the scale of his achievements.

The Driver Carousel

With an uncompetitive car and political turmoil swirling around internally at Ferrari, the biggest task in what turned out to be Mattiacci's short-lived tenure as day-to-day boss of the racing team would be away from the race track and revolved around its driver lineup. Räikkönen had underwhelmed in his return to the company but was already signed up until the end of 2015 – plans were in place to draft Ferrari's academy prospect Jules Bianchi as his replacement. So priority number one became Alonso's long-term future.

Given the turmoil Ferrari had faced that year, Mattiacci felt a big contract signing would assuage some of the growing anxiety behind the scenes. If he could get Alonso, who had a contract until 2016, to commit to a long extension to the end of the decade it would be a ringing endorsement of his new leadership and a signal that one of the grid's best drivers had not lost faith in Ferrari's ability to win further down the line.

The problem was . . . he had. Having narrowly missed out in 2010 and 2012, the setback of 2014 had been a bitter blow to Alonso. He had joined convinced his talent, Ferrari's long history of technical innovation and the political clout of the Italian team would be a winning combination. It had not turned out like that. Now he faced the prospect of waiting two or three more years before Ferrari had a title-contending car again. Recalling Alonso's frame of mind Spanish journalist Carlos Miguel said: 'He had lost the love by 2014. He had dealt with a lot and when he saw that engine . . . it was difficult to think about a longer time with Ferrari after that.'

This feeling of disillusionment started to become clear in Alonso's negotiations. The Spanish driver started asking for exit clauses to be inserted into any new extension – hardly indicative of a man who truly is committed to the project, Mattiacci thought. Fortunately for the new boss, Alonso was falling out of love with the team just as another superstar was starting to wonder about his own next career steps. One of the biggest critics of the new era was the driver who had won four championships with V8 engines: Sebastian Vettel.

The Red Bull driver hated the muted tones of the new power units. Ahead of the opening race that year, he had been unequivocal in his view of the new generation of hybrid engines: they were 'shit'. Vettel had claimed a record number of wins in 2013 but immediately looked uncomfortable with the new generation of cars and would struggle to replicate that form. His new team-mate Daniel Ricciardo had come into the team and would win three races, while Vettel went winless for the first time since 2007. Vettel had grown up in Germany watching his idol Michael Schumacher win titles in red and his poor start to the season and clauses within his Red Bull contract had opened up the possibility for a move in 2015.

Di Montezemolo and Mattiacci, who was being slowly sidelined as the new team principal, held conversations with Alonso and Vettel. As these developed, they suddenly saw one driver who had significantly soured on Ferrari and another in Vettel who could not have been more enthusiastic about the prospect of joining the team. As the spring became the summer, it became increasingly likely Alonso wanted out – he was now being strongly wooed by McLaren, which had an exciting new partnership with Honda set to start the following season.

Unlike a lot of drivers on the grid, Alonso had grown up dreaming of winning championships with McLaren (like his hero Ayrton Senna) rather than with Ferrari and he had unfinished business from 2007. Alonso's relationship with Mattiacci deteriorated as the months progressed, with some saying the new boss had made him an offer with significantly better financial terms, only to take the offer back immediately. While McLaren's deal came with significantly better terms, di Montezemolo maintains to this day that Alonso's wish to leave had never been financial. 'Money was not on the table with him, at least not in my discussions with him. Never.'

Alonso was offered his release in a tense meeting with Mattiacci at Maranello in early September. Technically, by this point the team had already offered a deal to Vettel, so certain were they that Alonso did not want to continue beyond 2014. Di Montezemolo remembers joining Marchionne, who was a few days away from formally replacing him as president, to call Vettel personally to say they wanted him to be racing for Ferrari the following year.

It meant Vettel left the Italian Grand Prix in September that year convinced he would be back the following season as a Ferrari driver. Ahead of the next race in Japan, Alonso visited Honda's factory at Sakura. The new deal with McLaren was a formality by that point, but was a little way from being sorted contractually. But then the story went public. Ahead of media day for the Japanese Grand Prix, Red Bull shocked the paddock by releasing news Vettel would leave the team at the end of the year for Ferrari. Alonso appeared in the press conference that day unable to confirm his move to McLaren, making it look as though he had been playing games behind the scenes and Mattiacci had called his bluff by signing Vettel and leaving him flapping in the breeze.

As Andrew Benson wrote, 'Alonso was angry. Not because, as some believed at the time, he had been tricked by Ferrari into signing a release he did not want to sign, but because he had lost control of the narrative. The fact Vettel was joining Ferrari was announced by Red Bull, and it came before Alonso had said he was going to leave. From an image point of view that looked bad for Alonso. The order of events in public made it look like it was Ferrari's decision and not his. The reality was that both had mutually decided that going their separate ways was the best solution. And that had come about because Alonso had lost faith in the team and decided he needed to leave.'

Alonso would go on to sign a deal reported at $40 million a year to rejoin McLaren, the team he had sensationally left after a rift with Ron Dennis seven years earlier. The move would ultimately strengthen the narrative that Alonso makes poor career choices – the Honda partnership was a nightmare, yielding no wins or podiums in four seasons for Fernando and Jenson Button, who left after three. Vettel, who had won for Toro Rosso with Ferrari power in 2008, aimed to do what Alonso had been unable to do – bring the drivers' World Championship trophy back to Maranello.

'The dream of a lifetime has come true,' Vettel said when the move was announced. 'When I was a kid, Michael Schumacher in the red car was my greatest idol and now it's an incredible honour to finally get the chance to drive a Ferrari. I already got a small taste of what the Ferrari spirit means, when I took my first win at Monza in 2008, with an engine from the Prancing Horse built in Maranello. The Scuderia has a great tradition in this sport and I am extremely motivated to help the team get back to the top. I will put my heart and soul into making it happen'.

Bianchi

When the Vettel and Alonso news unfolded ahead of the Japanese Grand Prix, media focus shifted towards a driver at the other end of the grid: softly spoken French rookie Jules Bianchi, who had scored a spectacular ninth-place finish for the little Marussia team at that year's Monaco Grand Prix. Ferrari had invested significantly in Bianchi and, having seen Sergio Perez sign a deal with McLaren the year before, the company was determined not to let another talented young academy talent have his head turned by an offer from a rival team.

Bianchi had impressed everyone who worked with him and the path had already been mapped out for him. He looked set to step up to Sauber, which ran Ferrari engines, in 2015, before replacing Räikkönen the following season.

'Jules was always at Maranello,' Domenicali remembered. 'Every day he came to the factory to nurture his dream of driving for Ferrari. Our idea was that, after Marussia, he should go to another team to grow and be ready for the big leap.'

It was a question of when, not if. But as happened with Ayrton Senna 20 years earlier, events would conspire quickly and tragically to prevent a dream Ferrari move from ever happening. That year's race took place amid a local typhoon. As the rain worsened in the closing stages conditions became close to undriveable in certain parts of the race track. Sauber's Adrian Sutil, the driver Bianchi would have likely replaced the following season, spun off while coming through the Esses and his car came to rest against the tyre barrier. It was an innocuous crash by F1 standards and indicative of how difficult drivers were finding it to stay on track. Sutil had gone off right by a marshal's post, meaning a 6.8 tonne recovery vehicle was nearby – it was promptly deployed trackside to remove Sutil's car.

Race control implemented 'double-waved yellows', which came with the instruction to drivers to slow their speed and to be ready to come to an immediate stop. This was often used to avoid neutralizing a race via a safety car, although Japan was quickly looking like a race which would need to be red-flagged altogether. F1's rules at the time were unclear about how much drivers actually needed to slow down and teams took advantage – the idea would be to lose as little time under double yellows as possible.

On that afternoon in Suzuka, most of the pack continued racing far too quickly for the conditions and considering there was a vehicle on the infield. Marshals had connected Sutil's car to ropes and had just started hoisting his Sauber into the air when Bianchi came around that part of the circuit. His speed still at 132 mph (212 km/h), he lost control as he reached the crest of the hill and spun out of the fast left-hander which followed. As Bianchi's car completed a full rotation it slammed into the truck. Because of the height of the car relative to the crane, the Marussia hit and went underneath the crane – an investigation later found Bianchi's head had absorbed much of the impact.

Andy Mellor, deputy head of the Safety Commission of the FIA, wrote in the report: 'The problem was the Marussia partly dipped below the stem of the crane and was therefore pressed from above against the bottom of the crane. That worked like a brake, with an abrupt deceleration. In this process we had the contact between the helmet and the crane. We had never seen something like this before.'

This was in the era before the Halo which is now mandatory on F1 cars, but the FIA believed the huge forces involved and the rapid deceleration of the car would have meant the outcome was much the same had the Marussia had a cockpit protection device fitted to it. The impact and rapid deceleration of his car meant Bianchi suffered a severe brain trauma called a diffuse axonal injury. He would remain in hospital until his death nine months later.

Bianchi's crash robbed Ferrari and Formula 1 of one of its most exciting young talents, in whom di Montezemolo had recognized traits of his two favourite drivers. 'Jules was fantastic. He grew up with us. What happened to him cannot happen again. Jules was a very nice guy: intelligent, quick, and very good at working with the technicians. That was one of the main characteristics in the past of Niki and also Michael. When we decided to do the driver academy, he was the first young driver. We already decided when we hired Kimi – because we took Kimi for a contract for two years –

we said, at the end of the two years, Jules will be ready to drive for Ferrari. He was our driver of the future.'

The legacy of the Bianchi crash in Formula 1 was the introduction of the virtual safety car, which today's fans will be familiar with. It prompts drivers to significantly slow their pace in line with a certain lap time delta which appears on the dashboard of their steering wheel in front of them. The VSC, as it has become known, has given race control the option to neutralize the pace of a race for a shorter period of time to deal with certain incidents without needing to deploy the actual safety car on the race track.

When winning his first race for Ferrari at the following year's Malaysian Grand Prix, Vettel would pay tribute over the radio: '*Merci, Jules. Cette victoire est pour vous* [Thank you, Jules. This victory is for you]. You will always be in our hearts. We know sooner or later you would have been in this team.'

Bianchi's legacy to Ferrari lives on in some advice he gave. Before his accident, Bianchi had suggested the team's academy talent scouts take a closer look at his godson, a young karting prodigy from Monaco named Charles Leclerc. The young Monegasque would fulfil the story Bianchi was unable to complete, racing for Sauber in 2018 before replacing Kimi Räikkönen at Ferrari for the 2019 season.

Tone Shift

Vettel's signing was a huge feather in the cap for Mattiacci, but even he did not survive the new winds of change blowing through the company. He had facilitated operational changes below him in the organizational structure at the team, with engine boss Luca Marmorini removed from his role by mid-year. Engineering director Pat Fry and chief designer Nikolas Tombazis also left in Mattiacci's first few months with the team. By the end of the season, a complete restructure of the team meant the engine department was overseen by Binotto, while the technical operation was overseen by the highly respected James Allison. Harshly, Marco Mattiacci was also sent packing at the end of the season. It was a surprising move, given the clout he had behind the scenes prior to the appointment. Before accepting the job he had seemingly been on a rocket ship to great things within the Fiat empire. As Andrew Benson wrote for the BBC, 'The fact that this former protégé of Fiat boss – and new Ferrari president – Sergio Marchionne has left the company altogether hints at some kind of cataclysmic internal falling out'. Mattiacci always had the feel of an interim appointment, but most expected him to continue in 2015.

Marchionne's replacement was another largely unknown character, but unlike Mattiacci, was external to Ferrari. Maurizio Arrivabene, (whose surname literally translates to 'Arrives Well') was vice-president of global communications for Ferrari sponsor Philip Morris, when he got the call. The appointment was a clear departure from di Montezemolo's approach of trying to promote from within – had he stayed on, it's likely Mattia Binotto or Andrea Stella would have replaced Mattiacci. Arrivabene had at least been loosely involved in F1 in the years prior, as the representative of Philip Morris on the rule-making F1 Commission since 2010. Ferrari's F1 team was now in the hands of a man more comfortable in the board room than in a Formula 1 garage or on the pit-wall.

The silver haired Arrivabene shared some of the traits of Ferrari's new president: dogmatic and ruthless, he had built a reputation as a fiery operator who did not suffer fools lightly. His arrival signalled a new approach. On arrival, Arrivabene stated: 'It will be a real team. I do not believe that F1 is about the success of the individual but of the team . . . We will have a team that is working together because everyone feels part of a common goal. If we win two grands prix next year it is a success for us, and if we win three it is a triumph.'

In the space of a few months, Ferrari had changed completely and the team's rivals, such as Christian Horner, took note. 'Ferrari has always been old-school, traditional, respectful. Well, they certainly were . . . Things changed a little when the Marlboro Man came. Arrividerci . . .' Horner recalled. 'Mattiacci didn't have a fair run. It was him who persuaded Sebastian, with Luca, to go to Ferrari. Everything took on a different perception when Marchionne arrived as president.'

Seasoned members of the media also clocked the immediate tone shift at the team. Recalling Ferrari's traditional end-of-year Christmas media dinner, Reuters correspondent Alan Baldwin noted how much things had changed.

'Montezemolo's media Christmas lunches had become legendary when he was in charge. He would hold court for 30 minutes or an hour with us all, talking about all manner of things. We'd have dictaphones out, be going back and forth with him. He was a very warm and charming personality. Then there was a news embargo until the following day, so we all knew we could eat and have a glass of wine or two without worrying about filing until the next day. It was completely different under Marchionne. He kept the media dinner going, maybe he felt he had to, but I'll never forget how weird and different it was. You had Marchionne and Arrivabene on their own table, separate to the media, and we were sat almost behind a rope dividing their table from us. No questions, no interaction. It felt a lot more hands-off than Montezemolo's approach – it showed the old ways had changed. What had come in just seemed a bit awkward.'

After years of di Montezemolo's tried and tested approach, Ferrari had been pushed onto a new path. Marchionne's vision for the company was hugely different to that of his predecessor – Ferrari was soon floated on the New York Stock Exchange. On track, he promised a return to championship glory, but achieving that goal would prove to be a much trickier proposition than he imagined.

11

TWO SIDES OF THE SAME COIN

'If we were to somehow fail to win a title over a ten-year span, it would be a tragedy.'

Sergio Marchionne

Renewal was the name of the game for Ferrari coming into 2015. The drama and criticism of the team from all angles had stung. Mercedes had won the previous championship at a canter and the rest now appeared to be playing catch-up. New president Sergio Marchionne had declared when he took over at Fiat in 2004: 'I like to fix things' – fixing Ferrari was now his number one priority.

The Scuderia had a fresh energy about it. A jaundiced Fernando Alonso had left for McLaren and in his place was an enthusiastic Sebastian Vettel who had made his boyhood dream of emulating Michael Schumacher come true. New team boss Maurizio Arrivabene arrived to his first race in Melbourne with a swagger and confidence; beneath him was a new organizational structure, with long-time Ferrari man Mattia Binotto heading up the engine/power unit department, while the hugely respected James Allison led the technical team.

An impressive pre-season, where Ferrari had appeared to be second quickest behind Mercedes, meant the team arrived in a positive frame of mind at the Australian Grand Prix. Even the most optimistic member of the *tifosi* would not have dared predict early victories given how the previous two seasons had gone. In Melbourne, Vettel and Kimi Räikkönen qualified fourth and fifth. Mercedes was still a step ahead, but in the race Vettel managed to score a first podium for the Ferrari SF15-T, albeit half a minute behind.

Having dominated so completely the year before, Mercedes publicly welcomed the idea of a Ferrari challenge. 'I hope we can have a good fight. That would be awesome,' said winner Nico Rosberg in the post-race press conference, sat alongside his fellow countryman.

Vettel, buzzing after his first race as a Ferrari driver, was in a playful mood. Flashing a cheeky smile back, Vettel replied back: 'Be honest. Do you really hope so? Seriously? You finished 30 seconds ahead of us and you hope it's going to be closer? So you hope you slow down? Is that what you're saying?'

It was the first of a number of occasions as a Ferrari driver Vettel appeared to revel in getting under Rosberg's skin in the press conference format. As it turned out, Vettel would not need to wait long, nor would he need Mercedes to slow themselves down. The second race, the Malaysian Grand Prix, would immediately enter into modern Ferrari folklore.

Green Shoots of Recovery

Changes to Arrivabene's Ferrari were still taking shape behind the scenes: at the start of the year, the team signed Lotus head of strategy Ignacio 'Iñaki' Rueda. Lotus's failure to pay staff on time in previous years had voided his gardening leave, meaning he only had to work the Australia race for his old team before making the switch to Ferrari in time for Malaysia. But Rueda's arrival was last-minute, and so Malaysia's strategy was largely left in the hands of Ruth Buscombe, who since has become an analyst for F1 TV, and a makeshift strategy team.

Going through the various permutations, Buscombe and her team were sure it was a two-stop race – many others in the paddock thought the Pirelli tyres on offer meant the quickest way to the chequered flag was to stop three times. Buscombe can remember pitching the idea to Arrivabene, a man who had cut his teeth in board rooms rather than pre-race strategy meetings.

'We were the B-Team, in terms of strategy,' Buscombe told the *Pit Stop* podcast in 2024. 'We did our work and I said, "I think it's a two-stop". We did the presentation, went through safety car scenarios. People there said, "If there's an early safety car, I think it's a three-stop", because of the degradation and all that stuff. I said, "No, it's still a two-stop."

'Then Arrivabene, who is the scariest man I've ever met in my whole life – even when he was saying nice things, you were terrified – he went, "If I said, theoretically, I was going to cut your head off if you were wrong – would you still say it's a two-stop?"'

Even at the risk of a hypothetical beheading, Buscombe told Arrivabene 'Yes' – it was a two-stop all the way. Historical trends had suggested there would not be an early safety car, but Buscombe was confident it was the call regardless how the race played out.

Vettel had qualified second and held the position at the start. Shortly after Räikkönen got a puncture, Sauber's Marcus Ericsson spun at Turn 1 and got his car beached in the gravel – of all the years, this was the Malaysian Grand Prix to buck the norm and have an early safety car.

The majority of the field stopped as the safety car came out at the end of the third lap. Ferrari held firm with what had been discussed pre-race. As he watched other cars peeling into the pit-lane Vettel heard a confident call: 'Stay out!' It was completely against the grain of what the rest were doing and put Vettel onto an offset strategy to most other drivers. It turned out to be a race-winning call. Lewis Hamilton quickly had reservations about the hard tyre Mercedes had put him on and staying out had a twofold benefit for Vettel: he stopped once fewer and maximized his time on the more favourable medium tyre. After pitting out of sequence, Vettel caught and passed the Mercedes drivers late on for a memorable first win in red.

When Vettel crossed the line, Arrivabene declared over Ferrari's radio: 'Yes! Great drive. Ferrari's back, Ferrari's back.'

Vettel's reply was characteristically elated: 'Woooohooo . . . Yes! *Si ragazzi! Mi senti, mi senti? Grazie mille, grazie, grazie, grazie! Dai! Forza Ferrari!*' As his Ferrari tenure continued, Vettel would repeat '*Grazie ragazzi*' more often than anything else, while '*Mi senti?*' (do you hear me?) became a recurring gag.

As much as the result removed the shackles of the previous year and a half, it also felt hugely symbolic. As a tearful Vettel basked in the moment on the podium, millions of viewers across the world were finally able to hear the most familiar sequence of F1 national anthems again.

'When I was up here and I heard the German anthem, and then the Italian anthem, and dressed in red. I don't know, I connected so many things from my childhood, and Michael,' Vettel said. 'I know it was me, but to realize it was me up there . . .'

It was easy to draw giddy comparisons with what had happened nearly two decades earlier. The previous year had been a clean break from the glory years of the past, with di Montezemolo and Domenicali both parting company with the team, but the shadow of the Schumacher era still hung over everything Ferrari did. In this campaign of renewal and rejuvenation, here was a German driver who had embraced the Italian language and paid homage to Ferrari as the greatest racing team at every opportunity, bringing a feelgood factor back that had been missing for too long.

Vettel's win, his first since 2013, had come earlier than many predicted, but it fuelled the feeling of resurgence – it was Ferrari's first in 34 races, nearly two full years. Internally, it did something just as important. 'No one in the outside world believed we'd win [so quickly]. We hardly dared believe we could,' said James Allison.

Vettel's first victory since leaving the Red Bull family also felt significant for other reasons. In 2014 he had been comprehensively outscored by team-mate Daniel Ricciardo. Speaking to the BBC later that year, Eddie Jordan said: 'I think Vettel needed it because after winning four World Championships with Red Bull, we all thought it was the Adrian Newey effect, the Red Bull, that little group of people. I for one needed to be totally convinced. Malaysia did that for me. Bravo.'

Like Schumacher before him, it was almost as if winning with Ferrari had brought Vettel validation in the eyes of his doubters.

The Vettel Effect

The Malaysia victory was not the sign of an imminent championship fight – Lewis Hamilton and Mercedes would win both titles comfortably. But Vettel continued to bite at the heels of the silver cars, scoring three podiums at the next four races. Although the trend of Kimi Räikkönen being off the pace of his team-mate had continued for a second year, the Finn took a spot on the podium at the race Vettel missed out on, with a dogged drive to second in Bahrain. It included a vintage Iceman pass on Rosberg down the inside of Turn 1 in the closing stages. It was one of the frustratingly rare glimpses of the old Räikkönen in his second stint with the team.

After his Bahrain podium Räikkönen, famous for being wholly uninterested in the politics behind the scenes of an F1 team, pointed out the improvements internally. 'I'm very happy how the team is working' he said. 'The atmosphere is good and things are improving, so I'm sure as a team we'll get there and be able to be all the time fighting for wins, but it will take a little more time.'

By mid-season, Ferrari's race operation was purring. With newer arrivals like Rueda quickly settled in, the good times would keep rolling.

Vettel took a dominant win in Hungary as Rosberg picked up a puncture and Hamilton received a drive-through penalty for a clumsy collision with Daniel Ricciardo, but Mercedes was never really in the fight for victory that race anyway. It might even have been a one–two finish were it not for a late failure of the MGU-K component for Räikkönen in the closing laps.

After a memorable second-place finish at Monza, Vettel ticked off Arrivabene's pre-season wish for three wins with victory at the Singapore Grand Prix, where he also claimed the first non-Mercedes-powered pole position of the new era. The lights-to-flag victory which followed was one of Vettel's most dominant, a throwback to some of his most complete victories with Red Bull. Again, this created a tantalizing thought: 'Imagine if Ferrari can give this man a car to fight Mercedes all year'. Ferrari's positive trajectory was clear for everyone to see.

On top of his three victories, Vettel made nine trips to the podium in 2015, a flawless campaign from someone who seldom made mistakes behind the wheel. Strategist Iñaki Rueda told me it was his best year at the Scuderia. 'It was a very special year, because everything was on the up. We had James [Allison], who had full trust from Ferrari management, so he could do whatever would be needed. You had Sebastian, who was very, very keen on making the team grow. Sebastian is a driver who gets involved with everybody in the team – for good and for bad. And in 2015 it was for good, because he tried to understand what the weaknesses were. He was very persuasive. When it remains positive, that approach is really, really good. A typical driver says, "You do that", and then they go away and play tennis or something. But he was very involved in the whole process and very keen on letting everyone in the team grow.'

There is some foreshadowing in Rueda's quote about what happened next. While Ferrari had thrived under the harmony and positive vibes of 2015, things were about to change in a big way and the new organization would be tested. The following season would turn out to be one of Mercedes' most dominant – it gave up just two wins all year, both to Red Bull. While 2015 had felt like the reset Ferrari had been in desperate need of, 2016 would start another slow unravelling of the race team, which would take years to play out to a conclusion.

2016: Torpedoed

With Vettel's three wins in the back pocket Ferrari entered the 2016 season on a high. After seeing his first target met, Arrivabene raised the expectations again. At the launch of the team's SF16-H, he said: 'Last year the objective was three victories, we got it. But I think this year we need to push a bit more. So it's going to be the championship. At least we would like to fight until the end for the championship.'

Excitement was palpable. Allison had been given the opportunity to influence the design direction of a car from the ground up and early signs were good. Integration had been a key focus. Binotto's engine team had worked on slimming the architecture of the power unit, leading to a more compact car. Chief designer Simone Resta said the team had gone in a 'very ambitious' direction with the tweaks, all of which had one intention: creating a car for all circuits and conditions.

Ferrari then went quickest in five of the eight days of testing and appeared to be starting the season in a stronger position than 12 months prior. After qualifying third and fourth in Australia, a victory opportunity seemed to slip away with a poor tyre call during a red flag suspension which followed a huge Alonso crash. While frustrated with the outcome, Vettel left Melbourne confident Ferrari could spend the whole year in the fight.

But thoughts about performance and championships quickly took a back seat. The day after Melbourne, tragic news came from the UK as the team travelled back to Europe. James Allison's wife, Becca, had died suddenly having contracted bacterial meningitis, aged 47. Allison, who had been splitting family and professional life between two countries, was immediately placed on compassionate leave so he could return to the UK.

On track, things started to unravel slowly. On the formation lap for the next race in Bahrain, Vettel's car failed on the way to the grid, although Räikkönen was able to salvage a second-place finish. Vettel finished second in China, where he almost collided with the man who had replaced him at Red Bull, Daniil Kvyat. After the race, an annoyed Vettel told Kvyat he had driven 'like a torpedo'. It was a consequential collision – at his home race in Russia two weeks later, Kvyat then did the same thing again and took an apoplectic Vettel out of the race, hitting Seb twice to unleash a storm of swear words on team radio. It handed Christian Horner the perfect opportunity of ending the Carlos Sainz Jr. vs Verstappen friction Toro Rosso were experiencing by demoting Kvyat and promoting 18-year-old Max Verstappen to the Red Bull team.

At the Spanish Grand Prix, a rare opportunity to win presented itself when Hamilton and Rosberg took each other out on the opening lap. Finally, here was a chance for Ferrari to kick-start its season with another feel-good win, right? Wrong. The day belonged to the teenage Verstappen, who claimed a remarkable first F1 win on his debut race with the team.

Räikkönen harried him all the way to the flag, while Daniel Ricciardo beat Vettel to the final spot on the podium. It was a bizarre race, with Ricciardo and Vettel leading Verstappen and Räikkönen after the collision. While the lead pair tried three stops, the chasing duo were put on a two-stop – and the latter strategy ended up working. Frustrations bubbling up in Vettel were clear in this race – after a lunge from Ricciardo in the closing stages, Vettel had memorably asked on the radio: 'Honestly, what are we doing, racing, or ping pong?'

Ferrari's momentum had petered out. Vettel finished second in Canada but another misplaced strategy call had handed Hamilton the initiative and squandered the win. The tone established the previous season had all but vanished.

'I ask you to be a bit patient, a bit more patient,' Vettel said after the Montréal race. 'The team is on a great path, things are improving and I think we're seeing results quicker than anyone else so far in the history of F1 . . .'

'After 2015, I think in their minds it was like we'd already won 2016, 2017 and 2018,' Iñaki Rueda said, referring to the Italian media's coverage that year. 'There was no way, to them, we weren't going to win. So you enjoy 2015 but then you have to live up to, not the results, but their expectations. And that there is the bad thing of Ferrari. The expectations are too emotional. And once the Italian press has decided something is bad, it's the worst thing ever. That will always be one of the biggest problems the team has, it's two different sides of the same coin.'

After Canada came an intervention from on high. Sergio Marchionne had grown tired of the team's misfiring race operation. With the team seemingly losing its way on car development without Allison and making avoidable mistakes across different parts of its race operation, the route forward to Marchionne appeared to be obvious – everyone needed to be pulling their weight to right the ship, no matter what the excuse.

Allison Departs

There was something brilliantly understated about Marchionne, whose favourite outfit was a black pullover with a close-fitting neckline and a collared shirt tucked neatly underneath, which is how he looked on almost every public outing he made. But that outward exterior belied his ruthless and uncompromising reputation.

The Canadian–Italian, son of a military policeman, had risen through the ranks to enjoy one of the truly great careers of the automotive industry. After taking over Fiat in 2004, he had saved the company from bankruptcy.

He had then performed a minor miracle in 2009 by saving the ailing Chrysler company, which was made profitable again in a merger with Fiat. Marchionne was a true star of the Agnelli family empire and was considered a titan of the business. He had remained in charge of those other entities while moving over to Ferrari – his first item of business had been to float Enzo's old company on the New York Stock Exchange.

Famed as a tough negotiator, Marchionne had an utterly ruthless approach to management. As Mediobanca analyst Massimo Vecchio said in a 2009 *Forbes* interview: 'He's got a lot of American in his management style. The only thing that matters to him is results. If you don't deliver, you are out. He is quite ruthless. When Marchionne took over [Fiat], he was literally firing one manager a day. There was a leadership problem and nobody wanted to take hard decisions. He reduced the layers of management and gave his role a more direct view of what the business was doing. And, of course, his ego is very big and sometimes people who had clashes with him were basically fired. Looking at his style from outside it seems awful, but he delivered.'

People in Formula 1 put it slightly differently. 'Sergio was very dogmatic,' Red Bull boss Christian Horner said. 'He was ruthless, win at all costs. He was a bully.'

Marchionne's intervention in 2016 has become stuff of legend to those involved in the team at the time. As the pre-season promise evaporated, he started appearing at Maranello, visiting the floor unannounced and calling for one-to-one meetings with middle management – directly undermining team boss Arrivabene's leadership of the team. It was a sharp departure from the di Montezemolo approach of leaving racing matters squarely with Jean Todt. Marchionne led what the Italian media had been told were 'crisis talks' at Maranello with a host of people around the team ready to feed back information about where they felt the team was going wrong.

Publicly, Marchionne had created a rod for his own back. Drunk on the positivity created by 2015, he had spoken up the chance of championship titles and added it would be 'a tragedy' if Ferrari got to 2017 and 2018 with either of its title droughts still intact. Those comments had ramped up the pressure and then the subsequent dip in results had immediately aged the predictions.

One obvious area that needed addressing was car development. One of the cornerstones of Red Bull's dominance at the start of the decade and Mercedes' at the end of it was the ability to consistently develop the car in a positive direction. Marchionne was not alone in thinking the team had lost its way since the winter tests. James Allison had been away from the team since March and his methodical approach behind the scenes was sorely missed. When summoned back directly by the president, Allison requested more time off – he was not in the right frame of mind to return. Marchionne, single-minded in his approach to running organizations, declined. On 27 July, it was confirmed Allison would be leaving Ferrari.

Lorenzo Sassi became head of the technical department and Enrico Gualtieri became head of the engine department – both would now report to Binotto, who became chief technical officer overseeing the entire operation below Arrivabene. The bespectacled Swiss–Italian was immensely popular with the rank and file at Ferrari but the loss of Allison, regarded as one of the best technical minds in the sport, was a huge blow, and everyone at the team knew it.

'In the immediate aftermath, you are not going to find losing someone like James Allison, a man of his calibre, is going to go unnoticed in the team,' head of racing activities Jock Clear said shortly after Allison's departure. 'The team is going to have to work hard to cover the gaps – Mattia will need help and we have to pull together. There is no suggestion he can step into the role James was doing and cover the background, but Ferrari is committed to pulling together in the areas where James was strong.'

Those who have worked with Allison admire the calming influence he brings to an organization. Allison was not just a great mind – he was someone who fundamentally understood people and how to get the best out of them. Rueda, who had followed James from Lotus to Ferrari, felt his departure ripped away something Ferrari sorely needed behind the scenes.

'The biggest driving factor behind 2015 was James Allison,' Rueda said. 'He's a manager that very much knows people, lets people deal with things. That is something that at my time in Ferrari I only properly experienced with James. He's a very good architect of teams and people. He's not just an engineer thinking how the car works. He doesn't micromanage. In 2015 Maurizio was in love with James, but the next year it all changed.'

Worse still, the removal of Allison and the context around it left a bitter taste in the mouth to many in the paddock. It was already hard enough for Ferrari to try and tempt British engineers to relocate, without the potential threat of summary dismissal.

Respected Italian journalist Leo Turrini wrote in 2023, 'Quite a few foreign technicians hesitate in the face of Ferrari proposals because they know the Scuderia's recent history. Some debts are not paid immediately, but later.' The same year, Jonathan McEvoy of the *Daily Mail* concluded, 'James Allison is the brain Ferrari let slip away. Old hands at Maranello shake their heads at his departure seven years ago, as well they might given the perpetual state of turmoil there.'

There was a slice of déjà vu about what happened next. Like Aldo Costa in 2011, after being dumped by Ferrari, Allison joined Mercedes as soon as his contract allowed. As technical director he became one of the indispensable cogs in that team's continued dominance of the decade. Behind Hamilton, Niki Lauda and Toto Wolff, there is a case to be made that Costa and Allison are the next most important parts of that dynasty.

The Driver/Chief Engineer

It would be easy to say Ferrari never recovered from Allison's departure, but that would not be true. Ferrari's cars in 2017 and 2018 would both turn out to be championship contenders. The saga around the former technical director did hint at a shift in culture already taking place around the team. The micromanagement from above during Allison's absence had massively undermined the leadership of team boss Arrivabene.

Before long it was not just Maranello that hosted unplanned visits from the president. In 2016 and over the next year and a half, it was not uncommon for Marchionne to attend post-race debriefs with the drivers, engineers, strategists and Arrivabene. Some present in those meetings vividly recall the room filling with smoke – no-one in attendance, some six or seven levels removed from the company's most important man on the organization chart, had the confidence to ask the chain-smoking Marchionne if he could take his cigarettes outside. Those present remember his advice being largely unhelpful. Marchionne would verbally eviscerate people who had made a poor decision, but would then go on to offer platitudes that those in the room needed to 'be more brave' and 'more courageous' like the company founder. As two different people who recalled those meetings told me, they often left them thinking, 'So, does he want us to take more risks, or less?'

The micromanagement did not stop with the president. As Rueda alluded to, at the race operation level Vettel had been as involved as he could be since arriving. As had been the case at Red Bull, he took on something like a player–manager role at a football team – he would talk to engineers and mechanics like he was one of them, determined to understand their points of view and committed to making sure his point of view was reflected in the decisions which were taken at every level. It was a commitment to winning he had shown at both Toro Rosso and Red Bull and had made accusations that the latter was 'his team' easier for critics to throw his way. But it's undeniable how important this was to Vettel's success. There is one good example from 2011, when Pirelli introduced a new type of tyre compound. Company boss Paul Hembery said Vettel was the only driver who had taken time to visit the Italian manufacturer's headquarters to ask questions and observe. It might have been a small thing, but that Schumacher-esque attention to detail had been a fundamental part of the dream team's success.

As is always the case, that approach can be a double-edged sword. When times are good, a driver wanting to be involved at every level is welcomed; when results dry up, it can come across as patronizing or unhelpful. When done right, it was a great trait, but it is clear this quickly started to grate when results went in the opposite direction.

F1 correspondent Lawrence Barretto recalls Vettel's mindset at that time and felt it hinted at something much deeper – that team boss Arrivabene was slowly losing control of the race team. 'Vettel became more and more involved as the years went on,' Barretto said. 'He would make calls on the team radio and behind the scenes he would be like, "Are we doing this, are we doing that?" I think he was just trying to help himself and the team, it came from a good place. He thought, "This isn't going very well, I'm a four-time World Champion, let me try." But because Arrivabene wasn't running the ship properly, rather than working with him on it, he just criticized Seb for doing it publicly.'

The rebuke from Arrivabene came at the 2016 Japanese Grand Prix and caused a wave of headlines. Speaking to Sky Italia, he said: 'Today, times are a little changed in the sense that what worked with Michael might not necessarily work with Sebastian. Sebastian just needs to focus on the car. He is a person who gives so much and that sometimes means an interest in a bit of everything. He does not do it with polemical spirit, he does it because he's completely immersed in what people call family but I call the team.'

The press had a field day with the comment. Given that the question he was answering had been whether Ferrari would emulate the di Montezemolo/Todt approach of tying drivers down to longer contracts in difficult moments, as they had with Schumacher in the late 1990s, it appeared to many as though Arrivabene was suggesting Vettel needed to wind in his neck or risk being replaced as Alonso had been. Vettel was incensed Arrivabene had given that answer. Rumours had already been flying that Vettel's style was rubbing team members the wrong way, so by commenting on it Arrivabene had effectively given some credence to the narrative.

'It was disappointing because Ferrari had worked so hard to get Seb,' Barretto said. 'So for the team boss to not be able to articulate how he felt with Seb in private, given his importance to the whole team, it just drove a wedge between them.'

While Arrivabene's leadership of the race operation had helped make 2015 such a success, as the difficult times mounted up, his lack of motor racing experience was being exposed. The silver-haired Italian became increasingly hostile with the media – his aggressiveness in the face of questioning was a glimpse into how he operated behind the scenes. Not only was Vettel stepping on his toes by inserting himself into how the race team conducted its business, but Arrivabene could see a clear successor emerging from the wreckage of the 2016 season. Before his promotion, Binotto had got the engine department back on track after its poor start two seasons earlier. Marchionne's favour was starting to shift away from Arrivabene to the long-serving Binotto. That, and his increasingly tense relationship with Vettel, would provide a backdrop for why the next two seasons failed to deliver the championship.

Vettel's inner frustration was clear in other ways during this period. The four-time champion had a complete meltdown during the Mexican Grand Prix a month later after several incidents with Verstappen, whose aggressive driving backed Vettel back towards Ricciardo in the closing stages of the race. Vettel and Verstappen had several near-misses on track, with the Dutchman regularly blurring the lines of what was and was not acceptable.

On crossing the line in third, Vettel's race engineer Ricardo Adami told the German driver that long-standing and respected race director Charlie Whiting would probably be handing Sebastian a penalty after the race. Vettel, completely incensed, opened his radio channel to the pit-wall with an extraordinary response.

'Here's a message to Charlie: Fuck off!' And then he repeated it, 'Fuck off! How's that?'

It was a remarkable incident of unbridled anger. While he immediately apologized to Whiting privately, in public it had looked like a petulant moment from one of the sport's most established drivers. Embarrassingly for Vettel, the teenage Verstappen would later tell the media the Ferrari driver '. . . was on the radio shouting like a child.'

While easy to frame the Mexico expletives as a driver seeing red in the heat of the moment, it would become clear as Vettel's Ferrari career continued how difficult he found it to contain the impatience he felt behind the scenes. There would be more egregious examples in 2017 and 2018 – some coming from anger, others coming purely from a driver crumbling under pressure. Given how Vettel felt about Ferrari, and how desperately he wanted to call himself the team's next World Champion, what followed probably should not have come as a surprise.

12

VETTEL FALTERS

> 'It's an unbelievably dark day for Sebastian . . . surely one of the darkest moments of his whole career.'
>
> **Nico Rosberg**

Of all the drivers Ferrari hired after Michael Schumacher, Sebastian Vettel initially seemed the perfect choice to bring another title to Maranello – not just because of the obvious German connection, but as a former World Champion who appeared to still be at the peak of his powers. Unlike Räikkönen, he had kept his performance level, and unlike Alonso, he was thought to be above the political machinations behind the scenes. Yet as the next two seasons unfolded, cracks began to show: Vettel found himself increasingly entangled in internal struggles within the team, and his form spiralled, leaving echoes of both his predecessors.

F1 had a fresh feel to it in 2017. A regulation re-set had produced new, more striking cars – front and rear wing changes had given cars more downforce, tyres were wider, increasing speeds through corners. The rules tweak raised hopes that Mercedes might be pegged back after a near-unbeatable 2016. The German team had a new look, too, with Nico Rosberg retiring immediately after winning the previous year's title. Valtteri Bottas stepped in from Williams as Lewis Hamilton's team-mate.

Coming into the new season, Ferrari's car immediately made headlines – its car, the SF70H, a reference to the company's 70th year, was lightning quick, with Kimi Räikkönen quickest in Barcelona's winter tests. But the team was generating attention for different reasons too. After a challenging 2016, team boss Maurizio Arrivabene had taken an extreme approach to the new season, implementing a media blackout – he would only attend mandatory FIA press conferences, while Räikkönen and Vettel's press appearances were extensively scaled back. It was an attempt to batten down the hatches, but it went down badly – the Italian media, especially, was livid. *La Gazzetta dello Sport*'s Luigi Perna criticized the move, writing, 'Low profile is acceptable, but not complete silence'. *La Repubblica* was more scathing, calling it 'absurd'. Communications chief Alberto Antonini, the unfortunate point of contact with the press during this time, quickly earned himself the paddock nickname 'Anto-no-no' for his habitual rejection of interview requests.

While it was an unconventional and, to some, a confrontational approach, it is easy to see how Ferrari arrived at the decision. Fluctuating public perception and immense pressure are intertwined into the story of the Scuderia and the Ferrari team had experienced both good and bad in quick succession. 'In 2015 we were heroes,' former head of strategy Iñaki Rueda told me, 'and in 2016 we were idiots. Tip-tap, just like that. At Ferrari, that happens worse than anywhere else.' The blackout coincided with an exciting start to the year for Ferrari and, although it would not continue long into the new season, it hinted at the mindset of the increasingly irritable and gruff Arrivabene when it came to dealing with problems or outside criticism.

The curtain-raising Australian Grand Prix felt like a heavyweight bout with the underdog challenger coming out on top – Ferrari went toe to toe with Mercedes, near-unbeatable in 2016, and won. Vettel went longer on his stint than Hamilton, beating the World Champion and his new team-mate, Valtteri Bottas. 'We have a great car, and we are here to fight,' Vettel said after the victory. Hamilton labelled the result a 'wake-up call' for Mercedes after three years of intra-team battles. Ferrari's momentum would only pick up steam from there.

Hamilton then won in China, where he and Vettel engaged in a thrilling, all-out race to the chequered flag in what was seen as a ringing endorsement for the new generation of F1 cars at the time. Vettel won in Bahrain and Hamilton took the honours in Spain. In Monaco, Räikkönen beat Vettel to pole position, but the German beat him in the race, staying out on his first stint of tyres and emerging from his pit-stop ahead – known in F1 as the 'overcut'. 'Kimi did not really get involved much with the team like Sebastian, he just let us get on with it,' Rueda said. 'But that's one of the few times he got upset and thought the team was against him. We stopped Kimi first and Sebastian second. Everyone thought we did it on purpose so Sebastian would win. If we'd stopped Sebastian first, we felt he would clearly undercut Kimi, so we gave Kimi the better option. But Seb had been quite clever about this, keeping quite a bit of pace in hand, which we saw when Kimi pitted. The team principal told us, 'Let them race'. So we let them race, but everyone thought it had just been orchestrated which was not true.' Orchestrated or not, the victory kept the wind in Vettel's sails, but pressure internally to keep the season rolling was mounting.

A flashpoint came in Baku, while Hamilton led Vettel under a safety car. The German driver felt (mistakenly) that Hamilton had brake-tested him (in other words, slamming on the brakes when directly in front) while the pack was moving slowly ahead of a restart. In reaction to that, Vettel drove alongside Hamilton and turned into his car, his front right wheel making contact with the Mercedes' sidepod. Vettel's car was not damaged, but he did receive a penalty – a chaotic sequence of events at the end meant he finished fourth, with Hamilton dropping down to seventh. Lewis was not impressed, 'He disgraced himself today, to be honest,' Hamilton said after the race. For a driver of Vettel's calibre, it was a bizarre display of lost composure. The incident evoked memories of his heated outburst towards Charlie Whiting at the end of the previous season in Mexico. 'Baku changed much of the dynamic, showcasing the pressure that Vettel was under at a Ferrari that was demanding ever more success,' David Tremayne wrote in *The Independent*.

Ferrari's strong start would begin to evaporate. After claiming victory at Silverstone, Vettel won in Hungary, before Hamilton won in Belgium and Italy. Vettel held the championship lead going into Singapore and claimed pole position, with Hamilton down the order. It looked like a good opportunity to turn the screws. At the start Vettel moved aggressively to cover the fast-starting Max Verstappen to his left, unaware Räikkönen had surged up the inside between the wall and the Red Bull driver. In a flash of sparks and carbon fibre the three cars collided, spinning dramatically out of the race, handing Hamilton an easy win, 25 free points and a lead of the championship he ultimately never relinquished in 2017. Memorably, afterwards Ferrari's official Twitter account said: 'Verstappen took Kimi out and then he went into Seb'. The stewards had found none predominantly to blame, but Vettel's move had seemed to many to be the instigating moment, moving across on the Dutchman and leaving him nowhere to go except into the side of Vettel's team-mate. Ferrari's sassy follow-up was widely mocked: 'What we tweeted was a factual description of events. No need to speculate on this.'

Ferrari's season had come apart. While Singapore had been a gift for the Silver Arrows, Mercedes' car development had also clearly surpassed Ferrari's across the season. Behind the scenes, divisions within the team were deepening, with technical director Mattia Binotto increasingly becoming the favourite of president Sergio Marchionne for how he had unlocked creativity across the race team. Arrivabene increasingly found himself isolated. 'It was clear there was a big difference in leadership styles, that's all I'll say,' Binotto told me, cryptically, refusing to comment on his former boss any further. But at that time a major shift was occurring. Arrivabene's management style created a wedge between himself and Vettel and one between himself and Binotto. Ferrari's dour, hawklike leader had trapped himself on an island, having made rivals of the two most important people in the team's hope of becoming World Champions again. This schism would only continue to break the race team apart the following year.

Away from the race track, Ferrari also seemed to be hurtling towards another showdown with the sport itself. At the start of 2017, American company Liberty Media had taken control of the sport and promised sweeping changes for the next Concorde Agreement including a budget cap, standardized components (for parts such as gearboxes) and simplified power units. Underpinning Liberty's vision was a desire to bring costs down across the grid and help create parity in performance on track as a result.

Marchionne made his view on the proposed changes clear with a memorable soundbite in a conference call that November: 'F1 has been part of our DNA since the day we were born. But if we change the sandbox to the point where it becomes an unrecognizable sandbox, I don't want to play any more.' The following week, Marchionne turned up the pressure at an event welcoming Alfa Romeo back to Formula 1 as Sauber's title sponsor. 'The dialogue has started and will continue to evolve,' he said. 'We have time until 2020 to find a solution which benefits Ferrari. The threat of Ferrari leaving Formula 1 is serious. The agreement with Sauber expires in 2020–2021, right when Ferrari could leave. We have to find a solution which is good for the sport but we also have to be clear on the things we can't back down on.' Jean Todt, now FIA president, was called in to mediate between F1's commercial owners and his former team, but the discussions would stretch into the next couple of years.

Marchionne's was the most serious threat to leave Formula 1 since Luca di Montezemolo and the FOTA (Formula One Teams Association) teams had plotted a breakaway championship in 2009. As on that occasion, the idea of Ferrari's spending being curtailed by a budget cap was baulked at by the company. Marchionne showed his willingness to consider the same drastic action as his predecessor. Asked how he would feel being the first Ferrari president to take the company out of F1, should that happen, he replied: 'Like a million bucks because I'll be working on an alternative strategy to try and replace it. A more rational one, too.' It was very much in line with the way Marchionne had operated as an executive in the car industry – my way, or the highway.

Ferrari's lingering unease about Liberty Media's vision for the future of the sport can be seen in a smaller example around this time – the decision not to get involved with Netflix and the first series of what turned out to be the smash hit *Drive to Survive* series, filmed across the 2018 season and released at the beginning of the following year. Mercedes also did not take part, citing it as a distraction.

2018: Another Great Start...

Although recent revisionism might suggest otherwise, the 2018 season was one of the great blown opportunities for an F1 team to win a championship. Vettel came storming into the year once again, capitalizing on a virtual safety car for an expectations-setting win in Australia before claiming victory in Bahrain – a race also remembered for mechanic Francesco Cigarini breaking his leg. It was the first time Ferrari had started a season with back-to-back GP victories since 2004. Excitement levels were even higher than they had been a year earlier.

Hamilton fought back with wins in Azerbaijan and Spain, before Vettel won in Canada. Three races later came what seemed like it could be a decisive moment – at Silverstone, Vettel led Räikkönen home in a one–two at the British Grand Prix. Although a German manufacturer, both of Mercedes' F1 bases are in the vicinity of the Silverstone circuit – after about a million '*Grazie mille*' on the radio, Vettel declared: 'In their own home! Great work from all the team, great strategy . . . now we bring the English flag to Maranello!' Whatever that meant.

The result ensured that Vettel would go to his home race at Hockenheim in late July leading Hamilton by 173 points to 161. It seemed poised to be a year-long fight. Leaving Silverstone that Sunday evening, it was inconceivable to think Hamilton would wrap up the championship with three races to spare – it felt as though Ferrari had struck a significant blow to Mercedes at one of their superstar driver's favourite circuits.

Hockenheim would turn out to be the low point of Vettel's Ferrari tenure. Yet again it was a grand prix turned upside down by a rain shower during the race – Vettel was leading but, with Hamilton gaining rapidly, the unthinkable happened. Entering the Stadium section, where the vast majority of his German fans were seated, the Ferrari failed to take the corner, sliding off at low speed, tripping gently across the gravel and clunking terminally into the barriers. Television pictures showed Vettel angrily slamming his steering wheel as the car came to a stop, then cutting to the Ferrari mechanics with their heads buried in their hands. It was an unforced error at the worst possible time. It would be one of the most enduring images of his time with the team. 'It was a small mistake but a big disappointment. I had it in my hands,' he said after the race. 'I should have done better but it wasn't the biggest mistake I have done. It was probably one of the most costly ones but that's how it goes sometimes.'

As had happened in Singapore a year earlier, Vettel's DNF allowed Hamilton a 25-point gain and a championship lead he never gave up. From there, Ferrari would lose their way in development and make missteps on the track. Mercedes would sweep their way to the title – the 2017 and 2018 seasons were like rhyming stanzas in a poem in that sense. To many, the blame this time around was squarely on Vettel's shoulders. In Ferrari's press release after the race, Arrivabene made no mention of Vettel by name, but he did mention the car he had at his disposal. 'In what was a particularly fraught weekend for Ferrari, it would have been important for us to bring home the win. Our car had shown it was up to the job.'

Insiders say Vettel became an easy scapegoat for the season as a whole not ending in victory. 'Hockenheim was a great example of what the problem was,' Rueda said. 'You come out of that race and you have all the *tifosi* and everything, management, the top guys, they said we had the race won – you Seb, you, you've thrown it away. That didn't help Sebastian and it didn't help anyone else really. That's not team spirit in any shape or form. Team spirit would be coming back from Hockenheim and saying, 'Look, that was a tough race, but let's rally around this guy and do better in future'. But there was no way that was going to happen, not at Ferrari at that time anyway.' The blame on Vettel was not limited to people with the Prancing Horse on their chests. Rosberg, speaking on Sky Sports after the crash said, 'It's an unbelievably dark day for Sebastian . . . surely one of the darkest moments of his whole career.'

More worryingly for Vettel was that the crash seemed to be part of a growing trend when it came to his driving. Around this time, his mistakes had grown, and he had developed a curious habit of randomly spinning during races. A popular five-minute video can be found on YouTube titled, 'All of Sebastian Vettel's spins for Ferrari', and it does not even feature all of them. Those who knew Vettel pinpoint Hockenheim as a pivotal moment in this spiral in confidence. 'I think it's an insecurity that started in my eyes with the crash at Hockenheim in 2018, while leading,' said Helmut Marko, one of the men pivotal in bringing Vettel to Red Bull, in an interview with *Autosport* the following year. Hamilton took a different approach, crediting 'divine intervention' for the victory.

Whatever the reason for Hockenheim, bigger news concerned Ferrari in the week after the race. On 25 July, just three days later, company president Marchionne died following complications following shoulder surgery in

Zurich. Marchionne had experienced a sudden decline in his health and had given up his various roles in Fiat in the days before his death, aged 66. His legacy as the man who helped save Fiat and Chrysler had already made him a legend of the automotive industry. Eventual Ferrari successor John Elkann said in a statement: 'He taught us that the only question that's worth asking oneself at the end of every day is whether we have been able to change something for the better, whether we have been able to make a difference.'

Marchionne's sudden death took some of the friction out of negotiations with Liberty Media. Although Ferrari still pushed back in what were thought to be key areas, according to various sources within F1 the negotiations between Ferrari, Liberty Media and the FIA became slightly easier with the no-nonsense Canadian-Italian out of the picture. 'Marchionne obviously didn't understand Formula 1 that well and he just wanted to use Ferrari's strength politically to manipulate,' Horner told me. For the most part, Liberty's changes have been hugely additive to F1. For one thing, Liberty has since managed to implement a budget cap which, it has to be said, has worked wonders in bringing the field closer together.

Marchionne's legacy at Ferrari endured for a while: two major changes had been set in motion before he died. One was the elevation of Binotto from technical director to team boss, which was confirmed at the end of the season but had been decided in his final months. Binotto had been an advocate for the removal of fear behind the scenes, something which had gripped the halls of Maranello on and off for years. He had suggested applied management science to make it happen, something Marchionne had loved. Calling on his experience working for the team since 1995, Binotto had pushed for creativity and originality in the technical department and as a result both had been embraced by the team. Even though 2017 and 2018 had been unsuccessful, Ferrari had taken the fight to Mercedes with forward-thinking car designs and an engine which seemed to be getting better year on year.

Binotto's popularity behind the scenes was also in stark contrast to attitudes towards Arrivabene, who was seen as increasingly difficult and terse, both inside and outside the team. The operational failures of the race team were laid squarely at the feet of Arrivabene and the contrast between that side of the team, which still largely walked on eggshells, and the liberation felt by those working directly for Binotto was like night and day. Writing in *Motor Sport* magazine, Mark Hughes said that under Binotto, 'Ferrari became the most creative technical group on the grid after years of just following the lead of others. So we eventually arrived at the position in 2018 where the worst race team was running the best car. It wasn't the worst race team because of the people within it – but because of how it was being led. This also seeped through to the mindset of its lead driver.'

Vettel's belief in Ferrari had taken a battering, that year especially. Like Alonso at the start of the decade and Alain Prost in the early 1990s, years of carrying water for Ferrari without a title had worn him down. 'I think Sebastian's demise was 2018,' Rueda said. 'We started well, very good car, very good team. But the pressure got to us and as it did, we slowly crumbled in terms of development of the car. I think that 2018 was the first year Sebastian felt the real pressure of the whole of Ferrari. In 2015, he was the star, 2016, we messed it. In 2017, okay, pretty good. But then in 2018, I think the *tifosi* really started putting the finger of blame at Sebastian for everything going on. But there was so much beyond just the track. I think by then he was falling out of love with Ferrari for different reasons. He was someone who wanted to make the team stronger. He came from Red Bull, when he was bigger than the team – Sebastian Vettel was bigger than Red Bull. Now we have Verstappen we don't remember that.'

Some felt Vettel's mistakes came from the added baggage that Arrivabene's bizarre management style had brought operationally. Mistakes had been few and far between during his time at Toro Rosso and Red Bull, but they were frequent at Ferrari. It looked to many in the F1 media that he didn't trust the decisions the team was making. With Ferrari's longer-term confidence in Vettel shaken in 2018, another of the decisions Marchionne had set in motion soon came to pass. A week after Vettel had spun while chasing Hamilton at the start of the Italian Grand Prix, Ferrari confirmed Sauber rookie Charles Leclerc would replace Räikkönen in 2019. It was a great PR win for the team, having supported the highly rated Monegasque youngster through title-winning Formula 3 and Formula 2 campaigns. Leclerc gave Ferrari's long-term future a homegrown flavour, regardless of what happened when Vettel's contract was up the following season.

Ferrari's driver academy previously had only one obvious success story in Felipe Massa, but no other members had made it to the main team. Sergio Perez had picked up podiums in his Ferrari-powered Sauber in 2012 but was allowed to leave for McLaren when the Woking-based team offered him a race seat in 2013. Jules Bianchi would have made it through to the Scuderia were it not for his ultimately fatal crash in Suzuka. Leclerc was the extension of that story arc and his elevation was a positive news event following Marchionne's death and at a time Ferrari had lost its way on track again. More missteps followed in the remaining races of 2018. Then, after Ferrari ditched a mid-season upgrade package and went back to the older spec car, results improved again.

Kimi Räikkönen finally claimed the first victory of his second Ferrari stint at the U.S. Grand Prix. The Iceman had beaten Hamilton off the start and held the lead to the finish, ending a run of 113 races without a win. Arrivabene said Räikkönen's Austin win was 'a testament to the fact that the team does come back and does fight back and did understand some of the issues we uncovered in the second third of the season.' But by that time, the writing was on the wall.

Arrivabene was not an easy man to work for – although undoubtedly a character capable of giving a great soundbite every now and then, he made people in the race team scared to admit mistakes or face problems, which quickly turned small problems into big problems. He had needlessly made Vettel's life difficult – the spin at Monza had come a day after Arrivabene and Ferrari had refused to deviate from its qualifying policy of alternating which driver went out first and second in qualifying, even when that occasion meant putting Vettel at a disadvantage. Arrivabene's leadership seemed to amplify problems simply by not addressing them in the right way – at times, his team felt like a return to the stereotype of the same old Ferrari of decades earlier, when it lived under the potential wrath of *Il Commendatore*.

Marchionne and Arrivabene's tenures were more or less identical in length. On one hand, they pulled Ferrari out of the hole it was in coming out of 2014 and had put the team back into a competitive position – with five wins in 2017 and six in 2018, it was in a much healthier position. Marchionne had demanded results at all levels and that had been a double-edged sword – it had energized some people in the company to deliver, but it had created deeper problems. Marchionne's meddling in Ferrari's F1 team from 2016 onwards was counterproductive and left lingering divisions across the company.

As for Arrivabene, history does not reflect on him too kindly. His Ferrari team promised much but ultimately delivered no championship victory. There's an argument to be made that in the modern era there has not been a Ferrari team boss more ill-suited to running Enzo Ferrari's race team than the former Phillip Morris executive. During our interview for this book, Christian Horner repeatedly referred to him as either, 'the Marlboro man' or 'Arrividerci' rather than by his name, which speaks volumes. Seen as a yes-man to those above him, to those below he could be infuriating, an ill-tempered autocrat who lacked the kind of charisma or warmth that would have allowed loyalty to supersede any character flaws. Arrivabene went on to become CEO of Juventus but in 2022 he and the entire board resigned, implicated in a scandal. In January 2023, Arrivabene was suspended for two years from holding office in Italian football as punishment for capital gains violations.

Replacing Arrivabene with Binotto was a flip to the other side of the F1 spectrum, replacing a fiery man from a corporate background with a methodical, logical and much-liked engineer. Binotto's lengthy career with the team also rejuvenated the rank and file – one of their own was finally getting the top job. After stints with Marco Mattiacci and Arrivabene, two men who had come from outside the F1 operation, it gave them an obvious link back to the glory days in its figurehead staff member. Binotto's methodical approach would be a breath of fresh air going into 2019.

13

LECLERC, BINOTTO AND A THIRSTY ENGINE

'Charles Leclerc may appear to be Harry Potter's polite younger brother but in combat his elbows have razor blades, he grows horns at 200mph [about 320 km/h], and his head appears to be as strong as the carbon fibre Ferrari chassis he steered to a glorious victory on home ground in front of the ecstatic *tifosi* in Monza.'

Martin Brundle

Charles Leclerc's elevation to a race seat and Mattia Binotto's rise to the role of team principal completely changed the dynamic of the team going into 2019.

After years of it being Sebastian Vettel's Ferrari there was a new, exciting and unpredictable edge to the team's driver line-up, while a Scuderia lifer was now back in charge of the company just as the popular Stefano Domenicali had been at the start of the decade.

Leclerc arrived in Formula 1 with a wave of expectation experienced by few others. A childhood banging wheels in karts with Max Verstappen, a prodigious race pedigree at the junior level, back-to-back Formula 3 and Formula 2 titles had led to his elevation to Sauber in 2018. He was so good at the Swiss-based team that Ferrari decided to promote him straight up to the Scuderia, a remarkably bold decision for a team with a pragmatic approach to drivers and a preference for experience and reputation in its line-up.

After a frustrating debut grand prix in red, Leclerc announced himself on the big stage, taking pole position in Bahrain, 0.3s ahead of Vettel. On Sunday he appeared to be cruising to his first F1 victory until 11 laps from the end, when his car slowed with an engine issue. Lewis Hamilton and Valtteri Bottas quickly passed him before further retirements brought out the safety car, meaning Leclerc at least got to hold onto a bittersweet third place for his first F1 podium. Hamilton consoled Leclerc post-race and in the cooldown room: 'You drove fantastic this weekend, man. You've got a long old future ahead of you. I know it sucks in this moment but you've got a long way to go.'

It felt like a classic F1 tale unfolding. Like Hamilton's breakout rookie season at McLaren against Fernando Alonso, or Daniel Ricciardo's 2014 debut alongside Sebastian Vettel at Red Bull, a new star had immediately announced himself as the coming man. There would be rough spots along the way. Two races later, in Baku, Leclerc created an instant meme when he crashed in the fortress section, saying on the radio: 'I am stupid!' At his home race in Monaco he felt confident of having the car to win, but Ferrari failed to send him out for a second run in Q1, thinking his initial effort was good enough. Leclerc was eliminated from the session and retired from accident damage on the Sunday trying to barge his way through the lower order. It would be the beginning of a painful few years around his home town streets.

Then came Austria, where Leclerc took pole and appeared to have another opportunity for his first win, only to be muscled off the track by Max Verstappen's Red Bull on the final lap for the lead. After a lengthy stewards' enquiry Verstappen's move was deemed legal and he kept the win. In the aftermath an old clip of the two drivers from their karting days went viral. It showed Verstappen complaining in an interview: 'I mean, he's just unfair. I'm leading, he wants to pass, he pushed me, I pushed him back. After he pushed me off the track. It's not fair.' The young Leclerc's reply, that it was 'nothing, just an incident', has become one of the most popular F1 memes of recent times.

Ferrari went into the summer break without a win but Leclerc would finally get his moment at Spa, although it was achieved against a tragic backdrop. Shortly after he had taken pole position for Sunday's race, Frenchman Anthoine Hubert – a long-time friend of Leclerc – was killed in a horrifying crash during the Formula 2 race which followed qualifying. It was one of those rare moments when the tone in the paddock changed immediately, everyone instantly aware that something awful had happened. Leclerc and Hubert had been friends from their karting days and it was a remarkably bittersweet occasion for his maiden victory to come just 24 hours later in a dominant performance from pole. 'First win . . . this one is for Anthoine,' Leclerc said on the radio as he pulled into the pit-lane. 'Feels good, but . . . difficult to enjoy a weekend like this. Thanks for everything, guys. You're the best.' Leclerc motioned to the sky as he climbed out of his car.

Hero status would follow a week later, as Leclerc cemented his status as the face of Ferrari by winning at Monza, taking pole and then beating the Mercedes drivers to victory. It was Ferrari's first win at the Autodromo Nazionale since Fernando Alonso's in 2010. 'Very difficult to put into words what I felt on the podium with hundreds and thousands of people underneath me yelling my name, yelling the Ferrari name,' Leclerc said. 'It was very, very special.' Leclerc's Italian win capped the team's 90th anniversary season in fine style and seemed to confirm that Ferrari was going into the new year with a car and a new lead driver who could compete for the world title.

'Monza was a tense thriller with a fairytale ending,' Martin Brundle wrote in his *Sky Sports* column after the race. 'Charles Leclerc may appear to be Harry Potter's polite younger brother but in combat his elbows have razor blades, he grows horns at 200mph [about 320km/h], and his head appears to be as strong as the carbon fibre Ferrari chassis he steered to a glorious victory on home ground in front of the ecstatic *tifosi* in Monza.'

Ferrari's future appeared to be in safe hands. But focus was about to shift from its new superstar driver to what was powering the car he had just taken to back-to-back wins.

Sensory Deprivation

Ferrari's engine gains had been massive in the years since Binotto had taken charge of the engine department. His success at getting the team's V6 turbo hybrid project back to Mercedes-challenging performance levels had increased his standing with former president Sergio Marchionne and put him on course for the team principal job. Marchionne's business mantra had put results above all else. 'I'm sure he put massive pressure on Mattia and so on to win at all costs,' Horner told me. 'He clearly had a sense that Ferrari could do what other teams couldn't.'

As early as 2018, suspicions had been raised by rival teams about data that they had legally acquired on the SF71H car. By 2019, with Binotto at the helm, the team had a car which could qualify better than it could race, although after the summer break Leclerc's back-to-back wins appeared to mark a change in performance.

'It was the peculiar difference in pattern of performance between Spa and Monza that elevated the matter from regular rivals' competitive paranoia to something that demanded a full investigation,' Mark Hughes wrote for *The Race* a year later. After Ferrari's sudden spike in performance, other teams sought clarity behind closed doors from the FIA. They suspected that Ferrari had found a way for its engine to momentarily exceed the mandated maximum fuel flow rate of 100kg/hour, which they alleged was being done by 'gaming' or circumventing the FIA's fuel flow sensor.

The data they now had from those tell-tale grands prix appeared to make a strong case.

'If you were somehow getting around the fuel flow limit,' Hughes wrote, 'you couldn't use it all the time without needing way more than the regulation 110kg [fuel load]. So you'd use it where it would bring the most lap time – out of the corners before the squaring force of drag made it less effective. The Ferrari's acceleration out of Parabolica was indeed quite startling.'

Eyebrows had been raised at both ends of the pit-lane, even with teams who were running the same engine. 'That's one where I still really don't know the details,' then-Haas boss Guenther Steiner told me. 'With this engine . . . it was like we never really spoke about it. We didn't know what the engine was, what we were running, how we were running it, it was just weird.' Even Steiner and Binotto's great friendship did not get him any closer to the truth. 'He would not tell me anything! There was no chance. It's like it was in a box – it stays in a box. So I don't know any details.' Adding to the intrigue was the fact that Alfa Romeo and Haas were not overly competitive. They finished eighth and ninth in the Constructors' Championship in 2019, raising questions about how differently the engine in the Ferrari car was run.

Mercedes would later estimate the Ferrari had a 60 brake horsepower advantage it could not account for within the rules as they understood them. As rivals' complaints mounted, Ferrari's stance with the FIA and any other team raising questions became simple: prove it. As Hughes wrote: 'The presence of something that could subvert the fuel flow meter reading isn't the same as proving it was used. It's rather like with Benetton's "Option 13" software of 1994 that allowed for the banned launch control but without any traces that it had been employed. Sure, why would it be on there if it wasn't used? But that's not the same as proof.'

After Red Bull sought clarification, a technical directive was issued to the teams ahead of the U.S. Grand Prix over what was and was not allowed regarding the fuel-flow meter, the device which monitors the fuel consumption. Ferrari's run of six straight pole positions suddenly ended as the performance dropped significantly that weekend. 'That's what happens when you stop cheating, of course,' Max Verstappen said in his disarmingly frank way after the race in Austin. 'But yeah, [the FIA] had a good look at it. So now we have to keep a close eye on it.'

Binotto was furious, responding: 'These type of comments I feel are completely wrong. It's not good for the sport and I think everybody should be a bit more cautious.' Even so, at the Abu Dhabi Grand Prix, a random weight check before the start showed that Ferrari had under-reported what they had put in the fuel tanks by 5kg.

Ferrari claimed it was simply an error, but rivals suggested a team would only put more into the car and under-report it if they knew they had a system which was burning more fuel. Mark Hughes wrote for *Motor Sport*: 'If a team was to make use of an ability to run an illegally high fuel flow, it could burn off any difference between declared and actual – but for that to work would require not being randomly weight-checked before the race. If the difference was small it could credibly be claimed just to be finger trouble. But if the difference was 4.88kg (as on Leclerc's Ferrari in Abu Dhabi), that's difficult to explain. That's 4.4 per cent of the total permitted fuel load (about three laps' worth) and around six litres.'

The issue would linger through to the following season. As 2019 became 2020, Ferrari and the FIA engaged back and forth over the issue. Pre-season started, with news stories bubbling away in the background about the coronavirus which had now reached Europe. F1's focus was very much on the winter tests and the potential on-track pecking order. And then it happened. In the final seconds of the final test, a press release was sent out.

'After thorough technical investigations, it [the FIA] has concluded its analysis of the operation of the Scuderia Ferrari Formula 1 Power Unit and reached a settlement with the team,' it read. 'The specifics of the agreement will remain between the parties. The FIA and Scuderia Ferrari have agreed to a number of technical commitments that will improve the monitoring of all Formula 1 Power Units for forthcoming championship seasons as well as assist the FIA in other regulatory duties in Formula 1 and in its research activities on carbon emissions and sustainable fuels.'

Button-pounding of laptops quickened around the media centre. Pre-season testing always has a certain amount of meaningless speculation to it – a lot of educated (and some uneducated) guesswork about the season ahead. This was different. The timing had felt prejudged, like a good day to bury bad news, dropping the release as the press focused on the final timings. And it was curiously vague. Rivals' reaction came swiftly. Days later, the sport's seven non-Ferrari powered teams – Mercedes, Red Bull, McLaren, Renault, Williams, AlphaTauri and Racing Point – went public themselves with a letter.

'We, the undersigned teams, were surprised and shocked by the FIA's statement of Friday 28 February regarding the conclusion of its investigation into the Scuderia Ferrari Formula 1 Power Unit. An international sporting regulator has the responsibility to act with the highest standards of governance, integrity and transparency. After months of investigations that were undertaken by the FIA only following queries raised by other teams, we strongly object to the FIA reaching a confidential settlement agreement with Ferrari to conclude this matter.' The letter went on to say the teams were considering legal options.

A good litmus test for how serious something is in Formula 1 is usually whether or not teams are aligned in agreement. For seven to have signed a joint statement showed the magnitude of the unhappiness behind the scenes. The open letter prompted a reply from the FIA, which confirmed what had been implied – the governing body simply had not been able to find the smoking gun.

'The extensive and thorough investigations undertaken during the 2019 season raised suspicions that the Scuderia Ferrari PU could be considered as not operating within the limits of the FIA regulations at all times,' it said. 'Scuderia Ferrari firmly opposed the suspicions and reiterated that its PU always operated in compliance with the regulations. The FIA was not fully satisfied but decided that further action would not necessarily result in a conclusive case due to the complexity of the matter and the material impossibility to provide the unequivocal evidence of a breach. To avoid the negative consequences that a long litigation would entail especially in light of the uncertainty of the outcome of such litigations . . . [the FIA] decided to enter into an effective and dissuasive settlement agreement with Ferrari to terminate the proceedings.'

World events would quickly overtake the Ferrari engine story. In any other year, the build-up to Melbourne's opening race in March would have been dominated by the settlement agreement. Rival teams – especially Mercedes and Toto Wolff – were furious at the settlement and the lack of transparency behind it. Melbourne would at any other time have been the stage for the next barrage in the story – Wolff and other team principals would have been probed on the penalty, their quotes only fuelling it further.

Something much bigger was taking place. On arrival in Australia, a McLaren team member tested positive for coronavirus. By the early hours of Friday morning, McLaren had withdrawn from the event as more positive tests flooded in. Behind the scenes Ferrari quickly indicated they were not willing to race in the circumstances, with the focus of teams shifting immediately to getting staff home as safely and quickly as possible. Some nine hours after McLaren's withdrawal, F1 announced the race had been cancelled.

'If the pandemic hadn't have happened, Toto would not have let go of that,' Steiner told me. 'You know Toto, you throw the guy a bone, he doesn't let go. When the pandemic hits us and all of a sudden we are all struggling to survive – who fucking cares about the Ferrari engine? Nobody spoke about it. In the meetings we had after Australia 2020 no-one was bitching about the engine of the Ferrari, it was "How can we keep this sport alive?" which of course is the right thing.'

As the world adapted to the new reality of Covid-19, Formula 1 teams joined the fight on the frontlines – Maranello started assisting in the production of ventilators for the Italian healthcare system. Focus shifted back to when F1 might be able to get going again. With a handful of teams staring at the reality of financial collapse, F1 managed to reboot in early July, earlier than most major sports around the world.

The Year of Living Dangerously

Before F1's truncated 2020 season started, big changes had happened behind the scenes. With time to kill and no racing to be done, the early months of the pandemic acted as an accelerant for the driver market. In May, Ferrari confirmed Vettel would leave the team at the end of the year. It was quickly confirmed Carlos Sainz Jr. would join from McLaren as his replacement in 2021.

As Leclerc had thrived in 2019, Vettel's signs of a collapse in confidence had been most evident. He had looked like a shadow of the driver who had arrived in 2015, both in terms of form and confidence. A collision between him and Leclerc at the Brazilian Grand Prix had only raised speculation that there was unrest behind the scenes, that Vettel had been struggling to adjust to his new, lessened importance in the eyes of both the *tifosi* and the team itself.

'The reason for the change was not the difficulty in managing Sebastian and Charles,' Binotto told me. 'It was the importance of renewing the team.

Sebastian, I have full respect for him, he was a great driver. In 28 years the two most difficult moments for me was the engine matter of 2019, the other was to communicate to Sebastian that we were making that decision.

'It's like when you engage Cristiano Ronaldo at Juventus to win the Champions League, after five, six years you have still not won it, it's time to change. When we engaged Sebastian at Red Bull it was with the objective to win. We missed it in 2017 and 2018. And sometimes – I'm not saying it was his fault, that's not the point – it becomes time to refresh and to start again.'

The quirk of that year's schedule meant there was a whole season to run before Sainz replaced the four-time World Champion – ironically, Sainz would be on the other side of that dynamic in 2024, when Ferrari announced Lewis Hamilton's signing before the first race on the calendar.

When the season started, it immediately became clear there had been a residual effect of the Ferrari and FIA settlement – some called it an engine penalty, although Ferrari have always insisted it was instead a clarification on what could and could not be done. Either way, Ferrari's car in 2020 was massively uncompetitive. Given the long lead times required for car development in F1 the SF1000 had been developed around what the team's strengths of previous seasons had been – straight-line speed. 'They no longer had their joker – the powerful engine' was ESPN journalist Laurence Edmondson's take. 'In that time they had become so reliant on that powerful engine that they had let slip some of the other departments that were key to performance.' With engine performance stripped back, the flaws of the SF1000, such as high drag and insufficient downforce, became more pronounced.

It was an extreme downturn. Leclerc took an unlikely second place at the opening race, the spectator-free Austrian Grand Prix, before grabbing another podium at the fourth race in Silverstone. He would score just once more, while Vettel would score his only podium (and his last while racing in red) in Turkey towards the end of the truncated season. Ferrari finished sixth in the Constructors' Championship, dropping behind the winner Mercedes as well as Red Bull, McLaren, Racing Point and Renault. They finished just 24 points ahead of AlphaTauri, Red Bull's junior team. It was one of the biggest year-on-year drops of performance the sport had seen since the McLaren switch to Honda power in 2015. This only ramped the frustration of other teams about 2019.

'The whole thing has left quite a sour taste,' Horner said during Ferrari's slump in 2020. 'I mean, obviously you can draw your own conclusions from Ferrari's current performance, but there are races that we should have won last year, arguably, [if Ferrari had run with the 2020 spec engine].'

The controversial engine had been doubly counterproductive. 'We were so challenged by Ferrari on the engine side last year that we went in new directions to find performance,' Wolff told *Auto Motor und Sport* in 2020. 'In some races last year, we saw more than 50 kilowatts of power difference. For us, the task arose: How much power can we actually extract? And you can only find gains in the internal combustion engine. All other areas are limited. We turned over every stone we could find.'

The consensus in the paddock was clear. Ferrari had been severely scaled back by the secretive agreement. Some rival bosses today will still tell you none of them would have been given the same treatment. Horner himself was annoyed years later when Red Bull's overspend of 1.6 per cent in the first year of F1's budget cap of $145 million – which led to a $7 million fine and a 10 per cent cut in its aero testing the following year – became a weeks-long news story.

Carlos or Daniel?

For 2021, Sebastian Vettel was gone, with Carlos Sainz Jr. replacing him. Ferrari had been following the Spaniard, the son of the former World Rally Champion for a while. They had also seriously considered Daniel Ricciardo.

Given his huge popularity, Italian heritage and ability to speak the language, Ricciardo seemed by many to be a natural choice. It was always the dream move of his father, Joe. Talks stretched back years, even before switching management over to CAA Sports in 2019, but Ferrari had never seemed truly sold on him. According to sources at the team, Maurizio Arrivabene once told colleagues he thought Ricciardo laughed and joked around too much to be a Ferrari driver.

'Everyone says it would be a good fit, obviously, with my name and all the background stuff, but yeah, I try not to get emotionally caught up in any kind of situation,' Ricciardo said in 2020. 'Daniel was considered,' Binotto told me. 'We did analytics comparisons and I think we simply decided for Carlos because he was, between all of them, the most consistent in the race. The one that in terms of Constructors' Championship would have brought the most points through a season. He was very close to Charles in his first year at Ferrari, just behind. With car development Carlos was probably stronger at that stage too.' Binotto's view would be vindicated in 2024, with Sainz's consistency through the season helping Ferrari mount a late challenge against McLaren for the constructors' title.

The decision to pick Sainz over Ricciardo was soon vindicated in 2021. Sainz provided stability and consistency in results and behind the scenes was credited with his ability to succinctly convey what the team needed to do to unlock better performance in the car. Ricciardo's move to McLaren turned sour – aside from a memorable win at the 2021 Italian Grand Prix, it was marked by a spiral in form which saw his time at the team cut short at the end of the following season, still with one contract year left to run.

Ferrari was slightly more competitive by the 2021 season – Sainz outscored Leclerc four podiums to one in their first year together as Ferrari endured another winless campaign, albeit with a more competitive all-round package. That season was all about the epic fight between Hamilton's Mercedes and Verstappen's Red Bull.

One bonus of the close fight out in front was that Ferrari and other teams found it easier to shift their full focus to the next project: the 2022 car. F1's new rule change had been pushed back a year because of the pandemic – it aimed at creating race cars which could produce closer racing by removing the phenomenon known as 'dirty air', which for years had made it difficult for one car to closely follow another.

For Ferrari and the *tifosi* there was another obvious bonus for the new rules – after two years in the wilderness, here was a chance to hit the reset button. Ferrari had emerged from F1's last rule change as title contenders in 2017. Pressure was high on Binotto's team to deliver.

14

FALSE DAWN

'We live and die with our results. Certainly it was felt that Mattia was putting together a very good group with the right spirit. Equally we missed some targets in that 2022 season, we didn't present ourselves ready enough for the challenge.'

Laurent Mekies

Charles Leclerc's car is stationary, its nose nestled into one of the crash barriers lining the outside of France's Paul Ricard circuit. There is no obvious damage – an advertising board has collapsed clumsily onto the front of his Ferrari, obscuring a good view of his car's front wing – but his race, one he was in complete control of moments before, is over.

The crowd erupts, dust still settling around his car. Dismay, anger and jubilation erupts around the circuit as the screen shows Leclerc's car now out of the race. What follows is sporting theatre befitting the most famous team in the sport.

After a moment of silence, a series of deep, haunted, pained breaths, before what sounds like a guttural scream from the driver in the car: 'NO!'

As if to twist the knife further, TV cameras pan to two men in a nearby grandstand leaning on a guardrail. They are simply spectating fans but their reactions say it all – one, wearing a black Mercedes shirt, grins, before looking at the forlorn friend on his left. The friend, wearing all red, removes his Ferrari cap, hits it repeatedly and theatrically on the metallic divide in front of them, before crumpling his body forwards in defeat and sinking his head into his hands. It's an accurate summation of Ferrari's imploding 2022 season.

David Croft, long-time voice of the Sky Sports F1 coverage, sums it up a different way: 'For the third time this season Charles Leclerc, when leading a race, won't go on to finish it!'

For a team that has delivered many examples of the exciting and breathless start to an F1 season followed by a bitter and crushing collapse, 2022 felt like the worst of all. At one point early on in that year it felt like Ferrari had everything in place. The look had changed again – the gorgeous F1-75 (referencing 75 years since the first Ferrari production car rolled out of Maranello) had retained the iconic red colours but had gone back to a more 1990s feel with striking black front and rear wings, but it also stood out in a field of brand-new race cars. 'If I look at the 2022 car and the 2022 power unit, believe me there is a lot of innovation in it,' Mattia Binotto promised ahead of the season. 'I think that the way that the entire engineering team has faced the new design, the new project, and the 2022 regulations, which were a big discontinuity, was certainly with a more open mind than before. I can measure it by looking at the car itself, the way it's progressing, and certainly with the amount of innovation we put in it.'

A sidepod which ramped gently down in lower regions and cooling slats which stretched along the top, a design only replicated by Aston Martin, immediately put the Ferrari at the top of the list of tech journalists writing about which cars had caught the eye in pre-season. Although Binotto played down talk of a title fight and ahead of the opening race, Leclerc insisted Red Bull were favourites with the eye-catching RB18, it was hard to ignore how strong Ferrari looked in pre-season testing. That view was fully endorsed in the early rounds of the season. In Bahrain, Leclerc stormed to pole ahead of Verstappen. Leclerc led and, after a late restart, Verstappen's car hit trouble in second place, eventually retiring with an engine fault – Sergio Perez's Red Bull would also fail in the final laps as Ferrari secured a one–two victory, ending a run of 45 races without a win, the second longest in the team's history.

Leclerc and Verstappen would fight for the win again in Saudi Arabia, with the combination of the Jeddah circuit, the three DRS (Drag Reduction System) zones and the added effect of DRS on the new big-winged cars creating a unique spectacle. The two exchanged the lead multiple times in a late fight in which neither of them wanted to be ahead at the final corner, where the DRS 'detection' line was positioned, as doing so would mean ceding that advantage to the car behind. It showed great nous on the part of both drivers. 'Charles really played it smart in the last corner,' said Verstappen, who went on to win after three attempts to hold the lead.

In Australia Leclerc led away from pole at the start, although Sainz, having qualified back in P9, spun off on the opening lap. Red Bull's reliability issues came back again at mid-distance as a fuel leak took Verstappen out of the race. Ferrari's car was quick and its race operation had started the season humming; Red Bull's RB18 seemed to have a higher performance ceiling but appeared fragile. Leaving Australia, Leclerc had a 34-point lead over Mercedes' George Russell and a 46-point lead over Verstappen. It was early days, but at that point the consensus was Ferrari had plenty more wins left in the tank.

Sainz crashed out of the Emilia-Romagna Grand Prix early at Imola, before Leclerc spun late on chasing Perez down for second place after hitting the kerbs too aggressively. He dropped to fifth by the finish as Verstappen scored another win. The Dutchman then beat Leclerc at the first Miami Grand Prix and from there the season started to unravel.

Leclerc was leading when his engine failed in Spain, before a nightmarish Monaco Grand Prix which encapsulated the growing feeling that this

Ferrari team was still not ready to compete alongside Red Bull. Qualifying in Monaco is everything and Leclerc and Sainz had locked out the front row ahead of Perez and Verstappen. But come race day a rain shower delayed the start. When the grand prix got underway Ferrari was in complete control. Leclerc led Sainz comfortably until Perez pitted from wets to intermediates on Lap 17 as the track dried out. The Mexican driver began slashing the sector times on his out-lap on new rubber. Ferrari then split its drivers, bringing Leclerc in for the same tyre swap a lap later and keeping Sainz out on wets. But in that one lap Perez had gained enough time to pass Leclerc on track. When Ferrari pitted both its drivers to switch to slick tyres on Lap 21, Sainz (who had not taken on intermediates) stopped before Leclerc and Perez moved into the outright lead of the race.

This is when the infamous radio exchange took place . . .

'Box now, box now, for hard [tyre],' said Leclerc's race engineer, before suddenly offering a different instruction the moment his driver had turned into the pit-lane. 'Stay out, stay out, stay out . . .'

An incensed Leclerc replied: 'Fuck! Fuck! Why? Why? What are you doing?!'

Ferrari suddenly realized they would lose time double-stacking the two cars. Leclerc had made so much time back on his team-mate that he was now right behind Sainz. But the call had been made, he followed Carlos into the box.

Charles' misery only deepened a lap later when he saw Verstappen emerge from his own pit-stop in front of him, meaning the local favourite's comfortable lead had turned into fourth position in a handful of laps. Starting from P1 and P2 they had dropped to second and fourth. With overtaking almost impossible at Monaco, Perez held off Sainz to win the race. On the radio after the finish, Leclerc said: 'No words – the season is long but we cannot do that.' He added after the race: 'The win was clearly in our hands: we had the performance, we had everything. I just don't really understand the call that I had and I need explanations for now . . . We need to get better.'

The farcical radio exchange became emblematic of the issues within the strategic operation at Ferrari, although by the point of the double-stack pit-stop the race had already slipped out of the team's control.

'We were leading comfortably but we weren't sure whether it was going to rain or not for a long time,' Iñaki Rueda, at the time Ferrari's head of strategy, told me. 'We had enough margin that we weren't going to make the first decision. We saw Checo stop and that he was coming fast. We fell prey to what we were suffering all year – which was that Charles had a big lead but as soon as we had that car on a cold track, it was slippery and his pace dropped much more than we imagined. So we thought, "Red Bull is going to catch up by three or four seconds maybe, but we've got time in hand". But Charles really struggled to bring that car in and we lost something like 10, 11 seconds on one lap. That's where we lost the race, on the in-lap. The whole, "Stay out, stay out" was different . . . that was just a confusion in the heat of the moment. We wouldn't have changed the result had he stayed out. We had already lost the race by then. I was head of strategy at that point and I held the responsibility to not have brought the car in at the right time and I didn't do that. The complication of calling the car in sounded like shit from the outside but the car still came in one lap late irrespective. Everyone just used that clip afterwards but the race had already gone.'

In the days which followed, Rueda became a target for criticism for a video on the team's official YouTube channel, where he appeared to downplay Ferrari's strategic problems. 'When Mattia had become team boss he said, "Let's open up the team". He wanted us to do something like Mercedes was doing with James Vowles, a strategy briefing after every race. It was difficult to answer on races like that . . .' especially when faced with the ferocious Italian press.

'I couldn't go into one of those videos and say we need to do better and we'll need to work on estimating how to do our race strategy better. We said the "Stay out" communication wasn't important in the result of the race. That's what we tried to express on that video. Unsuccessfully. People didn't want to hear it.'

After Monaco, Leclerc's car failed again while he was leading in Baku. Charles had taken pole position, but his engine started billowing smoke on Lap 21. He was the second retirement – Carlos Sainz had already exited the race on Lap 9 with a hydraulics issue. Optimism returned after Silverstone, where Sainz claimed his maiden grand prix win, although that victory came after Ferrari had already blundered on Leclerc's strategy, failing to bring him in for a tyre change during a safety car period.

Leclerc claimed a win in Austria, although Sainz's engine failed in the final laps when he was closing in on Verstappen's second place. Leclerc was leading again at the Paul Ricard circuit in the south of France and looking to edge back into the title fight with Verstappen, only to spin out completely on his own. 'He was not consistent,' Binotto told me. 'He has to be more consistent. That is the biggest thing with Charles. I think more recently we have seen an improvement there but that was always the thing we saw, very up and down.'

'Obviously it's extremely frustrating,' Leclerc said after his Paul Ricard crash. 'I feel like I'm performing at probably the highest level of my career since the beginning of the season, but there's no point performing at that high level if I am doing those mistakes. I think there are 32 points overall [lost with mistakes], 25 today. And seven in Imola with my mistake, so at the end of the year we will count back, and if there are 32 points missing then I know it's coming from me and I did not deserve the championship. But for the second half of the season I need to get on top of those things if I want to be a World Champion.'

Leclerc would finish behind by a far greater margin than 32, but that was part of the problem. After getting over the early reliability issues, Red Bull's race operation was turning into a ruthless winning machine, getting on top of the early car trouble and then steadily developing the car to a point it was clearly the fastest. On the flip side, Ferrari was lacking in all areas. Drivers were not delivering as they should, strategy was all over the place and the team once again had appeared to slip behind on car development as the season progressed.

The team's strategy failings would again be laid bare in Hungary. George Russell took pole for Mercedes ahead of Sainz and Leclerc, who both looked well placed to win, with Verstappen starting down in 10th. Leclerc stopped on Lap 22, with Ferrari switching his car from mediums to another set of the same tyre, before switching him onto the harder compound later in the race. The two-stopping Verstappen had done soft-medium-medium and carved his way back through the order to win – Ferrari's decision to use the unfavoured hard tyre drew further criticism of Rueda's strategy team. Unfortunately for Rueda, Ferrari chairman John Elkann, who had taken the role after Sergio Marchionne's death in 2018, and CEO Benedetto Vigna were in Budapest that day.

'That was one of the races I was summoned to see John Elkann, actually,' he told me. 'Vigna, Elkann, Mattia, Laurent, myself. Elkann said, "Why did we do that, why?" We were scared of the soft tyres that year, scared shitless, because in the colder temperatures more graining appears. So we started on mediums and that was the mistake because it cornered us – we were stuffed, you can't take the softs long enough at the end. Max starting on the soft is where they beat us. On Friday the hard had been working fine but the temperature had been higher. Stupidly enough, for whatever reason, nobody in the team thought the hard was not going to be working. We just didn't think. From there we put in a closer cooperation with the tyre team, try and characterize the tyres for different temperatures, but that week it hurt us. It annoyed me because from Elkann we got the typical answer like Marchionne – "No, what you need to do is to make more courageous choices!" So again you come out thinking, what does that mean? Someone five, six levels of management above you. You give them your answer at your level and they never understand it.'

Rueda's name had become a byword for Ferrari's shortcomings from the pit-wall that season. Over the summer break, multiple websites compiled articles of the number of points Ferrari had lost through mistakes – via drivers, reliability or strategy, and it pushed towards 100. After the summer break, Red Bull failed to win only once – in Brazil, where George Russell claimed his first F1 win with Mercedes. On the outside Ferrari's season appeared to have fallen apart, although the team was still able to hold off Mercedes for second place in the constructors' trophy by the end of the year.

'Whenever there's a change of regulations, Ferrari always makes a good car,' Rueda said. 'Always. Ferrari has really good engineers, really good facilities. And they always come straight out with a strong car. But as soon as that car gets handed over to the race team they're swayed left, right and centre. And because the pressure at Ferrari is so high that becomes even more extreme than any other team. Whatever long-term plan is in place goes out of the window as soon as things go bad.' Some might say that the numerous race strategies discussed over team radio with the drivers – Plan A, Plan B and Plan C – are a manifestation of this. 'It happened in 2018 to a greater extent. In 2022 we made a lot of mistakes – a lot were my fault – but we fell victim to the same thing.'

Binotto, hand-picked as team boss by the late Sergio Marchionne, was now in a weakened position as team boss. When Marchionne resigned days before his death, Louis Camilleri had been named CEO of Ferrari, with Elkann named chairman shortly afterwards. Camilleri had shared Marchionne's high opinion of Binotto and believed fully in his ability to lead Ferrari back to title glory, having seen how he had galvanized the technical operation under Maurizio Arrivabene. Camilleri had been a firm believer in patience and time but resigned due to poor health in late 2020. Binotto had put a lot of good things in place behind the scenes – he had led a fresh overhaul of the team's wind tunnel and had signed off the production of a state-of-the-art simulator at Maranello. The team had also made huge progress on the power unit since it had been cut back in 2020. But Elkann, and Camilleri's replacement Vigna, were less convinced in Binotto's abilities. Neither had picked him to be team boss, which ultimately was his biggest downfall, and both found it frustrating how Binotto would insist on looking at the bigger picture when giving interviews in the press – Binotto had learned from Jean Todt and his formative years at Ferrari that the job of team boss was to protect everyone else from criticism. By the end of the year, his future seemed to be hanging in the balance.

'In 2022 we started so well, expectations were so high . . . but we never said before the season that was a year we could have won,' Binotto told me. 'The plan we had in place was that we were building to a win down the line. But because we started so well, even the ownership was expecting it by the end. When I would say in interviews that our ambition was not to win the title but to keep finding continuous improvement, they were like, "Oh come on, this guy has no ambition," which was not true. We had a plan to win.'

Binotto knew the 2022 season was being framed in a negative way, rather than Ferrari returning to a measure of success after two winless years. They had fared considerably better than close rivals Mercedes with four wins (which should have been more) compared to the solitary victory for the Silver Arrows. As the season neared an end, whispers started that Ferrari was sounding out replacements for Binotto. A meeting with Elkann ahead of the Abu Dhabi Grand Prix left the team boss feeling as though he would be given 2023 to see if the Scuderia could win the championship.

After that meeting, Ferrari put out a statement saying reports of Binotto's imminent sacking were 'totally without foundation'.

The situation changed after the season finale. Binotto now met with silence from senior management about the future and realized the ground was shifting around him. Reports in Italy since have suggested Elkann was mulling over a replacement for Binotto from as early as 2021, not convinced the engineer-turned-team-boss was the right man for the job. The 2022 unravelling only reinforced his view.

On 29 November, nine days after the season finale, Mattia Binotto resigned. Sources at the time suggested he knew he was about to be removed from his post. It brought to an end a 28-year tenure at Maranello. Many at the team were surprised Binotto had walked away, given his insistence that Ferrari was in a longer term cycle which would lead to a championship.

'It was certainly a very, very strange time, because obviously we had gone through the disappointment of the title fight, but we felt we had made a step forward compared to the previous years,' former Ferrari deputy team boss Laurent Mekies told me. 'There were some interesting baselines there for the future. So even though it had been a very tense season we were under the impression the project was continuing, the programme would continue and the team would be put to the test the following year.

'So of course it came as a shock when Mattia decided to stop. But it's the way Formula 1 is. It has very long lead time for success . . . much shorter for failure. It's the way the sport is. We live and die with our results. Certainly it was felt that Mattia was putting together a very good group with the right spirit. Equally we missed some targets in that 2022 season, we didn't present ourselves ready enough for the challenge.'

After Todt had stepped back from a hands-on role in 2008, a series of company men had taken the reins. The chosen one, Stefano Domenicali, had been unable to bring a championship back to Ferrari. Two corporate hires in Marco Mattiacci and Maurizio Arrivabene, parachuted into the alien environment of an F1 team, had been unsuccessful. Now Binotto, a quiet and methodical engineer, the face of Ferrari longevity and a man who had rejuvenated Ferrari's facilities and culture behind the scenes, had also left without winning a title.

It had taken a Frenchman to lead Ferrari to championship glory all those years before, so maybe it needed another one now? On 13 December, Ferrari announced that Sauber boss Frédéric 'Fred' Vasseur would be taking the job. Elkann had his man. Respected across the paddock for his long career in the sport, Vasseur had cultivated a brilliant reputation for leadership despite never controlling a front-running F1 team. Now, he was in charge of the most famous team in motor sport, with a race operation loaded with talent, some of the best facilities in the world and a race car that was in touching distance of Red Bull's dominant car.

15

RED FRED

'He's very emotionally flat and that is a really good thing for a team like Ferrari. That's what is needed in Ferrari, so I'm completely confident and I have full trust in what Fred does.'

Charles Leclerc

There are some parallels you can draw between the arrival of Jean Todt at Ferrari in 1993 and the arrival of Fred Vasseur 30 years later. Both came with a no-nonsense reputation. Both were known for being staunchly principled in the way they go about the business of racing. Both had forged reputations as unflappable leaders in less-fancied roles, far outside the orbit of F1's greatest team: Todt had risen through the ranks at Peugeot, while Vasseur had excelled as a team boss with junior team ART before a long stint as boss of Sauber/Alfa Romeo. Both were the first proper hire of the man upstairs – Todt was di Montezemolo's, Vasseur was John Elkann's choice. Both arrived at a team facing long championship droughts.

Vasseur's immediate job seemed obvious: smooth out the edges of the race team. For all of the criticism and negativity of the second half of 2022 he had inherited an operation that had won races the year before, yet had underperformed in every area. The most obvious first place to address was strategy. Iñaki Rueda – often staunchly defended by Mattia Binotto despite numerous strategic gaffes – was shuffled away from the race team operation, replaced by Ravin Jain.

Recalling this decision, Rueda told me: 'When Fred joined, he asked me to come to the office and he said, "Look, there's too much negative press against your name, I want you to stay in the team but you shouldn't come to the races any more." So at that point I moved back. Fred asked if I wanted to do strategy from the factory but I didn't want to ruin the succession plan we had for Ravin. I don't know if Fred had a chat with Vigna and Elkann and they said, "This guy is a complete idiot, just get rid of him". But clearly there was a mood in the team for me to move on.'

Rueda initially did not mind his demotion back to the factory, where he oversaw sporting matters, as he felt it followed a logical succession plan and enabled Jain to move up into the top job. He would leave at the end of 2023 to rejoin Mattia Binotto at Sauber. There were other high-profile changes Vasseur had to contend with, too. Head of vehicle performance David Sanchez left after a decade with the team, bound for McLaren. Italian media reports early in the Frenchman's tenure suggested something close to turmoil behind the scenes. Vasseur very calmly played those rumours down, addressing it head-on in the media and saying personnel turnover is 'the life of a team'. It might appear like an irrelevant thing on the surface, but Vasseur's no-nonsense approach to dealing with media reports was a breath of fresh air after a string of people from within the Ferrari orbit.

Binotto's deputy team boss, Laurent Mekies, was also soon confirmed to be leaving, having been offered the top job at AlphaTauri. While it could have been seen as a slow implosion behind the scenes, it was simply an offer the Frenchman found impossible to turn down.

'When Fred came at the beginning of the year, we clicked straight away, probably because of our common background,' Mekies told me. 'Very different management style, but that's neither good nor bad, it's different for every person. It was very, very tempting to stay and start the new chapter with him because we had a great structure in place. I learned a lot from Fred even in a few months.

'But an opportunity like AlphaTauri, especially after spending ten years there earlier in my career . . . it would have been very difficult not to jump on that train with them.' The departures gave Vasseur the chance to continue reshuffling internally, bringing the team more in line with his own vision. In a reshuffle after Mekies' departure was announced, Diego Ioverno was promoted to sporting director, a popular move within the team.

On track, Vasseur's tenure started in tricky circumstances. It was immediately clear Red Bull's RB19 was a step ahead of the rest, but an unlikely team had emerged as second quickest – Aston Martin, with the wily Fernando Alonso spearheading the challenge. Alonso would be a regular on the podium in the first half of the season.

Charles Leclerc and Carlos Sainz struggled with an unpredictable car that showed excessive tyre wear, which significantly limited the team's chances of strong results. It was not bulletproof either, with a reliability issue costing Leclerc a strong result at the opening Bahrain Grand Prix. Ferrari scored just two podiums before the summer break, through Leclerc in Azerbaijan and Austria. There was a continuation of the trend of the drivers' partnership – Leclerc's form was up and down, while Sainz's performance level was consistent. Leclerc might even have had a shot at that elusive first trip to the Monaco podium had a qualifying penalty not dropped him from third on the grid to sixth, which is where he ultimately finished.

Ferrari's season flipped around after the summer break as the team got a better handle on the SF-23. Sainz finished fifth at Zandvoort, third at Monza and then claimed a memorable win at the Singapore Grand Prix. At Marina Bay, Sainz used the DRS zones to keep the third and fourth-placed cars from mounting a challenge. Leading the race from the McLaren of Lando Norris, Sainz held his car back when he could have dashed clear. Carlos realized that Norris could not overtake him, but would have been passed by George Russell and Lewis Hamilton had the Ferrari driver not dawdled, allowing Norris the benefit of the DRS. Overtaking is hard enough at Singapore, so it showed incredible tactical awareness from Sainz to pull it off. Russell crashed out in the closing moments as Sainz secured the win, the only non-Red Bull win of the year.

Sainz then inherited a podium in Austin when Lewis Hamilton was disqualified alongside Leclerc. They were both thrown out after post-race inspections revealed excessive wear on the car's rear skid blocks. The teams put it down to the bumpy nature of the Circuit of the Americas race track (subsequently relaid for 2024). Leclerc bounced back with an impressive podium in Mexico, before he almost beat Verstappen to victory at a thrilling inaugural Las Vegas Grand Prix.

Ahead of that race, the fiery side of Fred Vasseur's personality had come to the fore, after Sainz's car had been ripped apart by a drain cover on the new Vegas circuit during practice. Driver errors that caused accidents had to be taken on the chin, but this was a circuit error that had laid waste to Carlos's floor and damaged his energy store, the replacement of which would mean a 10-place grid drop.

Vasseur, often cagey but rarely animated in front of the media, went to a press conference after that session and it was immediately obvious from his body language how upset he was. 'I think it's just unacceptable,' he said. 'We had a very tough FP1 . . . we won't be part of the FP2 for sure, we have to change the chassis, half the car, to set up the car, okay the show is the show and everything is going well but I think it's just unacceptable for F1 today.' It was a memorable moment because it went against the calm demeanour Vasseur so often displayed, showing the inner steel.

Despite the slow start to the season, at the final race, Ferrari had a chance to beat Mercedes to second position in the Constructors' Championship. They fell short by three points, Leclerc finishing second with George Russell taking third place by a whisker in front of Sergio Perez. Vasseur was satisfied with his first year at the helm. 'The performance is coming from everywhere in the company, we are able to produce parts quicker, we have a better reliability,' Vasseur said at the end of the season. 'We gave up too many points this season for different reasons, for reliability, for disqualification in Austin, for impeding in quali, but this is clearly where we have to work. We have to improve on aero, on engine, on every single topic. It's not that we have something wrong and something good and you fix something and you are making a step of four or five tenths [in one go].'

One of the most obvious takeaways from the first year had been the calmer feel around Ferrari. Although Binotto had done a lot to remove the culture of fear and install a no-blame attitude, his Ferrari team still appeared to be jittery and prone to emotional reactions. Vasseur's first year had come with a new degree of calm which seemed like the Ferrari of the Brawn era – Jain's strategy team had avoided the major mistakes of Rueda's time in charge and, although not perfect, appeared to have made a clear improvement.

According to one source at the team, Vasseur has a combination of traits from three of his predecessors – the leadership qualities of Stefano Domenicali, the sometimes direct and abrasive nature of Maurizio Arrivabene and the calm, logical approach of Binotto. On top of that, there is something refreshingly un-Ferrari about him. One viral video filmed at the end of the year, of Vasseur attempting to push Sainz's head into a birthday cake as he went to blow out the candles, seemed to sum up the new man and the culture that he and his predecessor in the job had helped to cultivate. The idea of Ferrari showing its team boss behaving in such a way a year earlier seems highly fanciful.

'Fred is a very direct guy,' Ioverno said in 2023. 'He is straight to the point. He knows the business, knows motor sport. He knows Formula 1. So, it's quite easy to work with him. It's easy to understand what he wants. You don't have to make your own conclusions – he tells you. He knows also how to enjoy himself but I think it is better not to upset him. Because I think he can be also hard.'

Vasseur's management style in F1 has not changed since his arrival in Maranello. 'Taking on the biggest job in motorsport could have forced a change in that approach,' Lawrence Barretto wrote at season end: 'He could have become more corporate, straight-laced and humourless. But after a year in the job, Vasseur hasn't changed one bit.'

Nationality is an unavoidable factor when it comes to Vasseur. Domenicali, Mattiacci, Arrivabene and the Swiss–Italian Binotto had all grown up and advanced their careers understanding and working with the expectation and pressure-cooker environment of Ferrari. While Binotto brought stability behind the scenes, his own undoing ultimately was borne out of politics, with John Elkann unconvinced he was the right man to lead. Sources have suggested to me that Elkann, the maternal grandson of Gianni Agnelli, was being advised by other people within the team about some of Binotto's weak points. It's a tale as old as time at Ferrari, perhaps reminiscent of Niccolò Machiavelli. Although he had a stint at the Ferrari engine customer Sauber, Vasseur is free of a lot of the nonsense that can waste time behind the scenes.

'The biggest two things for Fred were that he was hand-picked by Elkann, but he's also not been around too long to be messed up by all the politics there,' Rueda told me. 'For a lot of those guys, Ferrari is their life. It's all they've talked about for 10, 15, 20 years. When they go to lunch they talk Ferrari. When they go home they talk Ferrari. When they are at the race they talk Ferrari. People in management roles make friends and enemies very quickly. I think that's a big bonus for Fred, he's not really got that same baggage holding him down.'

Like Todt decades earlier, Vasseur has been seen as a leveller to that very environment, someone whose highs are never too high and whose lows are never too low.

'I think Fred has changed quite a few things, which made a really big difference,' Leclerc told *Beyond the Grid* in 2023. 'Whenever you are having a really good race with Ferrari, everybody feels so good, so happy, and Fred is always the balance of saying: "Yeah, it's great, but now let's re-centre a little bit because it's only one race and we've got many other races", and exactly the same in bad moments when everybody feels down, Fred is always there to give us the positives in a difficult situation to re-motivate everybody. He's very emotionally flat and that is a really good thing for a team like Ferrari. That's what is needed in Ferrari, so I'm completely confident and I have full trust in what Fred does.'

And yet like Todt and his famous meeting with di Montezemolo, where his love of Ferrari shone through (despite him arriving in a Mercedes), Vasseur is someone who understands and loves the brand as much as anyone. 'Where Ferrari is a bit special is everything that comes with it,' Vasseur told me in Las Vegas in 2023. 'It's an iconic brand. We have Enzo, the team, the car factory, the technology of F1. This combination is a good one. It's a good feeling to be a bridge between the two. We have a kind of responsibility with the past of the brand and Enzo, while still focusing on the future. The next race is always the most important, by definition.' You won't hear Vasseur talking about a race victory or a championship until he has his hands on the trophy, which seems ideal when hype can be such a debilitating factor.

At the final race of the year in Abu Dhabi 2023 several things happened which set in motion the big news story of 2024. Leclerc and Sainz were both going into the off-season hoping to secure contract extensions – for Sainz, this had been a lingering bugbear throughout his career, with multiple teams declining opportunities to sign him to long-term deals. By that final race, it appeared as though a bumper extension for Leclerc was being drawn up, but the Sainz camp felt in the dark about the status of his own deal. Several team bosses were speculating that a big change might be coming, with Elkann making it clear privately he felt Ferrari had to go back to having two superstar drivers.

During the weekend, Williams boss James Vowles met Sainz and pitched him a vision for the team's future. Vowles would later say he had no inkling of the conversations that were intensifying between Lewis Hamilton and Ferrari, but it was clear a growing feeling in the paddock was that Sainz's future at the team (even with his Singapore victory so fresh in the mind) was unclear. When Sainz left Abu Dhabi, he was unsure what was going on behind the scenes, but he had an uneasy feeling about where things were headed.

Even then, no-one could have predicted what the next stage of the Ferrari story was going to be.

16

'AMILTON

'This was the moment when he and Ferrari found each other. He wants to win the eighth title. Ferrari wants to win and with Lewis, they are stronger.'

John Elkann

It was natural that a superstar as big as Lewis Hamilton would be linked with Ferrari at various points in his career. But it was still a genuine shock on 1 February 2024 when, seemingly out of nowhere, Ferrari announced they had reached a deal with Hamilton to race for them in 2025. As bombshell announcements go, it was hard to top it, even if it was a full season away.

Most surprising was that just seven months earlier Hamilton had signed an extension with Mercedes. 'In the summer [of 2023] we signed, and obviously I, at that time, saw my future with Mercedes,' Hamilton said mid-way through the 2024 season. 'But an opportunity came up in the New Year and I decided to take it. It was obviously the hardest decision that I think I've ever had to make. Obviously I've been with Mercedes for, I think it's like 26 years they've supported me, and we've had an absolutely incredible journey together. We've created history within the sport, and it's something I take a lot of pride in and I'm very proud of what we've achieved. But I think ultimately I'm writing my story and I felt like it was time to start a new chapter.'

Ferrari had played a blinder, pulling off two bits of business to kick off 2024. Just weeks earlier, Charles Leclerc had signed a new deal, one which reportedly locked him down all the way through until 2029. Hamilton's deal was believed to be in the region of $87 million for 2025 with an option to extend into 2026.

'Some things happen very quickly,' Ferrari CEO John Elkann told *Corriere dello Sport* during the Paris Olympics in mid-2024. 'This was the moment when he and Ferrari found each other. He wants to win the eighth title, Ferrari wants to win and with Lewis, they are stronger.' A firm believer that Ferrari should always look to have the best drivers in the world in their cars, Elkann had been a long-time admirer of Hamilton's abilities. He had tried and failed to get him into a red car before.

Timeline

The biggest splash the Italian media had ever made about Hamilton – whose name, in that part of the world, will likely be pronounced without the 'H' – came in the closing months of 2019. Hamilton was in the first year of a two-year contract which would take him into the pandemic-shortened 2020 season, where he would win a seventh world title and hit 100 race wins, with Mercedes. But true to Ferrari's old philosophy of signing drivers as early as possible, the prospect of bringing him in for 2021 seemed a tantalizing one.

A big headline story in Italy's *La Gazzetta dello Sport* ahead of the 2019 Abu Dhabi Grand Prix, the final race of that season, suggested Hamilton had twice met with Elkann, who was attempting to 'Chat him up'. The paper went on to say: 'Elkann is a big fan of Hamilton, so too is Ferrari vice-president, Piero Ferrari, who is in Abu Dhabi this weekend. This is a courtship that has lasted for years. Even from the times of Luca di Montezemolo and Stefano Domenicali, the interest in the English champion has been constant and is still very strong today.'

Di Montezemolo admitted conversations had taken place during his tenure, although that is not out of the ordinary in Formula 1. Things never worked out, with di Montezemolo's final two driver decisions being to sign Kimi Räikkönen in 2012 (for the 2014 season) and helping to finalize the Sebastian Vettel deal in 2014 for the following year. 'We talked with him and it was clear he had a great respect for Ferrari,' the former president said about Hamilton during our interview. 'I think he's one of the best drivers in Formula 1, at the very least modern Formula 1, because he has been fantastic. A lot of people say, "Yes he was fantastic because he has got the best car, Mercedes." But if you see the difference with the drivers in the team, if you see how good he was, for sure he is a super champion.' As for 2019, it is also true Binotto's Ferrari explored the option. By this point Sebastian Vettel's goodwill at the team had eroded slightly after missed opportunities in 2017 and 2018. 'Discussions with Lewis started quite a few years before,' Binotto confirmed to me. 'He was interested, definitely.'

Ultimately, Hamilton stayed put and shortly after racing resumed during the pandemic signed a one-year Mercedes extension which would set up his thrilling 2021 title fight with Max Verstappen and Red Bull. After the controversial finish in Abu Dhabi that year Hamilton effectively disappeared from the public eye, no-showing the FIA awards gala and then going to ground for weeks over Christmas.

It was only ahead of the team's car launch in February 2022 that the Silver Arrows confirmed he would race that year. 'I never said I was going to stop,' Hamilton clarified. 'I love doing what I do. It was a difficult time for me, a time I needed to take a step back. I had my family around me and created great moments.' The new regulations would mark an immediate end to Hamilton's domination with Mercedes' singular interpretation of the technical rules leading them down a design cul de sac. Lewis did not win in 2022, his first winless season since he started in F1, and neither did he win in 2023, but that did not stop him signing what was reported to be a two-year contract midway through the latter.

Despite this extension, in 2023 there were more rumblings he might be looking for a change of racing colours. Ahead of the 2023 Monaco Grand Prix, Jonathan McEvoy of the *Daily Mail* had reported Hamilton and Ferrari were in advanced talks. Hamilton and Fred Vasseur shot the story down immediately afterwards and sources have told me the two parties were actually a fair way apart at this point. Elkann was still interested and Hamilton was intrigued by the new element in the negotiations – his old racing boss from junior categories, Vasseur, with whom he had always maintained a good relationship. But despite the presence of the Frenchman in the equation, most in the sport, including this writer, dismissed it as the same old rehashing of a move most assumed would never happen. But the rumours persisted. At Silverstone ahead of the British Grand Prix a month later Lewis's commercial agent was seen walking in and out of Ferrari hospitality on at least one occasion. On the grid ahead of the Belgian Grand Prix, Christian Horner approached me and *Autosport* journalist, Ben Hunt, to ask, with a smirk why 'None of you are asking Toto about Lewis going to Ferrari'. Given Horner's history of trying to wind up Mercedes boss Toto Wolff at every opportunity it was easy to dismiss his comments as being more of the same. But clearly, the story had more substance than it ever had before.

What appeared to have pushed Hamilton into Elkann's arms, so to speak, was the nature of his negotiations with Wolff. It would later emerge the deal he signed in 2023 had been a one-plus-one deal – a contract with options baked in to it which gives driver and team some flexibility and always suggests some longer-term uncertainty on one or both sides of the deal. Hamilton's options had left the door ajar for another team to come and make a final pitch.

Even those directly involved had no idea what was brewing until 2023 had rolled into the off-season. Wolff found out from an unlikely source – Carlos Sainz's father. 'I heard the bells ringing two weeks before,' Wolff told the *High Performance* podcast. 'The old man Sainz called me and said, "This is what's happening". (Sainz Senior's eagerness to deliver bad news to Wolff's door may shed light on the antagonism between the Verstappens and the Sainzes at Toro Rosso in 2016).

'Then there were a few drivers that rang me up that didn't before so I thought, there's something going on here. Then I sent a text to Fred Vasseur saying, "So you're taking our driver?" Didn't get any response. Very unusual for Fred, he's a good friend. So I saw it coming.'

Wolff got the big reveal the next day, 30 January 2024, when Hamilton visited him – shortly after telling the driver that Mercedes had just poached well-respected car designer Simone Resta. The following day, news filtered out of Italy. That morning a WhatsApp message to the Sainz camp was enough to confirm the news for ESPN. By midday most media outlets around the world were leading with it, once it was made official by Ferrari.

Clearly, the 2023 reports had a kernel of truth to them – going so far as to suggest Hamilton's plan was always to finish at Ferrari in some way. 'In 2023 we won more races than Mercedes, and the beginning of the 2024 season was good also, so it was not too difficult to convince him that Ferrari would be a good project,' Vasseur said in November 2024. 'And I think he had the project to drive for Ferrari in his mind for at least 22 years, or 23 years, because we were discussing about this in 2004. It meant that it was not too difficult. I think sometimes it's also a matter of coincidence, or to align all the planets, that he is on the market and that Ferrari has a seat available, and so on. But the contact was an easy one. We started to discuss one year ago, and it was not difficult to convince him at all.'

Neither side wanted to over-publicize the move at the time. Hamilton still had what would turn into a fairly awkward final year with Mercedes, while Ferrari were very conscious they had just yanked the rug from under the feet of the popular Sainz. Paddock sympathy for the Spaniard rolling into pre-season was huge. He had been a star performer of 2023, claiming the only non-Verstappen victory of the second half of the season at the Singapore Grand Prix.

Sainz Jr. has always come across as a classy individual and he exemplified that in how he dealt with the news, despite years of clawing his way through stints at Toro Rosso, Renault and McLaren to get to Ferrari, only to have it all snatched away. Asked if he could understand the call, Sainz told *Beyond the Grid*: '100 percent. I understood it almost right from the beginning. I think if it would have been someone else, I would have taken a lot longer to understand. But when you understand Lewis Hamilton, the seven-time World Champion and one of the best – if not the best in history – is going to replace you at Ferrari. And Lewis has decided to do the last part of his career in Ferrari, and that you need to be one of the two drivers sacrificed for that to happen – I understand. I also understand why it was never going to be Charles. Charles has been the project of Ferrari ever since he's been a junior driver.'

Lewis vs Charles

'I think for Formula 1 it's fantastic,' Horner told me in December 2024. 'I mean, Lewis Hamilton in a Ferrari . . . Ferrari are the most iconic team in Formula 1 and you've got the driver that's achieved the most in Formula 1 going there. Can he still deliver, going up against Charles Leclerc? He's one of the fastest guys on the grid. It's going to be fascinating to see how it plays out.'

There are so many intriguing elements to Hamilton's move – Leclerc is one of the biggest. At 40, Hamilton will be facing up against one of the grid's brightest talents. Many aspects of the Ferrari move are bold from the seven-time World Champion: taking on Charles Leclerc in Leclerc's house is one of them. For Leclerc, it will be a yardstick of just how good he is. 'For me to be able to drive the same car as Lewis is, first, a huge opportunity to learn from the best ever, as well as a huge motivation to show what I'm capable of,' Leclerc said in 2024, adding: 'It's definitely going to be a big moment of my career to be against Lewis, working together to bring Ferrari back on top. It will be incredible to see where I am compared to Lewis.' By the end of January 2025, Hamilton will have had his first pre-season test with Ferrari, but it will be another seven weeks at best before he gets behind the wheel at the Australian Grand Prix. That is the nature of Formula 1 for anyone changing teams and it only adds to the fascination of the early dynamic with his new team-mate.

There are multiple schools of thought here. Brazilian journalist Julianne Cerasoli said this has happened to another F1 academy product before: 'I think they are risking doing to Charles what they did to Massa by saying, "We love you Charles, *Il Predestinato*, but we still need someone bigger than you". It's easy to view it as a negative for Leclerc – after all, Elkann signing a superstar in the evening of his career suggests he does not think Leclerc is yet at that level. Others, like former F1 boss Bernie Ecclestone, think Hamilton is walking into a trap. 'I do not think it will be easy for Lewis,' he told the *Daily Mail* in 2024. 'Especially in that team. They will back Charles Leclerc. He is quick and has grown up there. They will not dump him for anyone.' Others might suggest that, beyond the remuneration and the obvious allure of racing for Ferrari, Hamilton's decision to ditch the comfort of Mercedes for the risks associated with Ferrari shows a supreme self-confidence.

The question of which version of Hamilton Ferrari is getting will also linger at the start of the year. Even the Briton seemed to have some self doubts about his own abilities towards the end of 2024. After his superb win at the British Grand Prix, Hamilton's final months at Mercedes were a painful rollercoaster ride. 'I'm just slow. Same every weekend,' he said ominously after a disappointing sprint qualifying in Qatar. When the interviewer pointed out Hamilton has more pole positions than any other driver and suggested the lack of performance could not solely be down to him, he replied: 'Who knows. I'm definitely not fast any more.' However, the momentary lapses into pessimism have always been there. How many times has the message: 'These tyres aren't going to last, Bono' been relayed on team radio, only for Lewis to nurse them to the finish? Hamilton did sign off with a strong drive to fourth, which included a well-executed overtake on team-mate George Russell on the final lap of his Mercedes career.

One person who does not buy that pessimistic approach is Vasseur. 'He had very good races in Vegas, in Abu Dhabi, and I was never, really, never, never, never worried about the situation,' Vasseur said in December 2024 'I'm really convinced that it was the situation, and I don't want to blame Lewis or Mercedes, but this position, it's not easy to manage and I can understand that if it's not going very well. But he also did very, very well on the last couple of events. I'm not worried at all.'

Writing off Hamilton at this stage of his career would be foolish given his track records. Lewis is a driver who is defined and guided by his emotions and the thrill of finally racing at Ferrari will surely kick-start whatever passion he may have lost in 2024 with the capricious Mercedes W15.

He is certain to be compared against other big names to join in the last 40 years. Nigel Mansell won on debut in 1989, Kimi Räikkönen won on debut in 2007, and Fernando Alonso repeated the feat at Bahrain in 2010. Sebastian Vettel won his third race in 2015, but significantly Michael Schumacher required seven races before he stood on the top step, and he was the most successful of them all. Ultimately, if Hamilton wins a championship for Ferrari at any stage, it won't matter when he tasted his first victory.

But until those wins start coming in, doubts and apprehension will be justified. The best summary on Hamilton's move might be from the man involved in trying to sign him in 2019, former team boss Mattia Binotto. 'Lewis is a fantastic driver, no question . . . 100 and something wins, seven championships. I don't think we are here to discuss his career.

'But personally, I don't think it's the right choice for Ferrari. He is a driver maybe at the wrong side of his career. I would say if you would not have signed Lewis today, Max would have been in Ferrari next year.' Whether Max Verstappen would have been available is a very different story – he is contracted to Red Bull until 2028, although rumours did linger for most of 2024 about a move to Mercedes.

'I think Charles is very happy with the decision,' Binotto said. 'To beat Carlos is difficult, but it's expected. So you will never be, let me say, congratulated because you are beating Carlos. If you are beating Lewis, you are the one, you are the man. You can probably ask for a better salary! It's a great opportunity and I think he pushed for it, honestly.

'But if that's one of the main reasons you're doing the change I don't understand it. You cannot have two strong drivers, high ambition drivers. It's too risky, they will share the points. With Charles and Carlos it was a lot more manageable. Lewis is at the end of his career and you are starting a new era in 2026. If he is slower than Charles, you're paying him a lot to be slower than Charles . . .

'But of course, if he's faster than Charles? Wow . . .'

Hamilton's first message as a Ferrari driver hinted at his excitement, updating his LinkedIn page with a post labelled #newjob. 'I could not be more excited for the year ahead,' he wrote. 'Moving to Scuderia Ferrari, there's a lot to reflect on,' he posted on the platform where he is listed as an entrepreneur, investor and F1 driver. 'To anyone considering their next move in 2025: embrace the change. Whether you're switching industries, learning a new skill, or even just taking on new challenges, remember that reinvention is powerful. Your next opportunity is always within reach. Here's to 2025 – a year of embracing new opportunities, staying hungry, and driving forward with purpose. Let's make it one to remember. Andiamo.'

17

IL PREDESTINATO

'When we won at Monza and we got back to the factory, at 11 p.m. we still had had 1,000 people outside the factory doing the "Ole!" for the mechanics . . .'

Fred Vasseur

Charles Leclerc's new Ferrari team-mate had spent large parts of the previous two years working as an executive producer on the Formula 1 movie alongside Brad Pitt and Jerry Bruckheimer. *F1* follows a fictional character, Sonny Hayes, joining a fictional team, ApexGP, for an against-the-odds comeback tale. As exciting as that project is for Formula 1, since Leclerc's arrival with Sauber in 2018 the sport already has a better tale that any studio executive could dream of.

Blessed with the unfair combination of movie star good looks, prodigious talent and a lengthy contract with the most famous team in motor racing, the Monaco-born star's life away from the race track is one of high fashion, fast cars and yachts. F1 photographers will tell you he and glamorous girlfriend Alexandra Saint Mleux are the most photographed couple in the paddock by some margin. In the *Drive to Survive* era, few drivers have resonated as much with Formula 1 fans as Charles Marc Hervé Perceval Leclerc.

But his cheerful demeanour belies a poignant story beneath – his journey to this point has been tinged with tragedy. Leclerc's father, Hervé, gave him his first taste of motor racing at a young age, taking him to a kart track owned by best friend Philippe Bianchi, just the other side of the Monaco-France border. The Leclerc and Bianchi families were very close; Philippe's son, Jules, was named Charles' godfather, despite being only seven years older.

Bianchi had seemed destined for great things, arriving in F1 in 2013 with Marussia and scoring the team's first points in Monaco of all places. A Ferrari deal appeared to be in the works for 2015 or 2016 when Bianchi suffered a serious brain injury at the 2014 Japanese Grand Prix – he died from his injuries the following year. Not long before his accident, Bianchi had urged the Ferrari junior programme bosses to take a look at his godson.

'I was a good friend of Jules Bianchi,' Sky Sports Italy commentator Carlo Vanzini told me. 'He always talked about Charles, this kid that was incredible, phenomenal, something different.' Ferrari listened to Bianchi: Leclerc had finished runner-up to Max Verstappen in the 2013 KZ Kart World Championship (ironically, Charles was driving for ART Grand Prix, the team set up by Fred Vasseur) and with Bianchi's recommendation Ferrari began to monitor his progress. In 2015 he would finish fourth in European F3 with the same team, Van Amersfoort Racing, that had propelled Verstappen into the Red Bull driver scheme. At the start of 2016, Leclerc was signed to the Ferrari junior programme. 'If I'm here today in Formula 1, it's thanks to Jules,' he would say in 2024, explaining his decision to race wearing a Bianchi tribute helmet at Suzuka ten years after the accident.

Leclerc's rise from his arrival within the Ferrari family was rapid: he won the GP3 (now Formula 3) title in his first year, moving straight up to the rebranded Formula 2 for 2017. By that point the F1 paddock was buzzing about the Monegasque driver as he raced clear in the points that year. But another tragic setback occurred on 20 June, when Hervé passed away after a long-running illness. Three days later, Leclerc took an F2 pole position in Baku and won the feature race, showing his remarkable resilience in one of life's darkest moments. Backed by Ferrari, Leclerc had started negotiations to race for Sauber before his father died. That deal was signed a short time later, but not confirmed until December 2017. Speaking to F1 TV the following year, Leclerc said: 'My father has done everything for me to arrive here . . . Last year, before I signed, I told him I had signed in Formula 1 to make him happy. We knew the end was near. I'm very happy to have managed to do that.'

Leclerc has opened up about that conversation more recently, revealing the level of extra baggage it gave him during that Formula 2 season. 'I knew how much it meant for us and we had done all the journey together,' Leclerc told *The Gentleman's Journal* in 2024. 'It was very difficult for me to accept that he would go before I actually signed my first F1 contract. I was really angry with myself for lying to him at first but, then, luckily, I signed the actual contract right after he left. I was realizing my dream, but I was also very happy to not have lied to him.'

Years later, Leclerc's first win would be overshadowed by the death of Anthoine Hubert the day before. Leclerc and Hubert had been close in the junior categories.

'The people I've lost were the ones that wanted the best for me, and whenever I asked myself the question, "What would they want me to do?" the answer came up pretty quickly that my father would just want me to put the helmet on and go win races. You can get ready mentally for many things, especially in my professional life, like how to be focused and relaxed in intense situations. But nothing really prepares you for a very difficult personal moment that you need to go through.'

The Curse

On his arrival in 2019, Leclerc had quickly become the darling of the Italian media. As just mentioned, his first victory had come with a tragic backdrop of the death of Anthoine Hubert 24 hours before – a week later his victory at Monza felt like confirmation Ferrari had a mega talent on their hands. In the closing laps, Italian TV commentator Vanzini dubbed him *Il Predestinato* – 'The Predestined'. It was a label he had used at different points earlier in the young Leclerc's career, but after such a famous win, the nickname stuck.

Vanzini's moniker was borne out of a mock press conference he had hosted for Leclerc, when he was brought in by former Ferrari Driver Academy boss Massimo Rivola to help Leclerc with media training. 'We had a session, a simulation media session,' Vanzini told me. 'I asked him, "So, you're starting from pole position, it's the last race of the season, of course you will race to win but your team-mate is fighting for the championship – will you help him?" And he answered, "No, I race to win". So we told him that's good for journalists, for news, but maybe not for the team. Maybe it's better to say, "Of course, I will do what the team needs". At this time I knew him but not very well, he said, "Carlo, the question was incorrect. Because it's not possible at the last race that my team-mate is fighting for the title and I am not fighting for the championship." So I fell in love with him at that moment.'

Fate did not always appear to be on the side of *Il Predestinato*, though, especially at the Monaco Grand Prix. The connection with the famous street race went deeper than just his upbringing. Hervé Leclerc had raced there in Formula 3 in the late 1980s and had dreamt of a day his son would win the principality's famous event. While France has enjoyed a generation of mega talent in recent years – Bianchi, Hubert, Pierre Gasly and Esteban Ocon – Leclerc has always been staunchly and proudly Monegasque.

Even before Ferrari, the Monte Carlo circuit had been unkind to him – he failed to finish either the sprint or feature race in Formula 2, before he collided with Brandon Hartley's Toro Rosso in his rookie F1 season for Sauber.

In 2019, Ferrari had messed up qualifying and he was eliminated from Q1 – he picked up a puncture fighting through the lower order, eventually retiring. The pandemic meant the race was cancelled in 2020, but Leclerc took pole on its return in 2021, although in strange circumstances. His quickest time had been the first in Q3, with his second flying lap ending up with a heavy crash in the wall. Some thought he might have been doing a 'Schumacher at Rascasse' or a 'Rosberg at Mirabeau', setting the P1 time then bringing out the yellow flags on the final runs, but Christian Horner radioed to a frustrated Max Verstappen that the size of the impact was so great his gearbox might not survive.

Ferrari opted against changing that gearbox (which came with a grid penalty) but Leclerc's car suffered a driveshaft issue on the way to the grid and he did not even get to start. In 2022, Red Bull and Sergio Perez caught out the Ferrari strategists when teams switched from wets to inters, despite Leclerc enjoying a comfortable lead from pole position. In 2023 a three-place grid penalty for impeding Lando Norris knocked him from third to sixth, where he would eventually finish, meaning he did not even have a podium to his name coming to the 2024 race.

The mood at Ferrari by then was different. February's blockbuster announcement about Lewis Hamilton has raised the scrutiny on the team and its lead driver, but it had been Carlos Sainz who had performed stronger in the early rounds, winning the Australian Grand Prix two weeks after missing the Saudi Arabian Grand Prix with an appendix issue. In Saudi, Ferrari junior Oliver Bearman had deputized brilliantly in Sainz's absence, giving a glimpse at a potential future should one side of the Leclerc–Hamilton partnership not work.

After podiums at Miami and Imola, Monaco would be Leclerc's moment to kickstart his season. Even when he took another pole position, with the cloud of a hometown curse growing every year it was hard not to think something was bound to go wrong for him again. Holding off McLaren's

Oscar Piastri at the start, Ferrari and the *tifosi* held their collective breath for the rest of the race, refusing to celebrate until he had crossed the line. As he closed in on the victory, the magnitude of what he was about to achieve sunk in. 'I think where I struggled the most to contain my emotions was during the last ten laps of the race, more than on the podium,' Leclerc said. 'I started to feel the emotion two laps from the end. My eyes started to fill with tears. I realized I couldn't see anything any more. That's when I told myself, Fuck! Charles, not now!".'

As Leclerc rounded the Rascasse section and the bus stop where he used to wait before school, F1/Channel 4's Alex Jacques' commentary accompanied him home. 'The grandstands he saw built as a kid growing up now rise for him and for the first time in 93 years this fabled race is won by one of their own!' Race radio played Leclerc screaming out in delight. After so many near misses, it immediately became one of the most popular race wins in recent memory.

Leclerc's emotions were clear after the race. 'It was very difficult, those thoughts again of the people that have helped me get where I am today . . . Obviously Monza in 2019 was extremely special, but Monaco is the grand prix that made me dream of becoming a Formula 1 driver. I remember being so young and watching the race with my friends. Obviously with my father, who has done absolutely everything for me to get to where I am today. I feel like I didn't only accomplish a dream of mine today, but also one of his.'

Constructors' Challenge

After a double DNF in Montréal, Ferrari lost their way with an upgrade at the Spanish Grand Prix that seemed more like a downgrade – a phenomenon which affected many teams across the 2024 season. With McLaren's resurgence in Miami and wins for Mercedes in Austria, Silverstone and Belgium, it looked like Ferrari might slip behind Mercedes to fourth in the Constructors' Championship. But after the summer break there was a resurgence for the Scuderia.

At Monza, Leclerc created another famous moment. With the McLaren drivers operating under the bizarrely named 'Papaya Rules', an unclear racing code of which driver should be prioritized, Leclerc capitalized. After locking out the front row, McLaren CEO Zak Brown had told Lando Norris and Oscar Piastri not to take risks on the first lap. Piastri had a different idea and launched a move around the outside of his unsuspecting team-mate, forcing Norris into a defensive move which nearly resulted in a spin. Leclerc snatched second position from Norris and then was able to stretch his first stint longer than the McLaren drivers, helping him move into the lead of the race and into another hugely popular victory.

In Italy, the emotion poured out. Vanzini was the cheerleader again: '*Incredible, incredible. Signori e signore, cinque anni fa raccontavamo, la prima vittoria a Monza del Predestinato . . . e allora torniamo tutti insieme, a chiamarlo cosi – perché questa e una gara da Predestinato. Il Predestinato vince il Gran Premio d'Italia!*' ['Incredible . . . incredible. Ladies and gentleman, five years ago we were talking about the first victory in Monza of the predestined . . . we can come back and call him that again, because this was a predestined race. The Predestined wins the Italian Grand Prix!']

Leclerc's victory was met with jubilation and an explosion of colour – red flares firing up as the crowd poured onto the track to take their place under the podium. 'It's an incredible feeling,' Leclerc said. 'Actually I thought that the first time would feel like this, and then the second time – if there was a second time – wouldn't feel as special, but my god, the emotions in the last few laps, exactly the same as in 2019.'

Excitement in Italy was building. 'Ferrari is so special with the fans and the *tifosi*,' Fred Vasseur told me. 'When we won at Monza and we got back to the factory, at 11 p.m. we still had had 1,000 people outside the factory doing the "Ole!" for the mechanics. Each day we have people outside the gates waiting for pictures, autographs, and so on. This, it's only at Ferrari. It's a special feeling and the best motivation to everybody.'

Leclerc fell just shy of victory in Baku two weeks later, where Carlos Sainz had a late tangle with Sergio Perez, before Norris comfortably won in Singapore. At Austin, Sainz and Leclerc qualified on the second row but the race changed at Turn 1, where Norris was forced wide by Max Verstappen, again allowing Leclerc through. Sainz followed his team-mate and the team claimed a surprisingly comfortable one–two victory. Ferrari's whole operation was electric – strategy calls were working well and the car looked like one of the strongest in race trim.

Notably in Austin, Vasseur sent strategy head Jain onto the podium with his drivers. In the press conference after the race, I asked both drivers about the impact he had made since being put into the job. 'I mean, he's incredible,' Leclerc replied. 'I have really a lot of trust in Ravin. He's done an excellent job. He's pretty young, too, for a position like that. But he's always super, super calm. And that's really needed. He also manages the emotion super well, which maybe in the past was probably one of our weaknesses, speaking of strategy. So I think, yeah, we have a very strong track team at the moment.' Sainz added: 'Having a good car on race day always helps to make the strategy work. And I feel like this year, compared to last year, we have a very strong car on race day. So making bold strategy moves on race day [last year] wouldn't be as easy and you would look more crazy by doing them. And this year, having a car that degrades less the tyres and makes you more competitive on race day also allows you more flexibility and better opportunities to play with the strategy.'

Sainz and Ferrari would have a good race car again seven days later, when Carlos won in Mexico, another race which saw Norris and Verstappen have a moment together on track. Norris recovered to finish second and Leclerc's third-place finish brought Ferrari to within 29 points of McLaren in the constructors' title race. The result also brought some peace of mind for the man making way for Hamilton. 'Honestly, I really wanted this one,' the Spaniard said after the race. 'I really needed it for myself. I've been saying for a while I wanted one more win before leaving Ferrari and to do it here in front of this mega crowd is incredible. Now with four races left I want to enjoy it as much as possible and if another one [win] comes I'm going to go for it.'

Although F1 drivers often downplay the impact of momentum, going into the final chunk of the schedule Ferrari appeared to have it. 'This year we changed our focus a little bit,' senior performance engineer Jock Clear said. 'It was clear for people to see that certainly two, three years ago we were the kings of qualifying and really struggled on a Sunday. But even last year the balance wasn't quite right. I think this year the encouraging thing is that wherever the drivers qualify, they get out of the car at the end of qualifying and think, "Yeah, but I know that I can race from here tomorrow". In previous years Charles has got out of the car in P1 and thought, "Now I have to hang on to this in the race". And when he's got to spend 56 laps of hanging on to a position it's a different prospect. Now we go into the race knowing okay, we qualified P2, P3, we know we can win this from here, and that's a really good place to be. Psychologically and technically it's the right way to approach racing, for sure.'

The run-in would be tense. A headline-grabbing drive from Verstappen in the rain at Interlagos combined with a red flag, denied McLaren points but they still extended their constructors' lead to 36 points. Ferrari got it back down to 24 after the Las Vegas Grand Prix, where Sainz snatched third behind the Mercedes drivers. In Qatar, Norris was hit with a late penalty for failing to slow for yellow flags while running second. Leclerc inherited that position as Ferrari cut the gap to 21 points with one race to run.

In Abu Dhabi, Ferrari was the underdog. Hopes appeared to be dashed on Friday, when the team confirmed a penalty for Leclerc after engine changes, dropping him to the back of the field, before McLaren locked out the front row of the grid. Then came another helpful intervention from a rival, when Verstappen knocked Piastri into a spin after an optimistic overtaking move into Turn 1. Suddenly the title appeared to be there for the taking. Norris, to his credit, was faultless out in front and claimed the victory which was enough to wrap it up regardless, but Sainz and Leclerc kept the pressure on right until the end, finishing a worthy second and third – given that Leclerc had started the race from P19 it was an astonishing podium finish.

Asked after the race if he was happy with his recovery, Leclerc said: 'No, not really. I mean, I'm of course really happy about the race. But the disappointment is a lot bigger. You don't win or lose a championship in the last race. But obviously, it's over the course of the season and after every single race. And McLaren has just done a better job than us. And congratulations to them. But it obviously hurts when you get to the last race. You know there's an opportunity. It was a very difficult weekend, obviously, already with the penalty on Friday. It was never going to be easy. But after such a good first lap, the hopes were high. And yeah, we just came short of our dream, which was to win the constructors'. So it hurts.'

The feeling was doubly bitter for Sainz, despite his seemingly stoic nature in the media interviews after the race. When asked by a Spanish journalist how he was keeping himself from crying, he replied: 'Maybe I already have. And you just don't know. And you haven't seen it. Maybe it was in the helmet. Maybe it was in the in the ten minutes prior to a race when I was in the car. Maybe it was in the in-lap. Yeah. Maybe you'll never know. I can just tell you that I did get emotional at some point today. I'm not going to tell you exactly when or how. It's a feeling that I save to myself and for my team . . . today there were moments that I got emotional and luckily you guys didn't get to see it.'

Regardless of the outcome, the fact Ferrari had been in the hunt at all was significant. Luca di Montezemolo had taken great pride in the fact his Ferrari teams were usually in the running until the very end of the season, but that norm had disappeared after Alonso's 2012 defeat to Sebastian Vettel and Red Bull. Despite the encouraging years of 2017, 2018 and 2022, Ferrari had waited 14 years to go into the final race with a shot at a World Championship – hard to believe given the success of the Michael Schumacher-era team. Many at the current Ferrari team seemed invigorated by the challenge of fighting McLaren right to the wire.

'We've had two seasons where we're basically fighting for the championship,' Leclerc said after Abu Dhabi. 'Obviously, one was not for long enough, which was in 2022. And I think with that, we've grown a lot. When it's been such a long time, obviously, the people in the team, most of them have changed. And so for many people, it was also the first time fighting again with Ferrari at the top. So I think it's an important process.'

However Charles is not a believer in momentum, whatever pundits might say or write. 'Momentum is not really a thing. There's been quite a lot of examples on our side where we finished a year strong and then the beginning of the next year we've been struggling, so we really need to stay on it.'

Leclerc's three wins in 2024 showed how high his performance ceiling can be. In the latter part of the year, there was no stronger driver – from the Belgian Grand Prix onwards, he finished on the podium eight times out of a possible 11. For a time, it had seemed as though the frustration of Ferrari was wearing down the team's favourite son, as it had with Sebastian Vettel before him – many had wondered if his confidence had been eroded so badly he might look elsewhere. But Leclerc today has become as synonymous with Ferrari as any driver since Schumacher and the new contract he signed in early 2024 will keep him with the team until the end of the decade. Predestined to be World Champion or not, there's no doubt Leclerc is still convinced he can win with Ferrari.

'We've got a lot more hard work to do in the next few years, but I believe in the project,' he said in a post-season Pirelli podcast. 'I have to believe in the project 100 per cent. And I am sure Ferrari is the next team that will be World Champion.'

Whether that World Champion is him or Lewis Hamilton remains to be seen.

18

WINNING AGAIN

'I spoke to one mechanic, he told me, 'We have to work better now because Lewis is coming . . ."

Carlo Vanzini

Ferrari's late-season charge in 2024 showed the depth of talent that now runs through every level of the Scuderia. Charles Leclerc appeared to have found a remedy to some of the inconsistency which had plagued his earlier years at the team. At the end of 2024 he looked like a complete driver and having Lewis Hamilton alongside him as a yardstick and a motivator to push on even further is an exciting prospect. The scenario of Ferrari getting a hungry, fired-up Hamilton gunning for that eighth championship is tantalizing. If it works, it will quite comfortably be the strongest driver pairing on the current grid.

But what 2024 showed most of all was how emphatically the team has changed. The blundering, chaotic and emotional title-contending Mattia Binotto team of 2022 has given way to a calmer, more confident squad under Fred Vasseur in just two short seasons. Whether a championship is more likely in 2025, with the teams still converging together at the end of this current cycle of regulations is tough to call. Maybe it will come in 2026 when everyone will be working from a clean sheet of paper. Whichever side of the fence you fall on one thing is certain: Hamilton's signing was a signal of intent from John Elkann and feels like Luca di Montezemolo's decision to bring Michael Schumacher to the team in 1996. There is no point investing in a big-name driver if the team is not ready to give him the tools to finish the job.

'When Ferrari changed from Sebastian to Carlos, it was like they were saying, 'Okay, we are not able to win at the moment. It's better to have two younger drivers who are growing'. But now we have to see the step,' commentator Carlo Vanzini told me. 'I had an interview recently with Aldo Costa and I asked him about Lewis. You could see his eyes light up. He had great love for Lewis and for Schumacher, who he also worked with. And that's the level he's at. I spoke to one mechanic, he told me, "We have to work better now because Lewis is coming". So Ferrari has to do something more. Last year they came back to fight in the constructors' . . . they might not have all the means to win, like when you look at the new McLaren wind tunnel. But Ferrari always has to win. And when you get a driver like Lewis at Ferrari, it's time to win. No excuse.'

Stefano Domenicali holds a similar view: 'When Michael arrived in 1996 it lifted everybody. Any top driver going to a team does the same thing. Like Fernando [Alonso] going to Aston Martin. Lewis will have the same impact. It gives everyone a level to aim for.'

Hamilton's championship-winning experience will be a huge piece of the puzzle. The seven-time world champion is bringing two figures over from Mercedes – former performance director Loïc Sera has joined as the technical director for the chassis, having originally been brought in to report directly to Enrico Cardile. When Cardile's move to Aston Martin was confirmed last year, Sera's new role was tweaked to give him more responsibility. Former F1 driver Jérôme d'Ambrosio has also joined as deputy team boss and head of the Ferrari Driver Academy, mirroring the role he had with Mercedes' junior programme. Vasseur's early team-building moves have proved very successful, with Ravin Jain completely reshaping the perception of the strategy unit and the likes of Diego Ioverno proving to be popular.

Keeping the team Vasseur has built together will be important. At one stage during our interview, former strategy head Rueda told me: 'Fred needs three, four, five years but I don't think he will get it.' Stefano Domenicali added: 'What was key in the winning times was the stability. Through the bad times we kept the same team in place. No-one blamed each other. I remember all the bad times – Jerez, Michael's accident, but then I also remember when we finally won the title. It was all about staying focused on the final goal.'

Stability – the presence of it or the lack thereof – has underpinned much of this story of modern Ferrari. 'Formula 1 is a unique kind of sport in that you need experience, you need a knowledge of Formula 1, you need also to have a team that you build without changing too many people every year,' Luca di Montezemolo told me. 'Starting from the team manager... I'm proud that from 1992 when I built step-by-step I had a clear goal in front of me and we built a very stable team. A team not only with the president, but with the team manager, the technical director, the chief engineering, with everybody. For most of that period my team was strong and it was stable. So I hope Ferrari can find the next group like that – the key is to not to change too often and to work with a clear strategy for the next goal.'

The indications from his first two years is that Vasseur will be afforded time, barring a monumental failure in 2025. The signing of Hamilton to a multi-year deal and the imminent rule change in the middle of that contract will require a level of continuity and there has been no outward suggestion Elkann is particularly trigger happy when it comes to making changes. Elkann was looking to remove Binotto before the former team boss quit in November 2022, but understandably so after the FIA engine settlement saga, two winless seasons and the implosion of 2022. Everything

Vasseur has done has been positive and has pointed Ferrari on an upward trajectory and outwardly the mood has been clear.

'I think Fred has installed a lot of confidence back in Ferrari,' believes ESPN reporter Laurence Edmondson. 'While the highs are still celebrated, Vasseur keeps them in check. He doesn't let people get carried away with the success. But equally when they've hit lows he's made sure they haven't hit spirals as a result. By keeping that level-headed attitude from the top that's filtered down to the team. He's also made some important personnel and structural changes in the team – many of them which haven't fallen into place until right now, like Loïc Sera from Mercedes. He's now starting to get everything in place. It's a more organized team, it's a more efficient team, and it seems to be a happier team under Fred. Those are the basic building blocks you need to challenge for championships. Then of course you need the special people on top, the engineers and drivers, so it does appear Fred has both of those things in place as well. So that's why the team now looks like such a threat in both championships, whereas even two years ago it always seemed so unlikely they'd mount a full-on championship challenge.'

While some within Ferrari's sphere resent the suggestion that Italy's most famous team cannot win without Italians in charge, it is hard to ignore the fact that a Frenchman who had no previous ties to the business has come in and had such a quick and demonstrable impact. 'I think Fred is someone who will fight his corner with conviction, without worrying about the bigger picture of the Ferrari politics all around him,' F1's Lawrence Barretto told me. 'That's ultimately a good thing given what the history of that team has been.'

The biggest endorsement of that project and the event leading it was Hamilton's arrival. Given his multiple chances to join Ferrari in the past, the fact he has chosen now is significant. Hamilton is unlike any other driver Ferrari has seen before – he is the only driver on the grid larger than the sport itself, boasting a knighthood and the kind of global fame and reach any athlete would dream of. But, as is always the case with Ferrari, he will be measured in one way only: results on the race track. Hamilton and Leclerc together may be box office. It may be a disaster, the kind of move which tears apart the strong and ambitious team Vasseur has brought together. Knowing both drivers and the respect which goes in both directions, it is hard to see that happening.

But it is not just down to Vasseur. Elkann's vision to bring Hamilton to the team has to be credited, as does Sergio Marchionne for how he helped to revive Ferrari after the disaster of 2014 and reassert the fact that the Prancing Horse's only aim every year should be to win or challenge for the world title. While Ferrari fell short of that in 2017 and 2018, the work done at the end of that decade, especially behind the scenes with personnel and resources, have been vitally important. Binotto helped to rid the company's departments of the blame culture which has blighted Ferrari on and off since the beginning of time, and Vasseur has only helped improve that culture since his arrival. It has been slow and it has been painful, but Ferrari has finally moved itself into a position where it feels like championship success is in touching distance.

So much so, that it's convinced the last man to oversee Ferrari championships to start believing again.

'I think Ferrari can win again soon,' di Montezemolo told me. 'The talent at the team is big. We saw good signs in 2024. Lewis is arriving. Charles is a mega talent. I think it is a good time for the whole team to finally have that moment.

'We will see in 2025 if they truly are in the condition to be champions again. But I have a lot of hope they will be.'

INDEX

Abu Dhabi Grand Prix, *see* Yas Marina circuit
Alboreto, Michele 24, 31, 32, 36, 37
Alesi, Jean 44, 48, 50–2
Alfa Romeo F1 racing team 12–16, 20, 32, 191, 204, 224
Alonso, Fernando 2–4, 11, 23, 76–81, 85, 89, 92, 97–102, 112, 117–32, 134–9, 141–151, 154, 156–9, 162–5, 171, 177, 185, 187, 196, 201, 202, 226, 239, 252, 255
AlphaTauri F1 racing team 206, 210, 225, 226
Alpine F1 racing team 27
Arrivabene, Maurizio 169–74, 176, 177, 180–5, 188, 190, 191, 193, 194, 196–9, 211, 221, 222, 228, 229
Arrows F1 racing team 59
ART motor racing team 224, 243
Ascari
  Alberto 7, 12–15, 22
  Antonio 12, 16, 18
Aston Martin F1 racing team 122, 214, 226, 255
ATS F1 racing team 32
Audetto, Daniele 26, 29, 42, 84, 85
Auto Avio Costruzioni 12, 13
Autódromo Hermanos Rodríguez, Mexico City 185, 186, 189, 227, 249
Auto Union F1 racing team 13
Azerbaijan Grand Prix, *see* Baku City Circuit

Badoer, Luca 74, 116
Bahrain Grand Prix, Bahrain International Circuit, Sakhir 105, 143, 149, 157, 158, 175, 178, 189, 192, 201, 214, 215, 226, 239
Baku City Circuit, Azerbaijan 189, 190, 192, 201, 218, 226, 244, 249
Bandini, Lorenzo 7, 18
Baracca, Francesco 13
Barcelona 94, 188
  see also, Catalunya circuit

Barnard, John 31–5, 41, 45–7, 51, 53, 54, 59, 92, 93, 140
Barretto, Lawrence 184, 185, 229, 257
Barrichello, Rubens 48, 66, 73, 77, 86, 115, 117
Bearman, Oliver 19, 246
Belgian Grand Prix, *see* Spa-Francorchamps and Zolder circuits
Benetton F1 racing team 48, 49, 51–3, 70, 204
Benson, Andrew 51, 92, 144, 145, 161, 164, 169
Berger, Gerhard 24, 33, 44, 46, 48, 50, 51
Bianchi
  Jules 154, 162, 165–8, 197, 243, 245
  Philippe 243
Binotto, Mattia 50, 55, 56, 74, 91, 105, 112, 121, 157, 159, 168, 169, 177, 181, 185, 190, 191, 195, 196, 199, 200, 203–5, 208, 211–14, 217–25, 228, 229, 234, 240, 254, 256, 258
Bishop, Matt 66
BMW F1 racing team 138, 157
Bonnington, Peter 113, 239
Bottas, Valtteri 187, 189, 201
Brabham
  Jack 21
  F1 racing team 21
Brawn, Ross 9, 12, 49, 53–6, 59, 61, 70–2, 78, 93, 104, 106, 107, 141, 228
Brawn GP 113–5, 139, 156
Brazilian Grand Prix, *see* Interlagos circuit
Briatore, Flavio 49, 79, 99, 112, 115, 149
British Grand Prix, *see* Brands Hatch and Silverstone circuits
Brixworth, Northamptonshire, UK 156
Bruckheimer, Jerry 242
Brundle, Martin 60, 109, 111, 200, 202, 203
Button, Jensen 113, 118, 124, 128, 142, 143, 146, 165
Byrne, Rory 48, 53, 59, 62, 71, 72, 87

Cardile, Enrico 255
CART championship 59
Castellotti, Eugenio 16
Catalunya circuit, Barcelona, Spain 51, 57, 71, 76, 139, 144, 149, 178, 188, 189, 192, 215, 247
Caterham F1 racing team 156
Cerasoli, Julianne 91, 118, 238
Chinese Grand Prix, *see* Shanghai International Circuit
Chiti, Carlo 20
Chrysler motor company 155, 180, 195
Cigarini, Francesco 192
Circuit of the Americas, Austin, Texas, US 145, 197, 205, 227, 228, 249
Clark, Jim 17, 47
Clarkson, Tom 103, 138
Clear, Jock 181, 250
Codling, Stuart 25
Colajanni, Luca 37, 38, 40, 45, 52, 54, 55, 71, 79, 83, 93, 94, 125, 135, 141, 151
Collins, Peter 7, 16
Cologne, Germany 147, 148
Concorde Agreements 21, 22, 41, 75, 191
Constructors' Championship 1, 2, 5, 6, 9–15, 20, 31, 41, 49, 58, 65–7, 72, 77, 85, 99, 102, 158, 175, 204, 210, 211, 222, 227, 248–50, 254, 255
Costa, Aldo 55, 93, 140, 141, 151, 182, 255
Coughlan
  Mike 89, 92–4, 95–9
  Trudy 89, 94, 95
Coulthard, David 60, 62–4, 66
'Crashgate' 112, 117, 148
Croft, David 214

Dennis, Ron 62, 90, 96–8, 165
Domenicali, Stefano 10, 22, 25, 55, 56, 61, 89–91, 95, 110, 112, 113, 115, 118, 119, 131–3, 142, 158, 159, 166, 174, 200, 222, 228, 229, 234, 255, 256
Drivers' Championship 1–3, 5, 8–15, 17–20, 24, 29–31, 35,

259

41, 44, 49–51, 58, 60, 62, 63, 65–7, 70, 74, 77, 80, 84, 85, 97, 99, 101–5, 108, 110, 119, 122, 123, 127–30, 135, 138, 145–9, 165, 175, 184, 186–8, 193, 209, 218, 237, 238, 245, 252–4
see also, World Championship
DRS (Drag Reduction System) 130, 134, 215, 226, 227
Dutch Grand Prix, *see* Zandvoort circuit
Dyer, Chris 74, 80, 81, 101, 102, 105, 118, 122, 124–9, 131–5, 137, 140, 151

Ecclestone, Bernie 21, 42, 52, 75, 83, 98, 99, 114, 238
Edmonson, Laurence 209, 257
Elkann, John 195, 219–25, 229, 231, 232, 235, 238, 255, 256, 258
Emilio-Romagna, *see* Maranello
Ericsson, Marcus 173
ESPN, US sports channel ix, 5, 108, 109, 111, 155, 209, 236, 257
Estoril circuit, Portugal 50, 51
European Grand Prix 59, 65, 106, 144

Fangio, Juan Manuel 14, 22, 47, 74
Farina, Giuseppe 14
FDD (Ferrari Design and Development) 45–7, 53, 54, 93
Ferrari
 Alfredo 'Dino' 12
 Alfredo Jr. 12, 13
 Alfredo Sr. 13
 driver academy, *see* Maranello
 Enzo 2, 3, 8, 12–21, 24–8, 30–2, 34, 36–9, 41, 47, 59, 74, 80, 82–5, 132, 152, 153, 161, 180, 198, 230
 headquarters, *see* Maranello
 Piero 131, 132, 135, 233
FIA (Fédération Internationale de l'Automobile) 5, 14, 20, 21, 34, 56, 61, 62, 66, 74, 75, 77, 92–4, 96–9, 111, 112, 114, 117, 121, 149, 167, 188, 191, 195, 203–7, 209, 234, 256
Fiat motor company 25, 28, 29, 36, 37, 40, 41, 52, 133, 141, 160, 169, 171, 179, 180, 195

Fiorano test track, *see* Maranello
Fiorio, Cesare 35–7, 41, 42
Fisichella, Giancarlo 80, 116, 129
Forghieri, Mauro 20, 28, 39, 55
French Grand Prix, *see* Magny-Cours, Paul Ricard and Reims circuits
Frentzen, Heinz-Harald 59, 65
Froilán González, José 14, 141
Fry, Pat 141, 168
fuel flow sensor, controversy 203–8
Fuji Speedway circuit, Japan 30, 101
Fusaro, Piero 36, 37

Gasly, Pierre 245
German Grand Prix, *see* Hockenheimring and Nürburgring
Giannini, Rossella and family 85–7
Gilles Villeneuve circuit, Montreal, Canada 49, 59, 97, 100, 138, 144, 178, 179, 192, 247
Gislimberti, Paolo 68, 69
Glock, Timo 108–110, 121
Gobbato, Ugo 12, 13
Grosjean, Romain 145

Haas F1 racing team 39, 87, 204
Häkkinen, Mika 60, 62–71, 90
Hamilton
 Lewis 2, 6, 8–11, 90, 92, 97–102, 106–113, 118–23, 128, 130, 142, 144–6, 149, 150, 157, 158, 173–6, 178, 182, 187–90, 192–4, 197, 201, 209, 211, 227, 231–41, 246, 250, 253–8
Hawthorn, Mike 7, 16, 17, 22
Hill
 Damon 49, 51, 59, 60
 Phil 17, 18, 20, 22
Hockenheimring, Germany 20, 46, 65, 117, 123, 144, 193, 194
Honda F1 racing team 31, 77, 163–5, 210
Horner, Christian 11, 27, 33, 34, 75, 77, 83, 150, 159, 169, 170, 178, 180, 195, 198, 203, 210, 235, 237, 246
Hubert, Anthoine 202, 244, 245
Hughes, Mark 143, 196, 203–5

Hulkenberg, Nico 146
Hungarian
 Grand Prix, Hungaroring, Mogyoród, Pest 67, 72, 79, 97, 98, 105, 107, 114, 117, 144, 150, 176, 190, 219
Hunt
 Ben 235
 James 30, 84

Imola circuit, San Marino 19, 48, 49, 64, 69–71, 215, 246
Interlagos circuit, São Paolo, Brazil 2, 10, 33, 80, 81, 101, 102, 104, 108–111, 117, 118, 120, 121, 123, 146, 208, 220, 250
Ioverno, Diego 226, 228, 256
Irvine, Eddie 2, 49, 63–7
Istanbul Park circuit, Turkey 79, 105, 123, 209
Italian Grand Prix, *see* Monza, Autodromo Nazionale di

Jacques, Alex 247
Jaguar F1 racing team 65, 75
Jain, Ravin 225, 228, 249, 256
Japanese Grand Prix, *see* Fuji Speedway and Suzuka circuits
Jarama circuit, Madrid, Spain 19, 21, 29
Jeddah Corniche circuit, Saudi Arabia 215, 246
Jerez circuit, Spain 57, 59–62, 78, 256
Jordan
 Eddie 175
 F1 racing team 49, 65, 76, 77

Kehm, Sabine 67, 68, 70
Korea International Circuit, Yeongam, South Korea 118, 122, 123, 145

Lardi, Piero 84, 85
Las Vegas Grand Prix, Paradise, Nevada, US 227, 230, 239, 250
Lauda, Niki 1, 2, 18, 20, 22, 26–30, 39, 52, 55, 84, 85, 156, 167, 182
Leclerc
 Charles 2, 7–9, 11, 19, 85, 86, 168, 197, 200–3, 205, 208, 209, 211, 213–9, 224, 226, 227, 230, 233, 237, 238, 240, 242–254, 258

INDEX

Lotus F1 racing team 17, 92, 145, 156, 172, 182
Lowe, Paddy 45, 99

Magny-Cours circuit 44, 59, 74, 80, 105
Mansell, Nigel 23, 33–6, 40, 45, 48, 92, 239
Maranello, Modena, Emilia-Romagna 9, 11, 13, 19, 23, 26, 27, 30, 32, 33, 35, 38, 44–7, 53, 55, 71, 73, 82–8, 92, 103, 133, 138, 140, 144, 147, 148, 151, 158, 159, 165, 166, 180, 182, 183, 187, 193, 195, 208, 214, 221, 222, 229
Ferrari Driver Academy 19, 77, 85, 143, 162, 166–8, 197, 238, 243, 245, 255
Fiorano test track 47, 50, 83, 85, 86, 140
Marchionne, Sergio 133, 155, 160, 161, 164, 169–71, 179–81, 183, 185, 190–2, 194, 195, 197, 198, 203, 219, 220, 258
Marina Bay Street circuit, Singapore 106, 107, 120, 121, 148, 176, 190, 193, 226, 227, 231, 237, 249
Marko, Helmut 144, 194
Marmorini, Luca 141, 1684
Massa, Felipe 2, 10, 11, 77–80, 90, 91, 100–2, 104–118, 120, 121, 124, 126, 128, 138, 139, 142, 143, 146, 149, 151, 152, 155, 156, 158, 197, 238
Mattiacci, Marco 159, 162–4, 168–70, 199, 222, 229
McLaren
Bruce 96
F1 racing team 2, 5, 10, 18, 24, 30–4, 45, 56, 60, 62–4, 66, 67, 70–3, 75–7, 89, 90, 92, 95, 96–102, 105–112, 118–20, 124, 139, 141, 142, 145–7, 157, 163–5, 171, 197, 201, 206–8, 210, 211, 225, 226, 237, 246–52, 255
Formula E team 134
Mekies, Laurent 213, 219, 222, 225, 226
Melbourne circuit, Australia 91–3, 139, 142, 143, 157, 171, 172, 177, 188, 192, 206, 208, 215, 238, 246
Mercedes F1 racing team 5, 8–11, 13, 20, 22, 56, 59, 70,

95, 110, 125, 140, 146, 150, 154, 155–60, 171–7, 181, 182, 187–90, 192, 193, 195, 202–4, 206, 207, 210, 211, 213, 215, 217, 219–21, 227, 230, 232–4, 236–40, 247, 250, 255, 257
Merzario, Arturo 30
Miami Grand Prix, Florida, US 215, 246, 247
Miguel, Carlos 121, 129, 134, 162
Mille Miglia race 13, 17
Minardi F1 racing team 76, 77
Modena, Italy 12, 13, 16, 95, 152, 153
Monaco Grand Prix, Monte Carlo circuit, 7, 8, 11, 18, 19, 37, 49, 59, 64, 72, 73, 78, 86, 90, 94, 105, 107, 144, 165, 189, 201, 215–8, 226, 235, 243, 245, 246
Monteith, Gary 89, 90, 92, 94, 95, 102, 103
Montezemolo, Luca di 1, 2, 11, 24, 26–30, 36–50, 52, 53, 55, 56, 61, 65, 66, 71, 73, 76, 86, 102, 103, 110, 114, 116, 121, 131–5, 138, 140, 150, 151, 154–164, 167, 169, 170, 174, 180, 185, 191, 224, 230, 233, 234, 251, 255, 256, 258
Monza, Autodromo Nazionale di, Italy 3, 4, 9, 11, 15, 17, 18, 24, 30, 33, 58, 63, 65, 68, 69, 79, 88, 106, 149, 153, 154, 164, 165, 176, 190, 197, 198, 200, 202, 203, 211, 226, 242, 245, 247, 248
Mosley, Max 62, 66, 77, 94, 96, 98, 99
Moss, Stirling 52, 117

Newey, Adrian 28, 45, 62, 72, 139, 144, 147, 175
Norris, Lando 226, 227, 246, 248–51
Nürburgring, Germany 13, 15, 16, 20, 29, 30, 65, 67
Nuvolari, Tazio 13

Paul Ricard circuit, Le Castellet, France 213, 218
Perez, Sergio 85, 143, 145, 165, 197, 215–7, 227, 246, 249
Petrov, Vitaly 119, 120, 125–31, 134

Piastri, Oscar 247, 248, 251
Piccinini, Marco 31, 32, 41
Piquet
Nelson Jr. 106, 112
Nelson Sr. 85
Pirelli tyre manufacturer 72, 125, 139, 173, 184, 252
Pironi, Didier 19, 20
Porsche motor company 31, 157
Prancing Horse, Ferrari badge 4, 11, 13, 36, 53, 74, 82, 89, 103, 104, 142, 150, 165, 194, 258
Predestinato, Il, *see* Leclerc, Charles
Prost, Alain 20, 23, 34–7, 40, 41, 44, 48, 150, 196

Qatar Grand Prix, *see* Lusail International Circuit

Racing Point F1 racing team 206, 210
Räikkönen, Kimi 1, 5, 11, 23, 75–7, 79, 80, 81, 89–92, 94, 99–103, 105, 106, 109, 111, 113, 116–8, 122, 129, 134, 145, 149–51, 155, 157, 158, 162, 166–8, 172, 173, 175, 176, 178, 187–90, 192, 197, 234, 239
Ratzenberger, Roland 48
Red Bull
F1 racing team 2, 5, 11, 27, 33, 75, 76, 83, 106, 113, 119, 121–4, 126, 127, 132, 139, 141, 142, 144, 146–152, 158, 159, 163, 164, 175–8, 180, 181, 183, 190, 194, 196, 201, 205, 206, 209–11, 214–7, 219, 220, 223, 226, 227, 234, 240, 243, 246, 252
see also, AlphaTauri and Toro Rosso F1 racing teams
Red Bull Ring, Spielberg, Austria 201, 209, 218, 226, 247
Regazzoni, Clay 27, 84
Reims circuit, France 17
Renault F1 racing team 2–4, 20, 21, 76, 77, 79, 80, 106, 112, 115, 119, 120, 125–30, 134, 149, 155, 158, 159, 206, 210, 237
Ricciardo, Daniel 142, 163, 175, 176, 178, 185, 201, 210, 211

Rivola, Massimo 245
Ronaldo, Cristiano 85, 209
Rosberg
  Keke 20
  Nico 20, 107, 125, 143, 157, 158, 172, 175, 176, 178, 187, 194, 246
Rosso Corsa 8, 15, 94, 152
Rueda, Ignacio 172, 175, 176, 179, 182, 183, 188, 194, 196, 217, 219, 220, 224, 225, 228, 229, 256
Russell, George 215, 219, 220, 227, 239

Saint Mleux, Alexandra 242
Sainz
  Carlos Jr. 178, 208–11, 215, 216, 218, 219, 226–8, 230, 231, 237, 240, 246, 249–51, 255
  Carlos Sr. 236
Sakura, Japan 164
San Marino Grand Prix, *see* Imola circuit
Sauber F1 racing team 15, 75, 77, 90, 143, 156, 166–8, 173, 191, 197, 200, 223–5, 229, 242, 244, 245
Saudi Arabian Grand Prix, *see* Jeddah Corniche circuit
Scheckter, Jody 19, 20, 22, 24, 31, 40, 61, 65
Schumacher
  Corinna 60
  Gina Marie 65
  Michael 1–5, 9, 22, 24, 28, 47–53, 57–81, 83, 85–7, 89, 90, 91, 102, 105, 116–8, 122, 125, 131, 134, 141, 147, 149–51, 158, 163, 165, 167, 171, 174, 175, 184, 187, 239, 246, 252, 255, 256
Senna
  Ayrton 25, 34–6, 47–9, 69, 70, 92, 163, 166
  Bruno 142, 146
Sepang International circuit, Malaysia 66, 67, 73, 113, 117, 143, 157, 168, 172–5
Sera, Loïc 255, 257
Shanghai International Circuit, China 80, 101, 118, 143, 149, 159, 178, 189
Silver Arrows, *see* Mercedes F1 racing team

Silverstone circuit, UK 14, 15, 57, 64, 67, 96, 141, 144, 190, 192, 193, 209, 218, 235, 239, 247
Singapore Grand Prix, *see* Marina Bay Street circuit
Smedley, Rob 7, 10, 54, 91, 100, 101, 104, 106–115, 117, 126, 128, 140, 152
Spa-Francorchamps circuit, Belgium 49, 59, 62, 68, 100, 106, 116, 145, 151, 190, 202, 203, 235, 247, 252
Spanish Grand Prix, *see* Catalunya, Jarama, Jerez and Valencia circuits
'Spygate' 92, 95, 99, 117, 149
Steiner, Guenther 24, 39, 76, 204, 208
Stella, Andrea 55, 56, 119, 120, 127, 128, 143, 169
Stepney, Nigel 92–6, 99
Stroll, Lance 85
Surtees, John 20, 22, 27
Sutil, Adrian 166, 167
Suzuka circuit, Japan 34, 37, 58, 59, 63, 66, 67, 70, 71, 75, 80, 145, 154, 164–7, 184, 197, 243

Tambay, Patrick 20, 31
Todt, Jean 42–58, 63, 65, 66, 68–73, 77, 79, 101, 102, 141, 158, 180, 185, 191, 221, 222, 224, 229, 230
Tombazis, Nikolas 148, 168
Toro Rosso F1 racing team 106, 109, 142, 165, 178, 183, 196, 236, 237, 245
  see also, Red Bull F1 racing team
Toyota F1 racing team 76, 108, 148
Tremayne, David 117, 190
Trips, Wolfgang von 17, 18
Turkish Grand Prix, *see* Istanbul Park circuit
Tyrrell F1 racing team 31

United States Grand Prix, *see* Circuit of the Americas, Indianapolis Motor Speedway circuit
  see also, Las Vegas Grand Prix, Miami Grand Prix

Valencia Street circuit, Spain 106, 144, 147
Vanzini, Carlo 243, 245, 248, 254, 255
Vasseur, Fred 11, 43, 223–30, 235, 236, 239, 242, 243, 248, 254–8
Verstappen, Max 113, 121, 178, 185, 186, 190, 196, 200–2, 205, 211, 215, 216, 218, 219, 227, 234, 236, 237, 240, 243, 246, 249, 250, 251
Vettel, Sebastian 8, 11, 23, 83, 85, 106, 108, 109, 117–23, 127, 128, 130, 131, 135, 139, 141–7, 149, 154, 158, 163–5, 168, 170–9, 183–94, 196–8, 200, 201, 208–10, 234, 239, 252, 255
Vigna, Benedetto 219, 221, 225
Villeneuve
  Gilles 19, 31, 37, 59
  Jacques 51, 52, 59–62, 77
Vowles, James 217, 231

Weaver, Paul 124, 147
Webber, Mark 118, 122–30, 142, 144–6
Whiting, Charlie 186, 190
Whitmarsh, Martin 98, 99
Williams F1 racing team 2, 20, 25, 31, 35, 44, 45, 48, 49, 51, 59, 60, 62, 69, 73, 107, 143, 144, 152, 187, 206, 231
Wolff, Toto 22, 140, 182, 207, 208, 210, 235, 236
World Championship 1, 2, 9–16, 18–24, 26, 29–31, 34, 35, 44, 49–51, 54, 56–60, 63, 65–8, 70, 71, 74, 84, 85, 102–5, 108, 111, 113, 118–122, 127, 131, 137, 147–9, 165, 171, 175, 177, 186–8, 190–3, 230, 237, 238, 243, 245, 251–4
  see also, Constructors' Championship, Drivers' Championship

Yas Marina circuit, Abu Dhabi, UAE 11, 119–37, 140, 145, 146, 151, 205, 221, 230, 231, 233, 234, 239, 250, 252